LEGO

LEGO
a love story

JONATHAN BENDER

WILEY

John Wiley & Sons, Inc.

Library of Congress Cataloging-in-Publication Data:
Bender, Jonathan, date.
LEGO: a love story / Jonathan Bender.
     p. cm.
  Includes index.
  ISBN 978-0-470-40702-8 (cloth).
  1. LEGO toys. 2. LEGO Group. 3. Bender, Jonathan—Travel. 4. Journalists—Travel—United States. 5. Handicraft—Competitions. 6. Toys—Psychological aspects.
I. Title.
  TS2301. T7B46 2010
688.7'25—dc22

2009031387

For Kate and my family

Contents

Acknowledgments

Thanks to the AFOL community for welcoming me into the world of bricks as soon as I stepped into the room. I had an excellent building tutor in Joe Meno—any holes in my building repertoire are of my own doing. Dave Sterling demystified plastics, a testament to his ability rather than to my grasp of science. To Duane Collicott, Andreas Stabno, and their families: thanks for taking me into your homes and lives. Andrew Becraft was an excellent sounding board and gave invaluable feedback as a reader of an early draft. Dan Brown and his staff at the Brick Museum brought back my sense of wonder and reminded me that there is nobody in the world like the American entrepreneur. And thanks to all the fans who answered my questions without hesitation or irritation despite the fact that many were personal and definitely irritating.

The LEGO Group also made it easy to gain access to sources and places. LEGO Community Relations Coordinator Steve Witt helped facilitate relationships within the AFOL community as well as at the company. It still means a lot to me that he showed me his build room. Out at LEGOLAND California, Master Model Builder Gary McIntire convinced me to ride the third roller-coaster of my life through his enthusiasm for his job. Master Model Designer Bill Vollbrecht taught me about the park and what it takes to be a master builder; my thanks to him for the enjoyable afternoon I spent at a SandLUG meeting in his home. Serious Play consultant Gary Mankellow gave me a thorough walkthrough of the business side of LEGO—cheers to Jay Liebenguth for introducing us.

While I was in Billund, Denmark, Jan Christensen was an exceedingly gracious host/tour guide, and the head of LEGO Community Development Tormod Askildsen opened a number of doors. I am still amazed, and grateful, that Jette Orduna trusted me with LEGO's history in the Idea House.

Thanks to my agent, Jonathan Lyons, a consummate professional who continually exceeds my expectations. At John Wiley & Sons I'd like to thank Ellen Wright for steering the book through to production and my editor, Stephen Power, for making the editing process a discussion. He made my jokes better and the story stronger—all writers should have such an editor. And to Nathan Sawaya—an artist with LEGO bricks—thank you for opening your studio and using your talents to design an unbelievable cover.

My family is my support network: thank you, Mom, Dad, and Andrew. Dad, anytime you feel like putting together the Sears Tower for a third time, I'm there. To all of my family and friends who contributed bricks and encouragement, a heartfelt thank-you. As always, I want to thank my wife, Kate, for her patience and her willingness to build a life alongside me.

A LEGO cow carousel sits frozen in motion outside the Toy and Plastic Brick Museum in Bellaire, Ohio.

Back to School

Night has fallen in the school yard. Inside the chain-link fence at 4597 Noble Street in Bellaire, Ohio, a merry-go-round with cows the size of miniature ponies made of LEGO bricks sits frozen in motion on the concrete. A small tin sign to the right of the double doors at the front of Gravel Hill Middle School says the school grounds are closed after dark.

But the doors are open and the lights in the hallway are on. The trumpet notes of Buena Vista Social Club's "Chan Chan" echo softly off the tiled walls as a skinny blond-haired guy wearing a military-style cap stacks pirates, Star Wars characters, and superheroes on a six-foot folding table in front of a row of black and red school lockers. Tom Erickson is focusing on getting the minifigure display—an army of LEGO men—just right to greet several hundred attendees of Brick Show 2008, a LEGO fan convention that will open in about six hours.

It's the first weekend of September, but children haven't attended classes at Gravel Hill for half a decade, since the middle school was sold at auction in 2004. The building reopened in August 2007 as the Toy and Plastic Brick Museum. The brainchild of Dan Brown, a self-described "adult LEGO enthusiast," it contains a mishmash of LEGO sculptures and rare LEGO sets sprawled over three floors of the massive tan brick building. A computer recycler by trade, Dan has spent the last three years turning the former middle school into an unofficial LEGO museum.

It's three in the morning, and I've been snapping yellow LEGO bricks into a twenty-foot wall for the better part of six hours. I haven't seen a kid in the last four; instead, I've been building alongside Thomas Mueller, a thirty-two-year-old German transplant living in Los Angeles who is sipping Smirnoff Ice and handing me the bricks. He's clad in black shorts, a black T-shirt, black socks, and black sneakers. With his round glasses and close-cropped brown hair, he reminds me of the stage managers from my days in musical theater.

While building, my hands develop a rhythm all their own. I roll a brick into my palm using my index finger, which leaves my thumb free to keep grabbing more LEGO bricks from the red bin at my feet. The passage of time is marked by the different parts of my body that begin to ache as I sit cross-legged on the hard linoleum. Both of my legs have fallen asleep up to the calves. A joint or tendon on the side of my right knee has been making an odd popping noise every time I shift my body. But I am inexplicably determined to finish this wall.

It is the fourth and final castle wall that rings a twenty-by-thirty-foot classroom, rising eighteen inches to meet the chalk-rail banister. Dan has erected the first three walls out of yellow LEGO bricks, working into the early morning for several weeks before the convention. He is driven by a compulsion to top last year's Guinness World Record for "the largest LEGO image in the world." According to Dan, this will be the world's largest LEGO castle, even though Guinness isn't coming to measure.

He also sees this as a tribute to an elusive LEGO set: the Yellow Castle. In 1978, Set 375, Castle, was released in Europe as the first in LEGO's castle play theme. It came out in the United States three years later as set 375/6075. With a working drawbridge and fourteen knight minifigures, this kit has reached icon status in the adult fan community, with sets going for between $300 and $1,000 on eBay. Lost Yellow Castle sets are like Mickey Mantle baseball cards—given away by unknowing mothers cleaning out their children's closets. An important milestone in the LEGO Group's history, the Yellow Castle also represented a new direction for the company because it was the first in a series of sets that focused on a given theme.

"I'm feeling my age," says Dan, forty-one, as he puts down the plastic tub. "We should qualify for some sort of senior discount on LEGO."

He has the honor of putting the last brick in place, squatting down just as Tom strolls in carrying two blue 1 × 8 bricks (one stud wide by eight studs long) engraved with the words "Toy & Plastic Brick Museum. World Record Castle Build '08." I don't know it yet, but eight hours later I will be supervising close to a hundred kids as they build the interior scenes that will make up the castle courtyard, connecting the walls with large gray baseplates, the flat LEGO squares that form the ground underneath many brick structures.

It might make some cosmic sense that I'm morphing into an adult fan of LEGO at a former middle school, because it was right around that time in my life when I set down my bricks and didn't pick them back up for a long time. My LEGO building career likely peaked when I was ten.

When I was in fourth grade, I built a model of the Sears Tower using LEGO pieces and black spray paint with my father in our basement. It is the only thing we've ever built together. Neither of us is particularly skilled at home improvement projects. But for one glorious afternoon, using our tiny, primary-color plastic bricks, we seemed as talented as the men who build real skyscrapers.

The model was for the annual "state fair" held by North Stratfield Elementary School, in which each student was assigned a different state as a theme for a project.

"Dad, I got Illinois for the state fair. That's where Grandma and Grandpa live. And we're building the Sears Tower," I informed him, while spinning around a copy of the *Encyclopaedia Britannica* on our wooden table to point out the two pictures of the landmark monument.

"That's great. What did you have in mind?" my father asked as he took off his suit jacket and studied the photos. This was phase two of my plan, which secretly involved us using up all my LEGO bricks and then needing to go to the store to buy more.

"We're going to need a lot of LEGOs," I managed.

"I think you already have a lot of LEGOs," he countered.

"You're right, I do. And we're going to use them all," I concurred, showing him my rough drawing in blue ballpoint pen detailing the blocky rise of the tower. My plans ended there, and I expectantly waited for my dad to help craft the rest of the project. He agreed to help supervise construction.

We began construction on Saturday afternoon.

"Did you remember the LEGOs?" asked my dad when he came down to join me in the basement. I hadn't.

"Don't worry, I brought them down," he said, gesturing to the large blue bucket sitting on the shelf below his workbench. My name adorned the side of the bucket, spelled out in large letters formed by multicolor stickers. It was filled to the brim with LEGO bricks and miniature men.

I carefully smoothed out the sheet of paper with my ink blueprints on his worktable. They would not be consulted again. We spent the next two hours building the base out of blue, yellow, and white bricks. My father placed a small pile of rectangular pieces on the table about a foot below my eye level. My fingers grabbed the new pieces, snapping them together easily and watching the tower rise surprisingly quickly. We didn't talk while we worked, but the silence was comforting. We were building a monument to a monument. When the top of the tower was even with my nose, we began to look at how we might construct the top floors. My dad had brought down the encyclopedia, open to the page with the Sears Tower photographs. My hand-drawn blueprints were ignored as we attempted to match our building to the various photos of the skyscraper.

My father sat back and watched me lay the bricks for this final stage of building. I snapped on square pieces until I had completed the tiered top that helps shape the skyline of Chicago. After a brief pause we repurposed two tube-shape pieces from a LEGO police officers set to form the radio transmitters on top of the tower.

"Looks good," said my dad.

"It does," I said, surprised.

"But it's not done. We have to glue it."

I looked at my father with naked shock: Glue LEGOs? Was he crazy? You never glued LEGO pieces, because you always tore them apart to build the next jumbled assortment that was meant to be a spaceship, or a truck, or a castle, or something else.

"Otherwise it won't stay together. It could break," said my father. He had a point. I became excited about violating one of the LEGO taboos of my youth.

"Let's do it," I said eagerly. I ran upstairs to grab popsicle sticks and Elmer's Glue, the true hallmark of a successful school project. I smeared the glue along the side, and my dad blotted away the extra with a wet paper towel. It felt wrong—and I loved it.

We took a short break to let the glue dry and eat some sandwiches, then we returned to the basement. I barely felt the cold as my father turned on the lights and revealed our structure. I tried to pull it apart to test its structural integrity. It held. My dad handed me a pair of safety goggles. They didn't quite fit my face, and I kept my right hand over the side to make sure they stayed on over my glasses. My dad pointed me to a stool a few feet away as he shook a can of black spray paint, a gesture I have since learned would have sent LEGO purists running from the room. He hit the button and a glossy black sheen began to coat the primary-color toy building. In that moment, it became the Sears Tower. A few minutes later we left the basement coughing, the fumes stronger than my father had anticipated.

Waking up the next day was probably as close to a Christmas morning experience as a Jewish kid growing up in Fairfield, Connecticut, could have. I respectfully waited for my dad by the basement door after breakfast, dying to see how the paint had dried.

I was nervous going down the stairs. Nervous that the glue wouldn't hold or the building would somehow have fallen from the workbench and smashed on the floor. I don't know if my dad was nervous, I just know that he didn't say anything either before turning on the light in his workshop.

The light caught the glossy black paint first—a shining monolith in a dusty basement. It stood eighteen inches tall—a jutting series of rectangles that from across the room looked like a building, not a collection of LEGO bricks.

"It came out nice, Davey," said my dad, using an affectionate nickname that was short for my middle name.

"Thanks, Dad," I said.

It was one of the happiest moments of my childhood, though I didn't realize it then. But one rarely recognizes the memories that will last at the time.

Over the next two years, I gradually began to let go of my interest in LEGO. This was my time for oversize tortoiseshell eyeglasses and Benetton sweatshirts with prominent cartoon bears— in short, I made a lot of poor choices. My uncle bought us an eight-bit Nintendo system for Hanukkah one year, and I stopped building spaceships in order to battle Koopa. I was a soccer goalie until the goalposts were increased to regulation size in fifth grade, leading me into a six-year dalliance with musical theater. I flirted with a lot of new loves. And by the time I kissed my first girlfriend, the blue LEGO tub had been left to slumber in the closet.

I had entered what is known to adult fans of LEGO as the Dark Ages, the period of time when you don't play with LEGO bricks. Millions of children are entering the Dark Ages right now. Most never reemerge. Our LEGO bricks are sold at garage sales or are left in those plastic buckets in the closets of our childhood homes. It's a phenomenon that even the corporate executives at the LEGO Group have recognized by actively separating their community relations efforts into two categories: people over and people under the age of thirteen. I let go a year too soon, and I probably was a few years late in getting back.

But you never completely leave LEGO bricks behind. How could you, when LEGO products are sold in 130 countries, when there are roughly sixty-two LEGO bricks for every person on the planet? LEGO has seeped into every element of our popular culture. Nintendo sells LEGO Star Wars, Batman, and Indiana Jones–themed video games. Michel Gondry used LEGO bricks in a stop-motion animation music video that helped launch the career of the White Stripes. The LEGO collection is even on display at the Museum of Modern Art in New York City, where it is celebrated as a dramatic accomplishment in design.

Over the past two decades, there have been small signs that my interest in LEGO was returning. I have sought compromises, like a binging dieter. A hooded sweatshirt adorned with a LEGO cowboy hangs in my closet. It's a recent addition to my wardrobe, discovered at a LEGO retail store in a New Jersey mall, where I decided that an adult sweatshirt—not toys—was the socially acceptable purchase. LEGO men—snuck into my pocket while cleaning out my childhood closet—hide like garden gnomes in my office. But it wasn't until I was preparing to move with my wife, Kate, from Brooklyn to Kansas City that I was struck by what I was leaving behind. My mom asked me to drive out to Fairfield, Connecticut, to clean out the closet of my childhood bedroom before I left for the Midwest, and it was then that I came across the blue plastic bucket with my name on it.

"Those are your LEGOs—you can't give those away. You loved them," said my mom.

I promised I would keep them for her as yet unborn grandchildren, and she left me to finish my task. I reached to the back of the closet where the Sears Tower still sat, diorama-style, in a blue shoebox. I picked it up.

Seeing the tower after all those years made me realize that I still do love LEGO. I love it for all those things I built, but also for what it meant to build things with my dad. That tower held within it one of my childhood dreams, the idea that I could join the ranks of LEGO master model builders—men and women who construct giant LEGO sculptures for department stores and theme parks. It's a dream I left in the closet next to blue tub.

At the time, I was writing an essay for *Women's Health* magazine about why men need deferred dreams in order to deal with real-life responsibilities. The memory of wanting to be a master builder prompted me to search online for those who earned their living with LEGO bricks. I was surprised by the vibrant community I found. These weren't just master builders; they were minifig customizers and LEGO car clubs that existed solely to build miniature hot rods with working doors and hoods—and they were a community of thousands. And then I discovered the things they built: a twenty-two-foot-long *Titanic*, a mosaic of the *Mona Lisa*, round spheres from rectangular bricks. These were artistic works of incredible size built by adults. I began to think that it might be okay for a guy with no kids to start playing with a toy again.

Adult LEGO fans all have had a moment of awakening, something that brought back their love of LEGO. This was mine. For a true fan of LEGO, the bricks can never be put away forever. People have built their entire careers, relationships, and lives around this toy. They have developed a language and commerce, all in celebration of pursuing a childhood passion together. And I wanted in to that world. I wanted to build like they build. I also wanted to recapture what I used to feel as a child, while building.

From that moment on, I've been ready to dive back into the childhood world that I left behind, to discover what happens to people who never leave that world. I want to know how people can form such complex relationships around a simple brick, and what it means to pursue your dream when the potential for financial gain or even solvency is remote. This means not just meeting adult fans, but playing with LEGO bricks alongside them.

I'll need my own toys, however, if I'm going to play together with others. I've discussed with Kate the need to fill our house with toy bricks, but I don't think she quite has an idea of just how many we're talking about, as I've kept the pictures of the types of collections that adult fans amass to myself.

There are only two slight issues. I don't have any LEGO bricks at my new house, and I don't know how to build with them. The first problem is easy to solve. I've got a credit card, and LEGO is conveniently available at toy stores and superstores.

Regarding the second problem, my wife's former college roommate, Abby, voices my own fears: "Kate is the urban planner who builds all the furniture."

She's right. During the time Kate and I have been together, I have attempted to build one desk and one bureau. After multiple instances of screwing in the unfinished side facing out, both projects required some emergency assistance from my wife.

Even Kate admits to some skepticism about what I might build. "I could see you having trouble with three-dimensional visualization. It would seem that imagining things in 3-D would be critical to building."

But this problem can be solved, too. I'll seek out talented builders, at conventions and online, to discover what it takes to master building techniques. And I choose to believe that my abilities haven't regressed with age. I played with LEGO bricks once, and what I made was good. LEGO doesn't change—the bricks today are the same as when I was ten—but I've changed, and the adult me is better equipped. I'm smarter and physically stronger. I can do this.

As I anticipate learning to build again, I feel excited that I'll see the extremes of adult builders, including the Toy and Plastic Brick Museum, one fan's multimillion brick collection of LEGO sculptures and artifacts set inside a former middle school. I'm compelled to learn how a tiny LEGO man is transformed into a tiny LEGO Iron Man and how the *Mona Lisa* is recreated in a brick mosaic.

And in the center of everything sits the LEGO Group—a toy-maker that in recent years has tried to figure out how to court a small but vocal adult audience. It is not lost on me that their U.S. corporate headquarters are in Enfield, Connecticut—my home state—so I'll be making a mandatory stop to build again with my dad. Not to mention that I'll be going to Denmark in an effort to understand the culture of LEGO, and taking Kate with me.

I've got a year to build, and anything is possible.

AFOLs Duane Collicott (left) and Joe Meno play with DUPLO bricks the day before Brick Bash 2008 in Ann Arbor, Michigan.

2

I Need a Playroom

Before I can build with LEGO again, I have another milestone to contend with—turning thirty. It's my birthday, March 22, and I'm on my third cupcake—one for each decade. I feel a little sick, but happy. Guilt doesn't come until the doorbell rings and my in-laws arrive with a suitcase-size box to find me on the couch with frosting on my sleeve and wrappers stacked neatly on a plate.

I offer them cupcakes, and they sensibly share one between them as they wait expectantly for me to open my gift. I tear open the green wrapping paper and sit back admiring the LEGO set I have asked for on this, my thirtieth birthday. I haven't been this excited since I was in the fourth grade and my parents told me I could have my birthday party at a bowling alley.

"Do you like it?" asks Ann, my mother-in-law.

"The Trade Federation MTT. This is awesome," I gush.

An oversize brown ship that holds sixteen Star Wars droids dominates the 1,362-piece set—the floating ship was the attack vehicle used by the droid army in *The Phantom Menace*. It's the first major set I've ever owned with a retail price of $99.99. It's the kind of present I didn't know I wanted until I saw it.

"I didn't know that they made sets that big," says my father-in-law, Bob.

I flip the box over on the ottoman, trying to keep the conversation going as I stare at the various pieces and minifigures included in the set. It's funny because while my in-laws are there, I can only focus on getting started with building. But once I'm by myself, I'm unsure how to start, and instead I make a big production of washing and putting away the dessert plates.

After they leave, I realize I'm intimidated by the size of the LEGO set in front of me. I carry the box upstairs to our spare bedroom and lean it against the wall.

It is the room most often skipped when we give guests the tour of our house. My wife and I have been trying to conceive for a few months, and someday this will be our child's room. But for now, wrinkled clothing sits forgotten on the ironing board, and both of us try not to spend much time in the empty space. I'm not sure if I'm leaving the set here because it is a room of uncertainty, or if I'm hoping it will serve as some sort of good luck totem. *If you set out toys, then babies will come.* As if children were just available in the wild, ready to be ensnared by my commerce-inspired trap. At the end of the day, I put the set in that room for one simple reason—it is where I put things that I don't want to think about.

It works. Nearly a week passes before I think about the set again. And by that time, I'm 750 miles away in Ann Arbor, Michigan, to meet Duane Collicott, who is hosting the first LEGO convention of the calendar year.

Six days after my thirtieth birthday, I'm pacing inside the entryway of the Four Points Sheraton, nervous about meeting an AFOL, an adult fan of LEGO. I wish that I had built the MTT Federation so I could have at least one accomplishment to casually mention. But instead, all I can do is pace. The sliding door has a motion sensor that I set off repeatedly. I look back guiltily at the front desk manager, who is not smiling. I take a seat in the wingback chair by the entryway.

A white minivan pulls up, piloted by Duane, forty-four, a computer software programmer wearing jeans and a red-striped shirt, and a pair of squared-off glasses. Reddish-brown hair sprouts in tufts around his bald crown. He jokingly refers to himself as the "number-one geek" in Ann Arbor, after a local news reporter recently found him online by doing a Google search for the word "geek." Duane has an offbeat sense of humor and the propensity to announce what he is going to do right before he does it.

"I'll just wait at this light here because we're never going to be able to make the turn," he tells me before we pull in for breakfast at the Coney, an Ann Arbor staple that is half diner, half hot dog stand. Over eggs and coffee, he tells me about Brick Bash, the LEGO convention he organized for the first time in 2005.

"There are two types of AFOLs. Those that want the public exposure and the chance to show off what they have built, and those that just want to have a hobbyist convention," says Duane.

"Which one are you?" I ask.

"Well, the public is invited to Brick Bash. Which one do you think?"

Duane came home burning with the idea after attending his first LEGO fan convention—the now defunct Chicago House of Bricks—in May 2005. It was there that he unveiled his first large sculpture, a thirteen-foot to-scale re-creation of the Maumee River Crossing Bridge (now known as the Veteran's Glass City Highway) in Toledo, Ohio.

"I started out with one table and then I just took over another," says Duane, describing how he laid out the 260 white segments that frame the main expanse of the bridge, which in real life has a span of 1,220 feet. The bridge model features LEGO rope for the cable suspensions and translucent bricks along the central column. A commitment to using only LEGO parts is important to many adult fans, those I would come to know as "purists."

Purists don't cut or paint bricks. They don't make their own stickers to add details. If LEGO doesn't make it, they're not using it. And with those limitations comes a perverse pride in figuring out how to creatively use what is available.

In Chicago, Duane discovered the world of purists, who shared tips on building and wanted to know about what he had built. He was also fascinated by the science fiction convention that shared event space with the LEGO enthusiasts. "I came across a woman dressed as a pirate wench by the vending machine. I was glad I didn't bring my son."

He returned to Ann Arbor determined to organize a gathering that year for local LEGO fans. The first Brick Bash attracted just over three hundred people. He's organized the convention for the past four years because he loves the feeling of a few hundred people crammed into a poorly air-conditioned room sharing their love for a little plastic brick. It's not always fun to build alone.

"I remember a time when my dad and I are hanging out. We're the last ones there at Boy Scout camp. I hate the feeling. It's like old newspapers—they have no purpose. I don't like being the only one left at a place after it's over," says Duane.

After breakfast, the work begins. We head about two miles west of the University of Michigan campus before Duane pulls his mini-van up in front of the Courthouse Square Apartments in downtown Ann Arbor. He briefly wonders out loud if a pick-up truck is going to pull away from the curb before we come to a stop.

Opening the rear door, Duane asks me to help him move the nine translucent tubs filled with LEGO pieces. I reach for a storage tub and briefly stagger under its weight. It will take several trips to unload the van.

"This is heavy," I tell Duane as the first beads of sweat roll down my neck. He just grins. We stack six tubs on a hand truck, which Duane wheels over a black mat with a floral print outside the building. The mat says, "Welcome home."

The Courthouse Square Apartments is an affordable housing community for seniors over fifty-five. We enter the foyer, and the hand truck wheels sluggishly move across the deep red carpet. A receptionist stands up and slides back the glass partition separating her office from the hall.

"You gonna do something with all those little pieces?" she asks, eyeing the tubs skeptically.

Duane nods and stops long enough to invite her to the event. In the elevator, he explains that Brick Bash has outgrown its previous two spaces. The library was too small. The university was too expensive. The ballroom on the second floor of the Courthouse Square Apartments was priced right at $750 and was available.

The minivan unloaded, we leave for the airport to pick up Joe Meno, a fellow AFOL who is flying in from Raleigh, North Carolina. A short Asian man with glasses walks out of the sliding doors at Detroit Metropolitan Airport. A cell phone is clipped to his belt via a red case that resembles a LEGO brick. His white polo shirt matches his classic white sneakers. A graduate of the North Carolina State School of Design, he has dreamed of designing sets for science fiction movies and even had a six-week stint as an employee at a LEGO retail store. If Duane is a PC, Joe is a Mac.

This is the editor of *BrickJournal*, the magazine for adult fans of LEGO. One of his suitcases is full of the glossy magazines, which he intends to sell at the convention. I will buy one for $7, a discount off the $8.95 newsstand price.

Duane tells me right before Joe comes out of the airport that they've only seen each other in person a handful of times. I had wondered if adult fans would have difficulty interacting face-to-face, when so much of the community is dependent on online interaction. But they fall into an easy conversation on the ride back to the Courthouse Square Apartments.

The tubs we brought up earlier to the ballroom need to be unpacked; Duane turns over the first tub, and DUPLO bricks—LEGO elements intended for the toddler set—crash onto a six-foot wooden fold-out table in a primary-colored splash of noise.

"Imposter!" Duane shouts as he pulls a MEGA Bloks brick out of the pile. The popular plastic toys are manufactured by MEGA Brands, Incorporated, the main competitor to LEGO, based in Montreal, Canada. He keeps snatching up pieces and tossing them to the floor.

"How do you know?" I ask, fiddling with an oversize green brick.

"You can feel the difference, and when you drop it, it makes a different sound," says Duane as he drops a MEGA Blok and DUPLO piece in quick succession. I'm reminded of wind resistance experiments.

"MEGA Bloks sound hollow," says Joe.

The mixing of MEGA Bloks and LEGO is one of the major pet peeves of adult fans of LEGO. It's a common problem when you're buying at a garage sale or on eBay. The average person doesn't differentiate between the products because they technically can stack together and are interchangeable. But to an AFOL, it's like mixing premium goods with a generic store label, devaluing the rigorous quality control standards of the LEGO Group.

Duane continues to root out the offending blocks, while Joe and I unconsciously begin to snap together DUPLO bricks.

I stack together six bricks in rapid succession, excited to have built what I believe resembles an alligator. I hold it up to Joe and Duane.

"Very nice," says Joe, in the manner of a parent who is unsure what his child has built but wants to encourage him to keep building. Joe holds up what he has been working on for the past few minutes. It's a Tyrannosaurus Rex, made from the oversize child bricks.

"Wow," I exclaim, "that's awesome." I suddenly have the vocabulary and hero worship complex of a twelve-year-old.

Joe and Duane begin opening other translucent tubs, all of which are filled with various LEGO products. I continue to stack together DUPLO bricks in the hopes of building something that will impress the two men I have just met.

I am fully aware that I am building poorly with a product that was once known as LEGO Preschool. DUPLO bricks are twice the height, length, and width of a traditional LEGO brick. This makes them easier for small children to hold, and reduces the possibility that they'll swallow one. I guess I can consider it a small victory that thus far I can hold them and have managed not to choke myself. DUPLO appeared in 1969 with the recognizable configuration of two rows of four studs each— the classic LEGO standard of a 2 × 4. In true modular fashion, LEGO bricks can be stacked on DUPLO bricks.

"Bionicles," says Duane from across the room as a white top burps open. "I got them cheap because nobody else wants them." He is sitting cross-legged on the ballroom's thick carpet.

Joe lifts a second cover. *"Ehh . . ."* A small sigh of disgust escapes him. "It's such a fundamentally different building style. But it saved LEGO's butt."

The Bionicle line was introduced in Europe in 2000, and in the United States a year later. It's science-fictionesque, based on creatures that are part mechanical, part organic. It's the first LEGO line that comes with back stories and is actually registered as a separate intellectual property. Bionicle pieces aren't considered part of the LEGO system, since they can't always be snapped together with basic LEGO bricks. They seem like cooler versions of Transformers to me.

When I look over, Joe continues, "It's not studs. The building is based on ball joints." The heads and arms are all attached via circular plastic pieces the size of bullets in a pellet gun. Joe quickly builds a spiky red robot that he stands on a wooden table.

I hold up a yellow triangle that I have attached to red DUPLO bricks. "It's Pizza Hut," I joke. Joe and Duane laugh politely and I feel like a little brother who is about to be left behind by his older brother and friends.

A few hours later, I'm sitting across from Joe on the living room carpet at Duane's house. I'm struck by the absence of LEGO bricks in what amounts to an ordinary living room. A few coats lie on a wooden bench next to a comfortable couch and an easy chair. Joe is busy shaking LEGO pieces out of the T-shirt they were wrapped in inside his suitcase. They are the remains of a miniature laser of the type that would have been operated by the James Bond villain Dr. No. Joe had constructed the tiny laser as part of a villain's lair using LEGO pieces, even inserting an aftermarket series of LED lights that flashed rhythmically on and off. The Transportation Security Administration officials at Raleigh-Durham Airport were understandably concerned about the small flashing weapon in his luggage. It certainly appeared at least as dangerous as three ounces of liquid. The tiny laser is now in pieces, pulled apart by an overzealous airport screener who was not convinced that Joe's vignette depicting the evil lair of a Bond villain was harmless.

Duane kneels alongside us as Joe separates out the parts. He is excited to rebuild, trying to remember how everything went together. I would be apoplectic. When Duane hesitates to play, Joe encourages him.

"Go ahead, nothing is stopping you." Duane nods and picks up the tiny weapon. *"Pew, pew,"* he intones, the universal sound of a laser being fired.

Joe smiles as he reworks the base of the computer platform that "controls" the laser. He snaps on what he believes is the final piece, until he discovers an errant 1×4 plate. He has no blueprints. He is just building from memory. I watch his fingers work and notice that he confidently snaps together plates, even if moments later he changes his mind and breaks them apart. After a few minutes, he places the extra plate in his suitcase, satisfied with his makeshift fix.

Duane mentions casually that we might be able to go to Toys "R" Us after dinner, as his wife, Allison, peeks in from the kitchen and shakes her head slightly.

"Can we go to Toys "R" Us?" asks Joe.

"Please, please," I beg. I'm sort of joking, but I also really want to go and buy LEGO. I will have to settle for visiting Duane's personal collection. Just off the living room and down a flight of stairs in the ranch-style home is a cozy family room. It looks closer to what I imagined his living room would look like. Duane's younger son, Benjamin, is playing a video game on the LEGO Web site where you attempt to navigate your character through a series of obstacles in a Donkey Kong–like game. The games on LEGO's Web site are the only video games that Duane allows in his home.

"We don't have video games in the house. I really try to avoid them. In the summer or after school, when we hear there's nothing to do, the kids always end up picking up LEGO bricks," says Duane, who almost flunked out of Eastern Michigan University because of the video game Missile Command, which proved significantly more interesting than his classwork.

Plastic tubs line the wood-paneled far wall, and a table is covered with gray bricks as Duane's other son, William, a skinny ten-year-old with a shock of blond hair like his brother Benjamin's, feverishly works to finish his moon base for display at the convention in the morning. The moon base is under attack, and a host of spacecraft in bright red need to be completed as part of the scene.

I begin to wonder if there is a LEGO genetic connection. Are we destined to build what our fathers built? It was Benjamin and William who rekindled Duane's love for LEGO. When the boys were younger—two and four—the Collicotts bought a few DUPLO sets.

"I remember I was playing with the kids. I made a little boat out of DUPLO. I started to remember the aircraft carrier I had built as a kid, and the boat wasn't enough. I wasn't satisfied. It was then that I began to wonder if my mom still had the box," says Duane.

She did, and she shipped Duane the twenty-pound box, the kind that holds printer paper, filled to the brim with LEGO bricks. Not long after it arrived, Duane was in the living room with his two boys building a Space Needle out of every piece they had. But it still wasn't enough. That was when the idea for the bridge came about.

That need to acquire more pieces is easy to understand. A LEGO collection is quantifiable. You can physically see how many bricks you own. As I wander through the den, I start to think I'm not that different from Duane, because he doesn't appear to have that big a collection.

Then he calls me into the laundry room, and I see where the LEGO pieces are hiding. The left half of the cramped space is dominated by a series of wooden shelves. Plastic tubs the size of shoe boxes stretch six feet across and eight feet high. Pieces are sorted by color and element type. And just then he removes a section of the wall, across from the laundry machine.

"You have to see this," says Duane.

The four-foot-wide opening reveals a crawl space off the laundry room. Duane gets on his hands and knees, and as he disappears into the dark, I wonder if he's going to end up in John Malkovich's head, the size of the void being similar to the portal in *Being John Malkovich*.

Duane emits a small grunt, and a translucent box slides out onto the carpet: Duane's still with us. This is his other large project, the *M/V Stewart J. Cort*. He has constructed a nine-foot container ship, a scale model of the bulk freighter that plied the waters of the Great Lakes. There are thousands of pieces—and dollars—invested in the massive red boat.

"I'm using my brain beyond LEGO, especially with the scale modeling. You have to find a way to try and build the thing without using parts that are rare or cost a buck apiece," says Duane, gesturing to the overfilled racks behind me.

As nine sections come sliding out, Duane tells me the history of the real ship built in Mississippi. How it sailed up the Atlantic Ocean and Saint Lawrence Seaway in 1972 until it was cut apart in Erie, Pennsylvania, to be combined with seventeen midsection compartments.

The completed ship was one thousand feet long, destined to remain on the Great Lakes—too big for the locks on the Welland Canal. It makes Duane think about his great-grandfather, who worked the iron ore mines in northwest Minnesota after emigrating from Sweden, since iron ore was the main load carried by the first thousand-foot ice cutter on the Great Lakes.

But Duane's scale-model LEGO creation is ballroom-locked, destined to be whole only when it is on display at a convention. The nine-foot model always travels in sections. It is too big to display in his house, so it sits in modular pieces, the inner cargo hold built in the same fashion as the *Stewart J. Cort*, waiting to be connected. Duane will finish assembling it in the morning over at Brick Bash.

"I have a friend who is a magician. You don't make money with magic, but you do get to perform. I guess this is a little bit for the ego, and I guess I just have to get onstage once in a while," says Duane as he replaces the panel in front of the crawl space.

Duane admits that he usually doesn't even keep the ship and bridge in the house. A friend lets him use office storage space.

"How many bricks do you have?" I blurt out, unaware that this is the single most annoying question to adult fans. It's akin to asking someone how much money he makes.

"I don't honestly know. Not that many," says Duane. "But there is a guy with over a million bricks in his basement and garage in Columbus, Ohio. And you'll see guys buy literally pallets of sets after they go on sale at LEGO.com to sell to other fans."

The suggestion that Duane might have a relatively small collection floors me. I have one tub under my desk and a Star Wars set I'm ignoring. I thought that was a decent amount. I was wrong. He has two rooms half-filled with LEGO bricks and a crawl space stuffed with boxes, and he still needs a separate storage space.

This is what it means to be an adult fan. The slow, bloblike takeover of your home with tiny LEGO bricks that use up more room than I could have imagined. It is one thing to say that someone has a collection of hundreds of thousands of bricks; it's another to see that you need a few hundred square feet to store them properly. My thoughts turn to the empty third bedroom in our house and what kind of shelving might work. I know that Kate will suggest that the unfinished basement would be a better option. I don't need a man cave—I need a playroom.

"Purple" Dave Laswell stands behind his LEGO Millennium Falcon. It took him eighteen hours and forty-five minutes to build the 5,195-piece set, and that's a fast build.

3

My First Con

In the space of one day, I've met my first AFOL, seen his build room, and learned what it takes to set up a convention. But it wasn't always this easy to find fellow adult fans of LEGO, in part because guys like Duane represent the first generation of adult fans. For the initial three decades that LEGO produced bricks, the idea that a child's toy might become a touchstone for a grown-up community wasn't on the radar of the LEGO Group. Certainly nobody thought that kids would keep playing with their LEGO sets into adulthood.

The LEGO plastic brick debuted in 1958. By today's definition, the first "adult" fan (born the same year the brick was patented) technically couldn't have existed before 1971, since the LEGO Group differentiates between child and adult consumers at the age of thirteen. When you factor in the Dark Ages, that period when people's interest in LEGO goes dormant, and the time it takes for a toy to work its way into the culture, it becomes clear why the concept of adult fans doesn't appear until 1995. And even then, you'll find just a casual mention via an online newsgroup.

Initially, AFOLs were simply people who had an interest in talking about different LEGO sets, similar to Mustang or Coca-Cola enthusiasts. These connections were as much about the novelty of being able to chat with someone on their computer as they were about LEGO.

AFOLs gathered on the early ancestors of today's social media world: newsgroups. The first LEGO discussion board for adults was a text-based Usenet discussion group found at alt.toys.lego (referred to as ATL). It still exists today as a combination of actual discussion and spam messages. But then it provided a chance to share thoughts with people who might be kindred spirits. It was a place to speculate about the inner workings of LEGO and discuss upcoming product lines.

"I have this theory that lego is organized into several teams of designers, each working on a line. Every few years (say 3) the teams' new line comes out," wrote Paul Gyugyi on December 1, 1993.

But it wasn't until 1994 that the first inkling of a community appeared, when several active members of ATL formed rec.toys .lego (RTL for short). In contrast to the early discussions, where single posts lingered without a response for months, RTL users seemingly awoke to the idea that people could begin trading LEGO sets and even selling peer-to-peer. Perhaps more important, RTL gave birth to the "adult fan of LEGO." Jeff Thompson is credited with introducing the term in a post about the hobby on June 13, 1995. A day later, Matthew Verdier introduced the acronym "AFOL" (pronounced *eh-fall* or *ay-foal*).

"Anyone else notice this is an acronym of sorts. AFOL (Sounds like 'A FOOL') sorta like Adult Children of Alcoholics," posted Verdier.

RTL developed into a hybrid between a discussion board and an online marketplace. LEGO fans alerted one another to sales and talked about what sets were available at which retailers, in an attempt to make up for the company's fragmented distribution network in North America at the time. The users seemed to mirror the same professional types drawn to most newsgroups initially: male science heads with access to the Internet. In these early messages, there are plenty of references to software programming and e-mail addresses that correspond to labs, even NASA programs.

"This group almost restores my faith in humanity. And that's saying alot. . . . I think we can honestly say that it won't expand too much too rapidly, I mean look at us. We paragons, we know Lego is the coolest thing to hit earth and everyone else just thinks it's a silly plastic building block. They may never catch on. Which is fine because it means more Lego for us!!!!!" Jeff Hunt wrote on August 26, 1995.

But as it became more popular, RTL also became unwieldy. The posts were all kept on a single page, and the board was self-policed. Many fans seeking to talk about LEGO were frustrated that buying and selling now dominated the discussion. So adult fans Todd Lehman and Suzanne Rich Green launched a new online forum, the LEGO Users Group Network. LUGNET went live on September 28, 1998, and was specifically targeted to adults.

"We'd like to see an alternative area on the net that people can call home, and where they can have the opportunity to return to smaller focus groups but still be able to wander out into the greater community for a fresh change of scenery. I love RTL, but I think it's outgrown itself," Lehman posted the day after the launch.

LUGNET was the first community explicitly for AFOLs online. Members had to be over eighteen, as opposed to the earlier open message boards, which featured comments from computer-savvy pre-teens alongside those of older adult fans. LUGNET offered users the opportunity to create individual pages where they could display structures and sculptures they had built free-form. These constructions

were not based on sets provided by LEGO, but were instead called
my own creation (or simply MOC). The site was also broken down
into user groups, so fans could find information based on their
interests in building or find fellow users in their area.

Today LEGO estimates that there are a hundred active user
groups with twenty thousand registered fans online. From them
has sprung a proliferation of blogs and forums based on building themes such as space or castles. LUGNET is no longer the
center of the adult fan universe, but the threads it contains read
like a history of the important moments in the community's
development.

The Internet is where the heart of the AFOL community initially was found. But as users began to organize, they discovered
fellow fans in their local areas, and they started to connect offline,
often forming LEGO user groups (LUGs). Social events led to collaborative displays, where several fans would combine their structures to build, say, a Christmas scene in a mall or a local library.
Groups also began to form around members' building interests.
LEGO train enthusiasts formed LEGO train clubs (LTCs). These
were similar to model-train clubs in that the track was modular
and fans were able to build together in the same scale.

As various groups began to meet regularly, their discussions
turned toward organizing a convention for AFOLs. In 2000,
Christina Hitchcock, a member of the Washington Metropolitan
Area LEGO Users Group, decided to organize BrickFest. And that
August, sixty people came to the first convention, held on the
campus of George Washington University in Arlington, Virginia,
to talk about their love of LEGO.

Nearly eight years later, all of these resources were available
to me when I began searching for upcoming LEGO events in
February 2008. I found Duane's Brick Bash within ten minutes,
and was booked to go out on a plane not a week later. I was on my
way to Ann Arbor before I even really knew what to expect.

"You ready for the convention?" I ask Duane, a question I've
asked myself several times already.

"It's not actually a convention, it's a public display," he corrects me. When I raise my eyebrows, he continues. "Conventions are for adult fans. We get to interact and learn outside of being around the public. Public displays are about educating the public, showing them what we do."

There is a bit of "us" and "them" in what Duane says—something I don't immediately realize, as I still fall into the "them" category. Conventions, like BrickFest, are about getting together with other fans, learning new building techniques or debating the state of the community during lectures and seminars. Some feature "display" days, when the public is invited in for a few hours. This is often done to subsidize the cost of the event space, to please sponsors like LEGO, and to let adult fans (those who want to) have a few hours to show off to the public. Brick Bash, on the other hand, just focuses on the public and so doesn't fall under the rubric of a convention, although a few adult fans have come to set up a display or help Duane organize.

It's Saturday morning, and the function room at the retirement community downtown has been transformed. Underneath fantastic gold chandeliers straight out of Tony Montana's mansion, close to fifteen hundred people will come to see LEGO sculptures and let their children build something out of the giant piles of bricks that rest atop six-foot-long folding tables. A ring of buildings and MOCs are set up around the room.

The doors to Brick Bash open at 11 a.m., and within fifteen minutes the room is filled with more than a hundred visitors. LEGO pieces hit the red floral rug immediately. The boys I see in the ballroom at the Courthouse Square Senior Apartments look like I did when I was thirteen. They are too serious and wear glasses and have atrocious haircuts. They don't talk. They're too busy snapping together LEGO bricks.

The bricks have been put out for a simple reason. When you see LEGO pieces, you want to play with them. And since adult fans don't want people touching what they've built, it's often easier to provide an open play area. It seems to be a concession to the fact that although AFOLs have put together the show, the main audience seeing their creations and playing with the toys is children. Plus, this is a family event, in part designed to attract the next generation of adult fans.

As I watch the kids build, I notice that they tend to stack bricks directly on top of each other. That's a sensible approach to building. It's what I've done to start. The nubs on top of the LEGO bricks, known as studs, fit directly inside the tubes, the hollow cylinders on the bottom of each piece. That's how the design works; it's the reason that LEGO bricks stick together. But when I watched Duane and Joe build the night before at Duane's house, I noticed that they staggered and overlapped bricks to form new shapes or create a more stable creation.

I start snapping bricks together. I didn't think building would be hard, but the moment I realize that I'm stacking bricks like a two-year-old, I begin to rethink my method. A lot of time has passed since I last built, and I am reminded of the time my wife took me skiing. I hadn't been on skis in a decade. As tiny children in parkas snowplowed past me lying in a heap on the bunny hill, I began to think I had passed my prime.

Here there's a table where the kids will have a chance to display what they've built, along with a small card giving the description and their name and age. A blond teen who looks about twelve gets up and fills out his card. His creation is a mechanized robot in yellow and white with translucent yellow eyes and triangular yellow limbs that end in claws. It's very cool. I'm screwed.

Two mothers in their mid-to-late thirties stand a few feet away from the table. Their conversation naturally turns to LEGO.

"She's just turning three, she doesn't play with LEGO anymore," says the shorter woman in a blouse and jeans.

"Our whole basement is LEGO," says her counterpart in a green sundress. I don't think she's exaggerating.

"It's like that when they're in that creative stage of their childhood," says the shorter mom.

"Well, he's an artist, or he will be."

This is why mothers and fathers never throw away the LEGO bricks that their children loved. It occurs to me that those bricks might in some way represent the potential that you always want to see in your kid. The possibility that he or she will be a famous artist or politician grows smaller as they get older, but a part of that dream can be kept if you just don't give away the tub of primary-color blocks. Thinking about my own potential is mildly depressing, but I latch on to the idea of possibility because I need to believe that I can become better at building.

Some parents are doing more than just watching. A father is enthusiastically handing his daughter DUPLO bricks. She is determined to build a tower as tall as his lanky, six-foot frame. Halfway through the process, she has to stand on a chair to continue stacking. With one hand on her waist, the father steadies her and helps her build. They finish the tower, and they hug. I suddenly understand why my wife wants to have a baby. I like the idea of building with my daughter, experiencing the joy of watching her succeed with my help. And I wonder if there is ever tension for people who don't have kids and yet are playing with a toy that is firmly in the world of children. I don't have to wonder long.

It's around this time that I spot Purple Dave for the first time. Dave Laswell is a member of the Michigan LEGO Users Group. Dave has a Batman minifig on his nameplate, the tiny cape custom-built in Australia.

He is tall, but not imposing. A thick brown beard makes it hard to follow his words, and he absently touches a black fanny pack when he talks. He likes attaching strategy and story lines to what he builds. He is also a founding member of the Web site Mask of Destiny, a LEGO Bionicle fan site. True to his nickname, he is wearing a purple shirt.

He's standing in front of the Millennium Falcon—the LEGO set with one of the highest piece counts and prices of any set built to date. It is a Star Wars collector's dream and something Dave is likely to own, considering that he remembers falling asleep in the theater during the first Star Wars movie as a kid. Dave tells me about the build. He took Friday off work to run errands and take delivery of the set. It weighs forty pounds, shipped. That left Saturday and Sunday to snap together over five thousand pieces. Eighteen hours, forty-five minutes of building.

A man standing near the table leans over to talk to his son at a volume that I'm sure Dave can hear: "These are the kinds of guys that move their LEGOs one piece at time." The man is bronzed and wearing loafers without socks below expensive jeans—Ann Arbor's version of George Hamilton. He ignores a small hand-lettered sign that asks people not to touch the ringed binder of instructions. I want to slap his hand.

"Please, don't touch that," Dave says, a bit of strain creeping into his voice. Dave addresses his next comment to me. "It was already creased in the mail and I don't want it to get bent further."

The bronzed man moves away with his son, and I'm glad for Dave. This is the first bit of tension I have witnessed, and it's made me uncomfortable. I can see that Dave is struggling with wanting to display what he has built and yet not wanting someone to ruin all his effort by carelessly snapping off a piece or devaluing what he sees as an economic investment.

LEGO tends to make people happy. There is a pleasant buzz of conversation in the room.

But this interaction stands out. It's what sometimes happens when adult fans of LEGO come into contact with the public. Builders are faced with an endless litany of the same questions. In fact, every time I walk by Dave, I hear someone asking one of three questions. *How many pieces is the Millennium Falcon?* 5,195 elements. *How long did it take you to build it?* Two full days. *How much does it cost?* Five hundred dollars.

This is the holy trinity, and it would drive me crazy. How many? How much? How long? I immediately resolve to stop asking those questions right off the bat. In time, I'll learn that the number of hours in a build doesn't really mean anything, and not all pieces deserve equal weight.

At the end of the day, the convention is all but over and most of the crowd has left. Duane's wife, Allison, is absentmindedly grabbing bricks off the floor and tables while Duane wanders the room like an attentive maître d'. Underneath the DUPLO table, a sandy-haired four-year-old pushes a train that is ten cars long along the floor. He keeps getting it stuck around one of the table legs. I want to help until I realize that's the game.

The Michigan Lego Users Group is breaking down their town and train set. Train tracks ring the building display, which features landmarks from downtown Detroit as well as Pepsi and ACME manufacturing plants. Car models are removed and placed in storage tubs with streetlights, but the buildings are kept intact when possible. Chris Leach, the group's treasurer, has helped plan the layout of the club's display. He has close-cropped hair and an easy laugh that he lets go as he wheels a handcart full of train tracks. I offer to help Chris, and pick up a section of his four-foot tan building. The piece covers most of my chest.

"I wouldn't carry that down," says Joe, watching from a few feet away. "It has no internal bracing." LEGO buildings operate just like real skyscrapers. The higher they're built, the more support they need. As with any construction project, those internal bricks still cost money, so these buildings have been built without support beams. They can be broken down and built back up faster, but as a result are a bit wobbly when taken off a baseplate.

As if in response to his words, I feel the building sway inside my arms and realize that I am very close to dropping somebody else's creation. Even worse, I would have no idea how to rebuild it. I take short steps and tilt the building back slightly on my chest while riding downstairs in the elevator. It doesn't drop, but I don't volunteer to help carry anything else.

I walk back upstairs and see Joe standing next to a folding table near the front entrance. He's casually tearing apart the Bionicle creations from the day. I rip the head off a red figure and toss it back into the tub by Joe's feet. Everything has to be cleaned up before Duane can go home for the night.

I find Duane next to his oversize white bridge sculpture, carefully filing away the papers that explain the history and construction of the Veteran's Glass City Highway.

"Nobody ever actually sees how a bridge is made. But when the project manager of a bridge is giving a tour, they say that it went together like a bunch of LEGO bricks. People use that analogy all the time," says Duane as he stoops every few feet to collect a brick from the carpet.

"Everybody can snap together a piece of LEGO," I reply.

"Right, but some of us just can't stop," says Duane.

I smile, but that sentence runs over and over in my head on the plane ride back to Kansas City.

The first MOC (my own creation) I built, a delivery truck half the size of a stapler. It can only get better from here.

4

Stealing from a Thief

After returning from Brick Bash, I discover that a new stash of LEGO bricks is only another closet away. This closet happens to belong to my youngest brother-in-law, Sam, who is twenty-four. The closet in his childhood bedroom looks just like anyone's who has gone to college and not returned. In other words, it's an unorganized mess. My mother-in-law, Ann, helps me find the oversize blue storage tub, the kind typically reserved for sweater storage.

A musty scent burps up from the container as I pry loose the lid. It's not unpleasant—sort of a cousin to the dry skin odor that creeps into your grandparents' home. I figure that the tub hasn't been opened in at least a decade, so I'm curious to find out what's inside. There are thousands of LEGO bricks in every color, along with artifacts of the nineties: New Kids on the Block stickers, clear plastic Game Boy game cases, and Matchbox cars that change color.

A few days later, as my wife and I sift through the tub in our own living room, we discover interlopers among the bricks— plastic pieces that resemble LEGO, but are of inferior quality.

"You could always tell which ones were fake," says Kate. "They never snapped together right and they would never come loose from a real brick."

We also find disembodied minifigure parts—heads, torsos, limbs, and their minifig accessories. We start playing like children.

"Aah!" screams Kate in mock horror as she holds up a disembodied head from a LEGO minifigure.

"Aah!" I cringe as she waves the severed head.

"Here. I'll just put him on a body. Give him a helmet for protection."

"Right." I look at the torso to which she's attaching the yellow head. "But he still doesn't have any arms."

I dig down into the tub, but instead of arms, I find a large dried brown stain lurking on the bottom. I'm silently glad that LEGO bricks can be put in the dishwasher. I close the top and decide to ask my brother-in-law Sam if he has any idea about the origin of the stain. I e-mail him to ask if I have his permission to play with his LEGOs, and I'm surprised by his answer.

"No," he says, and I wonder if I was wrong to take them.

"What I mean to say is that I can't give you permission. The bricks belong to Ben. They shouldn't have been in my closet," admits Sam.

I have stolen from a thief. I reach my other brother-in-law, Ben, who seems surprised that their mom kept the bricks. He gives me his blessing, and I promise that he can have them back anytime. I make the promise only because I know he'll never ask for them back.

Now that I have loose bricks in the house, I feel compelled to build. I pull a few LEGO wheels from the tub and settle on attempting a delivery truck. I figure the boxy right angles will be easy, since most bricks are rectangular.

The wheels quickly snap together, connected by square 2×2 bricks. After that, I'm a bit lost. My dog, Charlie, sleeps fitfully on the couch next to me as I mutter continuously under my breath. I'm not even aware that I am talking until she gives a brief howl and sneezes before turning over to show me her belly.

Ben's bricks are close to two decades old, and they stick together. My fingernails aren't long enough to split apart pieces when I change my mind, and it's embarrassing that I don't possess the necessary finger strength to separate two plates, the flat LEGO pieces. I've resorted to using my teeth—a method that appears to have been tried by one of my brothers-in-law, based on the tooth marks at the corner of several bricks. I officially possess as much ingenuity as an eight-year-old.

Even though the truck is only four inches long, I continually tear it apart to try to make it stronger and simpler; hence, the muttering. I opt for an open-air door, reminiscent of a UPS truck, and apparently my LEGO driver will have to settle for some sort of telepathic method of steering and braking. The truck looks awful—and that's an improvement after three hours of construction.

I prepare to take a few pictures of my first creation. As my left hand reaches for the digital camera, my right hand inadvertently slaps the truck from my desk onto the floor below. The three-foot fall shatters the truck into an impressive number of pieces. It's small, so thankfully rebuilding only takes about twenty minutes. But I learn a lesson: Always photograph something before you move it.

In an effort to further build my collection, I head over to the local Target. I'm a lone, unshaven man in the toy section, and I attract a lot of attention. Mothers look at me questioningly, and several of the sales staff hover close by—to answer questions, whether

I have them or not. It probably doesn't help that I've been standing in the middle of the aisle for the past fifteen minutes, my mouth hanging slightly open as I try to mentally process how many choices LEGO is offering to the customers of Kansas City.

I happen to have been born in an important year for LEGO. In 1978, the company introduced a number of different sets based on two play themes: space and castle. The concept was to produce sets that, if purchased together, allowed the user to construct an entire world out of LEGO. Each box was part of a story—for example, a castle keep that could be set up next to soldiers attacking with a catapult. And within those themes, the minifigure (the iconic yellow LEGO man) appeared for the first time. But as a seven-year-old playing with LEGO bricks, I was unaware that the space police were an innovative concept less than a decade old. I just liked that they had translucent shields on their helmets.

This store has four shelves, fifteen feet in length, filled with LEGO Star Wars ships, SpongeBob SquarePants rockets, and the familiar blue buckets of assorted parts. I lift boxes and read the parts included, as focused as any child making his Christmas wish list. But I walk away without a set because I have no better idea of what I want to build than when I entered the aisle. I also experience a bit of sticker shock. The cheapest kit at Target is $4.99, but most fall somewhere between $39.99 and $149.99.

That might explain why LEGO pieces and sets don't often end up in garage sales. Sunk costs and sentimentality make pack rats of us all. So I don't have high expectations when I agree to accompany my wife to tag sales in our neighborhood the following weekend, despite her claims that "they might have LEGO."

Five garage sales later, and the closest thing I have seen to a toy is a jigsaw puzzle depicting Big Ben. The final stop doesn't look any more promising, with rusted-out lawn furniture being picked over by the latecomers to an estate sale just three blocks from our house. We first enter the garage, where a portly man in an ill-fitting cowboy hat is testing a handheld chainsaw. We don't linger. When my wife hesitantly asks, "Do you want to go in the house?" I say yes.

Inside we encounter close to twenty people milling around, picking carelessly through a lifetime's worth of collections. TWA prints and model cars are stacked haphazardly on folding tables. The stale air and pink carpet leave me feeling claustrophobic, but like someone bewildered in a blazing home, I wander away from the front door and head further inside the house. Clothes and price tags hang from furniture bunched together to leave narrow aisles that lead into the two bedrooms on the first floor.

"Plenty more upstairs!" declares the marker-stained sheet of paper taped onto the yellowing wallpaper. The temperature rises as we climb up to a wood-slatted top floor with a finished bedroom. My wife and I thread our way to the back of the attic, where another couple is testing the integrity of caned wooden chairs by repeatedly banging them into the floor.

I'm ready to pack it in, as I feel the first small bead of sweat form at the base of my neck. But then my wife says a magic word.

"Look honey, LEGOs."

Pluralizing the word "LEGO" is one of the most common mistakes made by the average mom buying a set or the dad talking about his kids. It is also one of the largest pet peeves of adult fans. AFOL Eric Harshbarger, a renowned LEGO mosaic builder who constructed a LEGO portrait of the actor Dean Cain atop a billboard on Sunset Boulevard for Ripley's Believe It or Not in 2003, explains the proper usage of the term on his Web site.

"The word 'LEGO,' when used as a noun, should only refer to the company that makes the product. Otherwise 'LEGO' is supposed to be used as an adjective. Thus, when referring to the pieces, neither 'lego' nor 'legos' is correct . . . rather one should say: 'LEGO bricks' or 'LEGO pieces.' "

I ignore that Kate has inappropriately pluralized the toy as I bend down to see a briefcase-size box containing four different LEGO sets: pull-back racers (the kind that are propelled by a buildup of tension), two Star Wars boxes, and an oversize container for Mars Mission—which features a series of interconnected tubes and LEGO aliens. The box promises over seven hundred pieces altogether, and has a $15 price tag on it. I immediately back away and pretend to be uninterested. The couple continues to smash the chairs into the attic floor. *Bang*. I squat down for a closer look at the LEGO box while telling my wife I probably am not going to buy it. *Bang.* This is what I do when I really want something. It's as if I'm negotiating with an invisible vendor. *Bang.* But in truth, my mind is whirring as I consider what will happen when I take it home.

I snatch up the oversize box and my heart races. Three minutes later we walk out into the cloudy afternoon $16 poorer—$15 for the LEGO sets, and $1 for a glass pitcher adorned with dinosaurs. My return to childhood is complete.

When rain starts to fall, we pack it in and head home, where I set about examining my haul on the ottoman in the living room, divvying up the pieces like Halloween candy. I now own two Ewok minifigs and a Chewbacca. In celebration, I utter Chewbacca's throaty animal cry of emotion, which makes our dog, Charlie, come running. I next pull out a light gray brick the size of my remote with two red buttons and what appears to be a USB port. I am stumped as to what it is.

I e-mail Duane a photograph of it, and he responds immediately with a series of links that describe the Technic nine-volt motor. Technic debuted in 1977 as the Expert Builder series (the name changed in 1984). As one might guess, it was designed for advanced builders, with lights and movable parts in working machines that had gears and motors. I click through the links and thereby discover the online marketplace of BrickLink, where millions of new and used LEGO bricks are bought and sold.

The "unofficial LEGO marketplace," according to the site's slogan, BrickLink.com is eBay for the AFOL community, and I am visitor 28,733,814. This is where the collectors and builders have come to shop since it opened its virtual doors in 2000 as Brickbay.

BrinkLink actually made national headlines in 2005, when William Swanberg, a Nevada resident and online seller, was charged with fencing stolen LEGO sets on the auction site. He allegedly used a barcode switch scheme in toy stores across the Pacific Northwest, tagging more expensive sets like the Millennium Falcon with cheaper bar codes, and then reselling the sets online at close to the true retail price. In just three years, he sold approximately $600,000 worth of LEGO bricks.

When I mention Swanberg's story to Duane, he says Swanberg was a big seller on BrickLink, even volunteering as an inventory administrator, cataloging the parts in sets.

"Sure, I bought some parts from him," says Duane.

"Really? What was he like?" I ask.

"Just another seller. He sent me what I ordered."

I'm not sure I believe him until I look at the feedback records for Swanberg and see Duane's account pop up three times in 2005. "Great deal. Thanks, I'll be back!" Duane wrote in April. Swanberg was arrested seven months later, pleading guilty to three counts of felony theft and receiving thirteen months in prison. U.S postal inspector agents had to rent a twenty-foot moving truck to haul away the evidence.

While reading about Swanberg on my desktop, I'm absent-mindedly snapping together white and black bricks. I'm using primarily 2×2 bricks (two studs wide by two studs long) to build what ends up looking like a two-humped camel. It's four studs wide with a slope for a head and yellow feet. It rests on my desk, and when my wife gets home she compliments me on what I've built. I smile, but don't reveal my secret. I, like balloon animal hacks everywhere, can only make one animal so far. It is a LEGO version of the Island of Dr. Moreau, wherein I have brick-engineered a pig-camel, a dog-camel, and a camel with wheels. These monstrosities are quickly torn apart, and I wonder if I have some unresolved camel issues.

BrickLink has the same addictive pull as eBay. You're looking at minifig heads and suddenly find yourself considering a bid on alligator tails. *Come on, they're only eight cents apiece.* I can see how it would be very dangerous to go to this site while drinking. When I search for local sellers, I come across the BrickScope store, which is based out of Lee's Summit, Missouri, about twenty minutes southeast of Kansas City.

The next day I'm at a local sandwich shop, where I'm to meet Andreas Stabno, the general manager of BrickScope. I'm flipping through a LEGO catalog when behind me, I hear someone say, "Jonathan?"

I look up and see a tall, slim man with close-cropped black hair. I'm not sure what I was expecting of a guy who has a five-hundred-thousand-piece inventory, but it certainly wasn't

Andreas Stabno. In an oxford shirt and pleated khakis, he is dressed just like the other five guys who entered the shop before him. Each of whom I gave a polite nod to in an effort to awkwardly determine if they were the person I was supposed to meet.

Andreas is, by all appearances, normal. Arriving exactly on time, he talks in the measured speech of an actuary, his day job.

"How's building going?" he asks.

"I think very early on, I've almost avoided building too much and tried to regulate a little bit," I tell him, "because I can see how it's like turning a switch and once the switch is flicked, it's too late. I think it would be very easy to be the guy at the cocktail party that for the first couple of minutes the conversation is really interesting and then after that nobody wants to hear what you're saying."

It's a half truth. The full truth would mention that I'm not sure I can build anything that I would want to show anyone yet. But he laughs knowingly in response, and I know that I like him.

Andreas was born in Hanover, Germany. He tells me about the first set he can remember. His father, a minister, returned from a trip with a small red double-decker bus; Andreas was hooked, and began to build and collect LEGO train sets. At thirteen he outgrew the hobby, just like me, wanting to sell his collection to purchase an Atari. But his mom stopped him, encouraging him to put the sets in storage.

"They both remember the memories and just how much time you spent with them," says Andreas.

"—how important it is to you . . . " I chime in. I don't even realize I'm responding in the present tense.

And seven years later, he was glad his mother had stopped him from getting rid of his LEGO sets. LEGO has a way of leaking back into your life, and Andreas found himself drawn to the few pictures that were on the Internet in the early nineties.

"It was harder because the community wasn't as established at the time. There was RTL, but people just exchanged information that way. There wasn't as much trading," says Stabno.

What's the harm in getting a few sets out of storage? he asked himself. Stabno sold the famed Yellow Castle set and began to trade for train sets, the ones that were missing from his collection.

"It started small, I was buying at garage sales and selling on eBay," he tells me. That sounds familiar. I tell him of my recent garage sale find. I'm delighted because he thinks I got a bargain. LEGO Star Wars minifigures always command a premium, plus sets at garage sales are rare, especially considering that the few local BrickLink store owners are always scouring the area on the weekends.

"You'll have to compete with me for sets," he says, and I can't tell if he's joking. I ask him if he ever worries about becoming obsessed again or if it's too late; but before he can answer, I offer a potential justification for why this might not be a bad thing.

"It always starts small, but then it grows. But you're not smoking or drinking or gambling. You're just addicted to LEGO. It's a vice, only one that's not bad for you."

"Well, it's a plastic. It's nontoxic . . . ," he trails off. We both laugh, but I'm slightly uneasy at the idea that buying LEGO could become a compulsive habit.

And with that, Andreas launches into his story of acquiring the Airport Shuttle set, which is considered the Yellow Castle for LEGO train enthusiasts. The red monorail on an elevated gray track was introduced in 1991. Set 6399, MISB (mint in sealed box), is selling for $1,600 on eBay at the time of our conversation. That's an average of $2.15 for each of the 743 pieces included.

So when he should have been studying for an actuarial exam, Andreas found himself traveling by train to pick up a LEGO train.

"The Airport Shuttle is kind of the Holy Grail of the town sets and train sets. People really like it, and it was one of the few things missing from my collection. I found an ad in the newspaper that somebody in Indiana was selling his collection. I called him and he had the Airport Shuttle. And the price he wanted for that set was $150, what I would have paid for just the monorail. I had to have it, and I asked if he could ship it to me. And he told me that he didn't feel comfortable with that, but would be in St. Louis soon. 'Would you meet me in St. Louis?'

"He was maybe eighteen, and his parents drove him to St. Louis. I met him in the parking lot of the train station. I had taken the train down from Kansas City with two empty suitcases and a check.

He opened the trunk of his car; we transferred all the sacks and pieces into my suitcases. I gave him the check in the parking lot of the train station and we said good-bye. I rode the next train back, flipping through all of the instruction manuals. So it seemed like a drug deal, which is what it really was . . . anybody watching would have thought, this is really odd."

The switch had flipped. Andreas began actively buying and selling. He found himself racing to the library to win a last-minute eBay auction for a train car that was missing from his collection.

But it's a funny thing when adult fans have children. They must make a choice about whether to let their kids play with the LEGO bricks on the shelves. Some collectors have piles of bricks for their kids and piles of bricks for themselves. Others consider every builder in the house to have equal rights to the pieces. Andreas, it turned out, was good at sharing.

"I was the collector wanting to display what I got, but kids change that a bit. I let the kids play with them and of course pieces get lost or broken, and so it really doesn't matter as much anymore," says Andreas.

When completing his collection became less important, he discovered that it was easier to sell. And after visiting a local BrickLink seller to save on shipping, Stabno began to compare prices on the Web site, calculating that there was a slight margin on loose brick he had bought in LEGOLAND Deutschland (in Gunzburg, Germany, about an hour north of Munich).

Since he was less attached to his personal collection, several of his unopened sets became the seed capital for him to launch a store, BrickScope, in September 2006. He can't help being precise; Andreas might be the only seller around with a formal business plan. Today, Andreas will buy anywhere from twenty to one hundred copies of a set, and he sold just over a hundred thousand pieces in April 2008.

"I miss the old days of not having to worry about the finance side and just building something for the fun of it. Maybe when the kids get a little older . . . ," says Andreas.

But sellers still aren't that far removed from the obsessive side of the hobby. As part of the research for his business plan, Stabno figures that out of the roughly two thousand sellers on BrickLink, there are only about ten stores that operate full-time. Most sellers are just funding their brick habit, parting out a set to keep what they need and selling the rest in an ongoing quest to break even. Many call themselves "hobby sellers" in order to avoid dealing with the Internal Revenue Service as a formal business online.

Hobby sellers are required to report income to the IRS, but many hobbyists choose to not report their transactions. And since it's likely not a significant amount of money, and they aren't required to possess a formal system of accounting, the odds of the IRS being concerned with those transactions are probably quite slim.

Conversely, the IRS sees hobby sellers as business entities when it is apparent that someone is trying to make a profit, has made a profit in three of the past five years, and is involved in regular business transactions.

At the same time, sellers remain adult fans, looking at what others are building, and at what sets LEGO is releasing, in order to keep track of the imperfect secondary market. New items on the shelf usually run around ten cents per piece, while the Star Wars or SpongeBob sets might be a bit more expensive because of the licensing fees attached to intellectual property rights. Bulk pieces offered in tubs by LEGO will likely be in the six- to eight-cent range, since there aren't as many specialty elements.

Unlike sets in retail stores, used or resold pieces don't exist in a vacuum. When an adult fan uses up a vast quantity of dark green bricks to build a scale model of a military helicopter, it can drive up brick prices substantially in just a week. Bricks that were four cents apiece could now be ten cents. When you need a thousand bricks, that means that your order has just gone from $40 to $100. Most store owners won't engage in profiteering; however, they do have to adjust their prices to reflect the supply.

And selling to collectors requires another level of customer service.

"The collectors have a higher level of quality control than the company itself does sometimes," says Andreas. It's a strong statement about a company that has built its reputation on the idea that the next brick they make can always be stacked with the billions currently in circulation.

But he tells me about recent orders that came in from France, both for the same types of pieces, 2 × 4 plates (flat pieces, one-third of the height of bricks, which are two studs wide by four studs long). One customer wanted the plates stacked in groupings of ten and twenty by color, while the other specifically asked that the pieces be shipped loose. Contrast those orders with some buyers who won't purchase rare sets outside the United States because of a fear that a customs agent will tear open the packaging while inspecting the box, ruining their investment.

Andreas sounds alternatively exasperated and amused as he tells me about the unique demands of his customers. It helps that he has been on the other end of the transaction, waiting for a set that feels like it might never come. Packaging is important. If Andreas has an order for minifig torsos, he'll wrap them individually in paper so they don't scratch. When shopping on BrickLink, you'll often see used bricks described as coming from a nonsmoking home, because collectors feel that the plastic absorbs the smell of cigarettes.

It reminds me of when my older brother, Andrew, dealt baseball cards. At fourteen, he was the youngest dealer in Fairfield County. At eleven, I was the youngest assistant, working the booth alongside him at local card shows. In 1989, people were becoming interested in baseball cards for two reasons: an obscenity written on the handle of Billy Ripken's bat handle, and the concept of mint condition. A small industry dedicated to producing soft and hard plastic cases appeared seemingly overnight, because a baseball card with a scuffed corner was instantly devalued.

It was the first time that I had seen grown men collect something alongside kids, and I remember that the fellow dealers and adults who bought from my brother were some of the toughest customers. Many had exacting standards, and almost all were reluctant to deal with a kid until they saw that he knew as much about card condition as they did. Perhaps more important, he had to convince them that he cared as much about the cards as they did.

When I tell Andreas about the lengths my brother went to to keep cards in mint condition, he immediately sympathizes. The left half of his basement has been converted into a storage and shipping facility with nearly all of his half a million LEGO pieces bagged and boxed. He says that I can come visit and see what it's like when a shipment of sets arrives at his doorstep.

"Is it like Christmas?" I ask hopefully.

"It *is* Christmas," he says, in the tone reserved for those who need to believe in Santa Claus.

I ask him how he breaks down the sets and organizes them for sale. Andreas tells me that he uses the same approach he had when he was a collector and was looking to sort pieces for whatever he was working to build.

"Everybody starts by just dumping everything in one bucket or bag. At some point they have too many pieces, and then there is almost an evolution of organization. People usually start by color and then they discover that they just can't find anything. So then they start to organize by piece or style of element and move away from organizing by color. But again, their collection will reach critical mass and they'll be forced to organize by color *and* type of piece. The key is to always be able to find things quickly."

I don't tell Andreas that I have my entire collection in one large plastic tub, because I've decided that by the time I go to visit his store in person, I'll have sorted all my LEGO bricks.

A week later, I'm sitting on my couch in a pair of athletic shorts and a stained Kansas State Wildcats T-shirt as the second consecutive episode of *Law & Order* drones on in the background. Someone has been killed, and Detective Frank Fontana is determined to find out why, even if he has to ruffle a few feathers to get it done. I wait apathetically with the rest of Kansas City to discover if it was the special guest star or not.

I haven't shaved in days, and I'm growing what must look like the beard favored by drummer boys in the Civil War. My uncombed hair is hidden safely beneath a Chicago Cubs baseball cap, but errant curls escape the sides and back.

It's eleven in the morning on a Wednesday in May, and I've been sorting LEGO bricks for the better part of an hour. Ben's tub of LEGO pieces sits open on the ottoman.

The buzzer on our doorbell sounds, and I look up at the front door guiltily. I can sacrifice the last forty minutes of sorting and quickly dump all the LEGO pieces back into the plastic tub, or I can open the front door and hope whoever it is doesn't have to come inside. I don't want to have to re-sort, so I walk the twelve steps to our front door. It's Edward, our air-conditioner repair man, ready to take a look at the leak in our basement. I encourage him to come in and lead him through my office on the right, hoping he doesn't notice the pile on the ottoman.

I forget that my desk is overgrown with a dozen Tupperware bins filled with LEGO bricks. A giant yellow shopping bag with a bright red LEGO logo rests on the adjacent file cabinet. I shouldn't have worried about the mess in the living room. I suddenly wish for the crying of a small child or a babysitter calling with an update—anything that would suggest to this stranger that my LEGO collection actually belongs to my kid. No rescue will come. My wife and I clearly don't have children, and based on my appearance, it's a good bet that I don't even have a job.

"The basement is this way," I mutter, because I don't know yet how to tell a complete stranger that I'm an adult fan of LEGO.

If not better, at least bigger. Here is
the biplane I created after turning to
Joe Meno for inspiration.

5

Color Changes
Everything

Sorting isn't fun, unless you're my wife. Kate finds satisfaction
in organization and detail. I view details as speed bumps to
creativity. My career as an editorial assistant was definitely shortened by my inability to develop a filing system beyond neat piles
stacked around my cubicle and sticky notes ringing my desktop
monitor. I hope our kids take after her; otherwise, our house will
be a disaster zone.

I sort bricks like a truculent child being asked to clean out his closet. Less sorting, more playing. I stop often to look at certain pieces (*LEGO makes tiny airplane turbines?*) and an hour later I'm still experimentally snapping bricks together. But building haphazardly is the creative equivalent of buttoning up your shirt after missing the first button. The end result is just slightly off.

I confess to *BrickJournal* editor Joe Meno that I'm stumped about what to do next. His suggestion is simple: "You need to build a plane," he writes at the end of one of our e-mail exchanges. I move the turbine across my fingers like a poker player rolling a chip and set myself to answering this building challenge.

To find inspiration, I begin rummaging through the Mars Mission box, where I come across a part that is meant to be a building support for a lunar station. A square plate connected by minibeams to a rectangular plate—a cross between a flying buttress and a stanchion that supports an oil rig.

And that one element inspires the design of my first substantial MOC (my own creation)—the building supports remind me of the struts that connect the wings of a biplane. I initially look online for pictures of the pontoon plane featured in *Indiana Jones and the Temple of Doom*, but my image search pulls up a black-and-white blueprint of a classic biplane of the same ilk as the one flown by the Wright Brothers.

Over the next seventy-five minutes, I secure a propeller to act as an engine and find that LEGO makes a variety of sloped pieces. I use these to make the body tilt slightly upward, suggesting that the plane is ready for takeoff. A biplane is essentially a flying rectangle with two sets of wings. It's just four studs wide, so I'll only need about a hundred pieces in total.

It's relaxing to build with LEGO, until you can't find a part—and then it is maddening. I rake my hands through thousands of pieces, occasionally wincing as the corner of a LEGO brick nicks the webbing between my fingers. After close to ten minutes of searching that would have made losing my house keys seem pleasant, I find a white steering wheel. *So, this is why you sort.*

The cockpit complete, my biplane needs a pilot. Only one catch—I've failed to provide space for his legs. Not a problem.

I pop the legs off the minifig I found and put a ladder on the side of the plane to hide my amputation. I send pictures to Joe, nervous to have somebody else judging what I have built; but as competitive as the world of adult fans can be, there is a lot of support for neophyte builders.

"Clever thoughts—removing the legs to make the fig 'sit.' Also, the wing supports—I would not have thought of that, because the supports I would associate with, well, buildings," writes Joe.

I feel the pride that doomed Job. Could creativity be my hallmark as a builder? I have thought of a new use for a part that a guy who would go on to build a fully motorized WALL-E Robot that summer didn't see. This is one of the main reasons that LEGO is so appealing. A novice can stack bricks alongside the professionals and find acceptance.

Joe brings me back from orbit by explaining that I'm currently building in what as known as "rainbow mode," where I'm just using the available parts and not worrying about color. It's the hallmark of those just getting back to the hobby. It suggests that either your collection is not yet large enough to support building monochromatically or you're not conscious of the concept of design. More experienced builders will look to match real-world inspirations for their creations or just add detail in the form of pinstriping or shading that matches actual building materials.

Rainbow building could also happen because you're color blind, I weakly offer back to Joe. I am slightly red-green color blind, but truthfully, not to a degree that I can't tell the blue plates from the white plates that make up the wing.

I'm slowly learning that the real challenge in building with LEGO lies in the details. I tell Joe that I think the difference between an acceptable model and one that really seems special is the ability to find the right parts to represent pieces.

"As the pool of parts you use expands and you get familiar with them, you will realize that sometimes there is too much detail in the context. Would the biplane look better if the engine was more detailed? A good builder is like a good artist—he/she knows how to steer the observer to places on the model and detail accordingly. A uniform level of detail isn't as effective—I think that is why I tend to not be impressed with buildings—a building by itself is dull, but the minifigs and little details are what makes them special," writes Joe.

I consider the pool of a few thousand bricks spread out before me, noting not just the number of pieces, but all of the different types. There are tubes and wheels, and nearly every geometric shape in a rainbow of colors. It's a big pile of detailed parts. It's completely different from the tub of bricks that my parents bought me as a child in the 1980s. Maybe I don't know much about detail building because it wasn't possible to build such intricate models when I was growing up. The play themes (castle, space) had just been introduced, and minifigures had only a single expression of simple happiness. LEGO was simpler then.

Yet LEGO in the 1980s would have seemed fantastic to the children who played with the first wooden toys to come out of the toy shop launched by Ole Kirk Christiansen in 1932.

That year, Ole Kirk's life was at a crossroads. His first wife, Kristine, had died giving birth to their fourth son, Gerhardt.

"Life is a gift, but also a challenge," Ole Kirk, a devout Christian, is said to have remarked around that time.

At forty-one years of age, he was a widower living in the largest house in Billund, Denmark—a house that he soon might not be able to afford. The Great Depression meant that demand had dried up for the stools, Christmas tree bases, and ironing boards that were the trademarks of his carpentry and joinery shop. The last three houses he had built were sitting unsold.

Ole Kirk guessed that even in times of financial strife, people would still be willing to buy wooden toys for their children. His shop, already known for producing wooden blocks, was given a new name: LEGO. The name was a shortened combination of the Danish words *leg* and *godt*, meaning "play well." (It later would be noted that the Latin word *lego* means "I assemble," or "I put together," a fact apparently unknown to OKC.)

The new name and toys debuted in 1934 at the Danish Trade Exhibition, the same year Ole Kirk remarried, wedding his housekeeper, Kirsten Sofie Jorgensen. The product line grew dramatically in 1937, when Ole Kirk purchased a wooden router, allowing him to build ducks, ships, and trains. At that time, wooden toys were seen as innovative, high-quality gifts for children, slowly eclipsing the tin tractors and mechanical toys from Germany that had dominated the market. Just five years later, LEGO officially became a family business, with Godtfred Kirk Christiansen, Ole Kirk's third son, working alongside his father.

The success of the wooden toys allowed Ole Kirk Christiansen to purchase an injection-molding machine in 1946, the first in Denmark. Less than three years later, LEGO had a catalog of close to two hundred different wooden and plastic toys that for the first time included bricks.

But these early "automatic binding bricks" were made of wood, and were available only in Denmark. Plastic bricks wouldn't be produced until 1953. LEGO applied for and received its first trademark a year later. The bricks were sold in barbershops as either singles or by the pack—packaged in a small box so that children could buy a brick just as Daddy bought a single smoke or a pack of cigarettes.

Godtfred had been toying with the concept of a system of play, in which all of the toys that LEGO produced in a given line could be used together. He settled on the plastic bricks, believing they offered the possibility for modular building. The LEGO System of Play began in 1955 and included twenty-eight different sets and eight vehicles.

Those initial bricks could stack, but they didn't lock together. So LEGO developed the stud and tube system to improve the clutch power of the toy. The first molds made twenty-four 2 × 4 brightly colored plastic bricks. The iconic 2 × 4 brick was granted a patent in 1958, the same year that LEGO founder Ole Kirk Christiansen died.

As the company expanded in western Europe with a large presence in Germany and Britain, Godtfred looked to sell LEGO toys in the United States. LEGO partnered with Samsonite Corporation in Denver, Colorado, granting them a distribution license from 1961 to 1972. The large-scale DUPLO blocks for preschoolers debuted in 1967, and ten years later, those onetime toddlers could build complex structures with the Technic line.

* * *

Thanks to Kjeld Kirk Kristiansen, who represents the third generation to rise to CEO, the LEGO of today is a vastly different company from the one that defined my childhood. The 1990s saw a series of themes that disappeared after several years, though they have recently developed small cult followings online: LEGO Ninjas, Wild West, Time Cruisers, Aquazone, Adventurers, and Rock Raiders. LEGO attempted to develop story lines based around exotic themes, trying to find the right tone. But LEGO wasn't hip, and Generations X and Y knew it.

By 1998, the company's number of elements had swollen to over fourteen thousand different pieces in a wide range of colors and sizes. LEGO had moved away from the concept of a system, where all the parts could fit together. With a ballooning cost structure and declining sales in the face of a market that seemed to have shifted toward video games and electronic toys, the LEGO Group reported its first ever annual loss, $27.7 million.

"I hoped that their 1999 plans would hinge on improving their core product," wrote adult fan Jeremy Sproat in a January 1999 posting on the forums of LUGNET. The adult community was worried that the company they supported was changing direction in search of a younger consumer, forgetting the attraction of their original products.

"Is lego [sic] just not making enough of the items that people want? I would love to see the return of some of the older 'retired' sets like the 8880 Super Car. Why spend money designing and tooling a new set when they can re-release a classic?" asked David Forrest in a LUGNET thread from the same year. Adult fans were always tending toward different building interests than children, although ironically, many would look back wistfully on the favorite sets of their own childhood.

But even in the worst year to date for the Danish company, its future identity and a considerable profit driver was being introduced: LEGO Mindstorms. The Robotics Invention System (RIS) was developed in partnership with the Massachusetts Institute of Technology's Media Lab. As part of a line of educational toys, Mindstorms came with two motors, two touch sensors, a light sensor, and a collection of LEGO Technic gears, axles, and bricks.

Children ten years and older were encouraged to build their own robots using the kits, with a second version introduced in 2006 as LEGO Mindstorms NXT. In the first twelve years, more than 1.3 million kits were sold.

But Mindstorms was not immediately the darling of the do-it-yourself community. The uncertain future of the company also led LEGO to look seriously at licensing opportunities, agreeing to create sets based on the Harry Potter and Star Wars series. LEGO was officially no longer just about bricks. The popularity of separate licensing lines convinced LEGO to offer a new intellectual property line that was completely outside the system of play. Bionicle ("biological" combined with "chronicle"), a product line of biomechanical beings from a science fiction world, appeared in Europe in 2000 and in the United States a year later. The figures would support a clothing line, a series of comic books, computer games, and DVDs.

LEGO was experiencing growing pains as the company sought to expand its identity. For every success like Bionicle, there was a Galidor: Defenders of the Outer Dimension—the short-lived action figure that didn't win over many adult fans.

"Galidor is nothing more to me than a huge ink stain on Lego's history, and signaled the lowest point in their dark ages (which I define to be from 1997 to 2004). The line was based on a failed TV show that lasted only one year, and was basically an action figure line with the Lego brand name slapped on. No studs, barely any technic pins, and pieces that are basically useless in any creations. I don't even consider the line real lego [sic], and I'm extremely glad that TLC learned a lesson," wrote the user Zarkan on the Bionicle fan Web site BZPower.

LEGO was about to discover the dark side of its adult fans.

"Fear is the path to the dark side. Fear leads to anger. Anger leads to hate," warns Yoda in *Star Wars Episode 1: The Phantom Menace.* Unfortunately, LEGO didn't have a Jedi Master on its payroll.

LEGO's financial struggles and disparate product lines made adult fans fearful that the company they had come to love was in danger of disappearing. They saw the classic story of a family business that just couldn't adapt to a changing business environment.

The fear developed into anger for a faction of adult fans who were frustrated by the company's new moves toward products like Galidor that didn't seem to hold any appeal for adults. The hate would follow shortly.

In 2004, the company faced a second crisis, losing $327 million. The Harry Potter franchise was tied in to the release of movies and failed to gain traction without a big screen offering to accompany new sets. The Bionicle line was thriving, but LEGO was having trouble predicting which sets would be successful, leading to shortages of popular models and overproduction of slower-selling sets.

Amid takeover rumors in which Mattel was mentioned as a possible suitor, the Kristiansen family made a decision to reinvest their money and hire a CEO from outside the family. Jørgen Vig Knudstorp, a former management consultant with McKinsey and Company and director of strategic development at LEGO, was tapped to revitalize the company. Drastic changes commenced.

Knudstorp identified two major areas that needed to be addressed immediately: the supply chain and the current cost structure. It was the back end of the business that was killing LEGO, not competition from video games or low-cost manufacturing in China.

The big-box retailer hadn't existed when LEGO first began shipping to small toy stores. LEGO had two factories and three packaging centers in five different countries. They were making too many products in too many places.

In an effort to cut costs, LEGO also looked closely at its product mix. Those few primary colors initially available for LEGO pieces had grown to more than a hundred hues. The customization of the minifigures, often the most expensive part in a set because of the stamping required to provide detail, became more elaborate as faces and uniform details were added.

For every plastics company, the price of colored resin is going to be a major expense. Under Jesper Ovesen, chief financial officer, LEGO instituted a pilot program that considered a change in the ordering and production of the base substance for the bricks. By narrowing the list of suppliers and developing a system to track the cost of each element, LEGO suddenly could get a better idea of the true costs of every brick to leave the factory.

In 2004, the company changed the tones of brown, light gray, and dark gray as part of a move to shrink the palette to sixty-three colors. The colors were focus-grouped with customers and major retailers; however, marketers didn't include adult fans in the development process.

"Focus groups will cheerfully run your company into the ground if they are leading your decisions. This goes for any focus group, AFOLs included," wrote Jules Pitt on LUGNET in May 2004.

The colors were relaunched as light stone gray, dark stone gray, and "new" brown. Adult fans nicknamed the new gray "bley" for its bluish-gray tint and the feelings of *blah* that it inspired. AFOLs had a laundry list of complaints. Anger bubbled over into hate.

Some suggested that the new colors resembled MEGA Bloks bricks, which is like saying your Rolex looks like it came from a New York City street vendor. AFOLs felt betrayed; they felt that their collections had been rendered worthless, as the new shades weren't visually compatible with the original gray bricks introduced in 1977. BrickLink sellers panicked, as the company's decision changed the market overnight, drastically reducing the price of the gray inventories in the secondary market. Over time, the price of old gray would skyrocket, according to the principles of supply and demand. In the wake of the backlash, LEGO designated the three new colors as universal, pledging that they would never change.

"There is no possible explanation you, or anyone else, could offer that would legitimize a change to colors that are not compatible with their original versions. These new colors make the old versions look terrible, and this could easily have been prevented! Are the Lego designers and executives color blind? Making these colors 'universal' is not the answer. Making the original versions of these colors 'universal' is the correct choice, but it is clear to me that this company has no idea what its own products are all about.

"Proof is in the financial situation that Lego currently faces. I am sure it will only get worse," wrote adult fan Greg Muri, who promised that LEGO had lost a customer.

With uneven profits and a declining toy market, LEGO couldn't afford to lose customers. Although adult fans might constitute only an estimated 5 percent of LEGO's buying audience, they have a dramatic impact on the other 95 percent. And that's when Jake McKee, the first community relations coordinator, got involved.

Jake is skinny with light brown tennis fuzz hair and a closely clipped goatee. The Dallas native started at LEGO Direct, where the company sold sets and merchandise via a catalog and a corporate Web site. Jake's experience working directly with consumers led to the creation of his new position in 2000, after which he spent six years as the main liaison between the North American adult fan community and LEGO. Better yet, the year earlier he had started building with LEGO again, reliving his own childhood through the LEGO Star Wars sets. Adult fans had a man on the inside. McKee worked to make the company understand the interests of adult fans and tried to explain to adult fans the realities of running a company.

"As I've said before, out of all bad things comes something positive. In this case, the positive is that there are many more people internally who understand your passion and interest," Jake posted to LUGNET in September 2004.

Herein lies the heart of the tension between the adult fan community and LEGO as a corporation. AFOLs would always form a minority of the toy company's customer base. But they would be a vocal minority, and just like Ross Perot, they wanted a seat at the table with the guys making the decisions.

Although LEGO might recognize that AFOLs were talented builders and, in many cases, tech-savvy brand loyalists, this raised an issue for the company: how do you value the contributions of customers who don't directly impact the bottom line?

To AFOLs, listening was not enough.

"Understanding is but a small step towards what really matters. Let us know when they start to care," was Purple Dave's response.

6

Brick Separation Anxiety

I used to make fun of my dad for caring so deeply about when the mail arrived at his office. Then I started getting freelance writing checks in the mail, and now I figure I owe him an apology. In our Tudor-style home that was built in 1938, we have a slot to the left of the front door where our mail-lady slides in letters and magazines. The box that catches these can comfortably fit a postcard, so retrieving the mail often involves the same maneuver that leaves children's hands stuck in Big Choice machines before the Claw gets them. I might not be completely ready to have kids of my own.

Working from home means that I'm the first to attempt this daily maneuver. After I hear the familiar plunk of a rubber-banded bundle, I reach in to find that my May issue of *LEGO Club Magazine* has arrived. I manage to get it out of the mail slot without ripping it, and start to flip through the pages. Based on the content, I can assume that I have raised the average age of their subscriber base significantly. It's tied to the release of the LEGO Indiana Jones video game, which, even to an adult, looks pretty fantastic.

It reminds me of the old *Nintendo Power* magazine, which was designed to complement the original eight-bit Nintendo. The *LEGO Club Magazine* is a mix of product announcements, sneak previews, contests, and a comic where the drawings have been given blocky, LEGO-esque features. There are a number of creations built by kids, and this again calls to mind the dispiriting effect of returning to skiing later in life. As on the slopes, it would appear that children are whizzing by me effortlessly, while I'm just trying to stay on my feet and not hurt myself in the process.

It is difficult to find benchmarks in the world of LEGO building. It's not as if you can build at a fourth-grade level or emerge with a certificate of completion. There are no formal schools for training or lesson plans. So in the beginning, I rely on the age range recommended on the LEGO set package.

Kate comes home to find a small blue-and-white tow truck on my desk. The tiny Creator set, seventy-nine pieces, has been put together between the time she left for work and when she came back. LEGO is proving to be an outstanding tool for procrastination. In addition to helping me avoid my work, I find that buying smaller sets prevents me from having to unbox the Trade Federation MTT—the massive Star Wars set in the spare bedroom that has gathered a fine layer of dust, but so far has escaped the interest of our cat, Houdini.

"You are getting better," says Kate, holding up the tow truck that evening.

"Well, not really. This set is rated for kids age six to twelve," I admit.

"Well, you build really well for a twelve-year-old," she says. I notice later that she picks up the instructions and considers the other two build options for the mini vehicle set. I tell her to feel free to build, but she declines, opting for a yoga class instead. Kate doesn't yet know that my plan for returning to LEGO involves getting her to build alongside me. Phase one is set for the third weekend in June, when the second annual Brickworld is being held in Wheeling, Illinois, a suburb of Chicago. Brickworld is a major AFOL convention, a three-day affair of building contests, lectures, and public displays. So, in two weeks I'll introduce Kate to the world of adult fans—leading her around on one of the public display days—hoping it inspires her to want to build more.

As I pack up my bag to get ready for Brickworld, I consider bringing something that I have built to the convention. As with baseball card or craft shows, table space will be allocated, with LEGO user groups given adjoining tables to set up collaborative displays. Organizer Bryan Bonahoom, a boisterous rocket scientist from Fort Wayne, Indiana, whom I met at Brick Bash, sends an e-mail reminding everyone to submit information for their MOC (my own creation) cards. An MOC card is a white piece of paper folded in half with your name and the name of your creation that will be put at the front of the table to identify what you've built.

I look at what I could bring and decide that I don't need an MOC card. My MOCs aren't really that impressive. The biplane sits on my desk, next to a rainbow mailbox and my first attempt at a self-portrait. A pair of purple arches from the Mars Mission set defines the mailbox. It has the familiar curved shape of a metal mailbox and even a red flag that can be articulated up and down. It can hold a half-dozen golf balls. It is an outstanding achievement only when compared with the self-portrait.

On a 32 × 32 green baseplate, I have laid a two-dimensional self-portrait that resembles Papa Smurf or Santa Claus, depending on the angle. I drew better self-portraits in elementary school. My auburn hair is represented by a bright red helmet, my jaw is outlined in white, and my mouth is a 1 × 6 red brick. Apparently in my mind's eye, I am the original Nintendo hockey player.

The concept of creating a three-dimensional picture of a two-dimensional sculpture is difficult to grasp, and this gives me a lot more appreciation for how hard it is to create a mosaic just using LEGO bricks. The best mosaics are LEGO-ized recreations of famous artwork—*Starry Night* or the *Mona Lisa*. Most people mock up sports team logos or pictures of their kids. Software programs let builders match bricks and colors to mimic the shapes and hues of a photograph.

I pick up the mosaic and the mailbox, placing them on a white shelf in the corner of my office. They won't be packed. I notice that my fingernails are getting a little long, and I'm happy about that. Prying apart LEGO bricks is difficult with short nails, and I've been purposely growing out my fingernails, to the mild disgust of Kate. I tell myself I'll build better when I have more bricks—a lie I'm sure most builders have told themselves at some point in the process.

Less than twelve hours later, I'm in the second conference room adjacent to the Ravinia Grand Ballroom in the Westin Chicago North Shore hotel. My hands keep shaking slightly as I try to apply a sticker to the torso of a minifigure using a cotton swab. The process is not dissimilar to the painting of tin soldiers. It's my third attempt.

We're forty-five minutes into Minifig Customization, with Jared Burks of Fine Clonier Decals, an online decal store for minifigs—one of eighteen classes being held at Brickworld. Behind round black glasses and slightly curly black hair, Jared sounds like a scientist as he describes the process of altering existing minifigures to represent superheroes and cartoon characters. His hands are steady and his movements are deliberate. It doesn't seem an accident that he is a researcher in College Station, Texas, working on understanding the chemical composition of leukemia.

The son of a screenprinter, Jared is one of the most visible members of the customization movement among adult fans of LEGO. Inspired by the Star Wars set released by LEGO, Jared started to modify minifigures; he figured he was on to something

when a Greedo head (a bounty hunter character from *Star Wars*)—
just the head—sold for $20 on eBay.

Jared's business has already matured. In two years, he's gone
from selling complete sculptured minifigures to producing decals
and accessories that let you create your own Teenage Mutant
Ninja Turtle or Superman. I'm fascinated by what amounts to
an entirely different secondary market from BrickLink—using
LEGO figures as spare parts.

"There are two camps when it comes to customization," are
Jared's opening words for his presentation. "Those who do it and
those who don't."

LEGO purists cringe at the idea of modifying LEGO pieces.
They argue that the challenge and beauty of LEGO come from
making something unexpected from the parts that are available.
Most customizers would answer that the LEGO market is like the
diamond market, where supply is at times kept artificially low.
LEGO doesn't batch parts, and rare pieces can rocket up in price
if they are in high demand. When LEGO produces approximately
eighteen male minifigures for every female minifigure, why drop
$40 on a feminine hairpiece when you can just make your own?

Cutting or painting bricks is also considered cheating. Anybody
can chop LEGO, but the best builders are the ones who use only
genuine factory bricks. And purists wouldn't even think of making their own accessories. Will Chapman isn't a purist. The owner
of BrickArms has one job: he runs an online store that sells military minifigures and tiny plastic guns, which he creates out of
molded plastic. LEGO as a company has made a decision not to create militaristic toys. The Pirates line, introduced in 1989, did include
muskets, and the Wild West sets later added modern rifles and pis-
tols. More recently, the licensed sets for Batman, Star Wars, and
Indiana Jones have all featured guns or laser blasters. Chapman
and one of his main competitors, BrickForge, which specializes in
medieval weapons, are filling the vacuum left by LEGO.

Chapman is busy setting up alongside other adult fans inside
the nearly fifteen thousand square feet of ballroom space on Friday
morning. The public won't be allowed inside until Saturday, and
it seems there is a lot to be done before the doors open. A few

tables down, purists definitely wouldn't like what Chris Campbell is holding. The computer programmer from Arkansas, who presented with Jared, is pointing out the glowing eyes and chest of an Ironman minifigure that is a custom creation. Campbell has used a Dremel rotary tool to drill a hole into the chest cavity of a minifig and insert an LED and battery. This isn't customization—it's surgery.

"That would take me years to get right," I suggest.

"It takes a lot of practice and you still end up with a lot of left arms and no right arms to match," says Chris, noting that plastic arms tend to crack under pressure.

Chris is showing me around the booth displaying the figures that he and Jared have created. Hundreds of minifigs stand on tan displays: superheroes and supervillains sculpted and stickered. The attraction is easy to see. Minifigs feel like something you collect. These are the real action figures of the LEGO world. LEGO itself has experimented with minifigs, adding different facial expressions with the Pirates line and spring-loaded legs for the National Basketball Association minifigs in 2002.

Just as on *The Simpsons*, yellow remains the dominant color for minifigures. But with the introduction of licensed characters for the Star Wars sets and NBA minifigs, LEGO began to reproduce flesh tones in order to more accurately represent people who actually exist. Scarcity is often the key to whether a minifig will appreciate in value over time—witness the $200 price tag on a limited-edition gold chrome-plated C-3PO, ten thousand of which were randomly inserted into 2007 Star Wars sets.

LEGO has a clear presence at Brickworld, sponsoring several of the build challenges and pushing its latest products, including LEGO Universe, described by the company as a "massive multiplayer online game." I step aside to let an eight-foot-tall minifigure mascot pass by me and resist the urge to take off his head to see if the person inside the blocky suit is a man or a woman.

I'm wandering down the first of four rows when I hear a low whistle. A small crowd is gathering around the sculptures of Adam Reed Tucker, a Chicago architect who is one of the co-organizers of Brickworld. He builds big, like seventeen-feet big.

That's the height of the scale model Tucker has constructed of the Burj Dubai, the tower that is the world's tallest building since opening in January 2010. A collection of to-scale architectural models has been set up in a circle near the center of the room, so that inevitably your eye is drawn to the twisting Chicago Spire or the tan Empire State Building. It suggests that Tucker has a healthy ego.

"If I could afford to buy windows by the case, I could build like that," a bald man remarks with a grimace as he snaps pictures.

I can understand the man's bitterness. The Sears Tower in my basement doesn't hold a candle to the fifteen-foot Sears Tower that looms before me. Windows are expensive. In fact, all LEGO is expensive. *Can wealth affect your place in the social strata?* An adult version of the guy who has the most toys wins. But with an architect's eye for detail, Tucker obviously has talent, which seems a more likely reason for the petty comment.

I accidentally bump into another fan while I'm snapping pictures. David Pace is also at his first convention. I ask him if he has anything to display, and I hear an echo of my own fears coming out of his mouth.

"I didn't bring anything. They'd sweep it off the table, say this guy has no talent," confesses David.

As I look around, that's how I feel. There is Chicagoan Beth Weiss, who builds elaborate totem poles and latticed national flags. Or Brian Darrow, a member of IndyLUG, the same LEGO user group as Bryan Bonahoom, who has brought the Blacktron Intelligence Agency: a thirty-by-five-foot space display that is a four-hundred-thousand-piece sprawling ocean of yellow and black, named for the sets released in 1988. Over in the corner is Steve Hassenplug, sitting at a white linen table adjacent to a series of Great Ball Contraptions, motorized LEGO setups that continuously loop miniature soccer balls via an elaborate system of levers and pulleys. Hassenplug is idly playing with a pneumatic pump that is making a headless robotic centipede dance with every push. It is mesmerizing. Here are my benchmarks. I've got a long way to go.

I feel better when Duane Collicott waves to me from the middle of the third row of LEGO creations. I'm beginning to understand his point about the difference between a convention and a public display. He's snapping together a red-sloped roof, putting the finishing touches on a model of the Grand Traverse Lighthouse that he has been commissioned to build. The real lighthouse sits on Lake Michigan, and Duane will drive his thirty-inch, six-thousand-piece version there later in the summer.

I place my hands on my thighs and squat down like a football coach watching an intense practice, unintentionally mimicking the stance of many builders as they critique other's work.

"Do you have to use jumpers? It looks like you have a half-stud offset—"

"Actually, I needed to offset it in two directions," replies Duane. He removes a portion of the roof, and we're suddenly discussing the placement of the green window frames and how Duane was able to avoid making the walls too thick. It feels good to use the language of building, and it goes a long way toward making me feel like I belong.

The first table inside the door belongs to the Toy and Plastic Brick Museum. Tiny gray bricks from the 1960s, a quarter of the size of standard bricks, sit under glass displays next to an eighteen-inch tall LEGO sculpture of Scooby-Doo. I'm hoping to meet the founder, Dan Brown, but the table is unmanned.

Dave Sterling, a Wisconsin plastics engineer for the aerospace industry, comes up next to me and admires some of the first LEGO bricks. He fidgets alternately with his short brown hair and the front of his Led Zeppelin T-shirt before inviting me to lunch with him and his wife, Stacy, and their friend, Abner Finley. It's like college orientation at the convention—you tend to stick with the people you meet first.

Over lunch at Quizno's, we talk about our LEGO collections. I explain that separating bricks that have been stuck together for years has left my teeth and fingers sore at times.

"It's kind of gross. I've got my brother-in-law's old bricks and they occasionally have a taste when I use my teeth. And that taste is something like ear wax," I tell Dave.

"You know, you don't have to use your teeth," Dave says.

"Your teeth and fingernails can even damage the bricks. I've bought used bricks that have teeth marks and that is not cool," adds Abner.

"What other option do I have?" I ask.

"LEGO makes brick separators," says Dave.

Sure, I think. *That's a great practical joke to play on the new guy. Oh yeah, Jonathan, there's a separator. There's also a group of elves that can finish whatever you're building while you sleep at night.*

"No way," I start to protest, but Dave interrupts.

"Yes, they're little green triangles. They're maybe two dollars," says Dave. He goes on to describe a slope with ridges. It latches on to a plate or brick in the same fashion as a bottle opener, allowing you to snap up or down and separate stuck together elements. I am suddenly self-conscious over the length of my fingernails. Dave has just made my weekend.

The Ravinia Grand Ballroom has been transformed in the few hours we've been gone. Hand trucks roll through the plush lobby in a steady stream, pushed by guys wearing shirts from the Greater Midwest LEGO Train Club. The parking lot is filled with trailers. LEGO creations have been secured in silver restaurant rolling shelves and storage tubs packed with paper to keep elements from breaking apart in transit.

People are still unloading when the opening ceremonies commence. This year, the convention has grown from 238 to 330 participants, with 80 percent between twenty and fifty years old. Tormod Askildsen, the head of LEGO Community Development, has been asked to give the keynote address. With light brown minifig hair and a trim physique, he gives off the vibe of a TV reality-show host. Albeit a host wearing a bright orange T-shirt that says "Mindstorms NXT" on it.

"So much has changed. It used to be that LEGO created value, but now value is being created across the community. It's nice to be together on the ten-year anniversary of the first dialogue between LEGO and adult fans of LEGO. We launched the Web site in 1998—we didn't even have an e-mail address because we were afraid that people would contact us." Tormod pauses as the room laughs along with him.

"We realized that we needed to find out where our future growth would come from. The LEGO mission is to inspire and develop the builders of tomorrow, and AFOLs are the builders of tomorrow. This is a very complex hobby that most people don't understand. It's so much more than a toy for kids. We need to work together to show people this," says Tormod.

Toward the end of the opening ceremonies, the crowd of several hundred is getting restless. The adult fans have been promised access to scratch and dent boxes and a special convention discount at the LEGO store in the Northbrook Court Mall.

Visiting a mall after all of the stores have closed is like walking into a zombie movie or a Kevin Smith flick. You never know if the undead or Ben Affleck is waiting around the corner. As I step on the escalator at the Northbrook Court Mall, the first thing I hear is a crackling, like a fire getting started. When the escalator steps reach the second floor, I see the beginning of the line into the LEGO retail store. The store is opening after hours for the attendees of Brickworld 2008, and the employees seem a bit overwhelmed by the crowd.

The group I'm with walks to the back of the line, which stretches for several hundred people and is growing at an alarming rate. The crackling noise is the buzz of conversation as adult fans of LEGO discuss potential set purchases—Green Grocer and Indiana Jones being popular choices.

The line begins to move briskly until the store reaches capacity, with a hundred fans grabbing and clawing through bricks. The LEGO employee at the door, wearing a bright yellow apron, operates like a club bouncer. One in, one out, under the watchful eyes of two of Northbrook's finest on hand for crowd control. I watch the frenzy as people grab discounted sets and fill boxes from the Pick A Brick tubs (loose pieces that you can grab and buy in bulk). And I want to get inside and join them.

I'm staring at a LEGO store employee who looks a lot like Dustin Diamond, better known as Screech from *Saved by the Bell*. While I'm trying to figure out what Screech is doing in a suburban Chicago mall, the employee at the door waves me inside even though nobody has yet exited.

I walk in, and I stop five steps later. The store is packed with LEGO fans carrying armloads of kits and cramming brick pieces into empty white cardboard boxes that they can fill up for $150 a pop. A forty-something mechanical engineer wearing a yellow LEGO T-shirt struggles to pick up six set boxes at once.

"It's like a shopping spree you always dreamed of as a kid," I say to him, stepping aside as a pair of teenage boys walk past, excitedly pointing to the Indiana Jones sets.

"Except you've got to pay for it when you get the bill next month," he responds, laughing, and he walks toward the back of the store, where a LEGO employee has just emerged with an armful of Green Grocer sets in an attempt to restock. The employee won't even reach the shelves in the front before he is empty-handed again.

I'm experiencing stimulus overload, so I mostly stand in the middle of the store like a child hoping he isn't really lost. I'm struck that, despite a lack of personal space, I don't see one angry face or hear a terse word. This is what bliss feels like.

Dave Sterling walks up to me, a big grin on his face.

"I thought you might forget these." He hands over two green brick separators. "You should have at least two."

"You weren't making it up," I say with a smile as he disappears into the crowd.

I eventually settle on buying a Pick A Brick cup, an oversize clear cup you can fill for $15 with whatever loose bricks and pieces are available. A savvy LEGO collector can stock up on parts well below retail or aftermarket cost. I am not savvy, but I pretend. I marvel over bright orange 1 × 4s and translucent blue 2 × 2s. I load up on white plates, window frames, and 1 × 1 headlight bricks. To paraphrase Mr. Barnum, I'm the sucker born right this minute.

An hour later, I've reached the front of the line. I place my Pick A Brick cup and two LEGO separators on the counter.

"What do we have here?" says the guy working the counter.

"That's everything," I shrug. The register reads $19.61.

"This is kind of anticlimactic," he says, gesturing to the two gargantuan sales bags that the person in front of me is still struggling to carry from the store.

"I know," I admit. "But we can pretend that I just helped you reach your sales goal for the quarter."

He half-laughs. "Shouldn't be a problem. Okay. Have fun at the convention." And he's on to the next customer.

On the ride home, I tell Dave a bit sheepishly that I wish I had bought more LEGO, I just wasn't sure what I wanted. He tells me about how his mom used to put LEGO bricks in his Easter eggs instead of candy.

"She thought it would be healthier than candy. She didn't want me to have so many sweets. Little did she know." He laughs before continuing: "But you have to careful. It's like gambling once you start, because you just keep buying. You think about a LEGO piece and it's just five cents. So you tell yourself, I'll just buy a hundred and that's only five dollars. But then you do that twenty times, and you've suddenly spent a hundred dollars."

I kind of want the rush that comes from spending a hundred dollars. I want my regret to be over credit card statements and embarrassing confessions to Kate. Because right now, I only regret that I haven't bought more.

7

Pink Skulls

It's the second day of the convention, and the volume is beginning to rise in the Elm Room at the Westin Chicago North Shore. A LEGO conspiracy—I didn't think such a thing existed. But I'm riveted as adult fans discuss the possibility that LEGO is leaking information about new sets. I turn my head to the back of the room to see who is talking, and I see the oversize figure of Bryan Bonahoom. With a mop of curly brown hair and a laugh like Chris Farley, he often can be heard before he is seen. But on this occasion, he just points to me and mouths one word: "Belville."

I nod my head and pack up my bag as my heart slowly begins to thud in my chest. I've been selected for one of the alternate build contests, the Belville challenge. The twenty other people in the room don't know I'm nervous. They are too busy debating the merits of seeing a Star Wars set early. Cold sweat forms, and I realize that I'm terrified. I briefly consider remaining in my seat, but Bryan is waiting at the back of the room and shuffling his feet impatiently. I walk slowly out of the room and try to control my breathing, but the ensuing moment of embarrassment is dominating my thoughts.

Building contests are featured at most LEGO conventions. When you get a few hundred men in a room for a few days, competition is inevitable. The two most popular types are alternate building and speed building. In the alternate build, everyone is given the same bag of parts or pieces and told to work in a particular motif or vignette. In the speed build, each of the competitors is trying to build the same set and whoever finishes first is the victor.

Earlier in the day, I dropped my name on a small slip of paper into two of the six challenges being offered at the convention. The first was a LEGO Chess tournament, and I believed that even if I had been picked, it would have been mercifully short. I am not a crack chess player. It also had the advantage of being the only challenge to not feature competitive building of any kind. The chess pieces were already laid out and constructed. That seemed right up my alley.

The Belville challenge sounded interesting to me. I doubted there would be many entrants, and ideally the other competitors would be as clueless as I am, because Belville is the line of LEGO products specifically aimed at little girls. It features predominantly pink and purple sets with fairy princess and horse riding themes.

Belville has "sunshine homes" and the "Blossom Fairy"—the antithesis of what interests the average thirty-year-old male. So when I dropped my name in the bucket, I was figuring that guys who love Star Wars and architectural structures would be just as mystified as I by a LEGO kitten or a pink tower piece.

I severely underestimated the creativity of my fellow convention attendees.

The five competitors are brought to two folding tables in the hallway adjacent to the lobby. My anxiety level rises as I realize that we will be building in front of not only other AFOLs, but also any member of the public who happens to walk by. One of my fellow competitors is a dad, Chris McDonnell, a Kentucky native who has accompanied his son Noah to the convention. I feel slightly better about my chances to finish fourth until I learn that he and his son often build together.

The organizer, Esther Walner, lays out the rules of the challenge simply. We have three small sets to use for parts: a Belville Blossom Fairy set, an Aqua Raiders set (think underwater James Bond), and a Castle set. Since this is the Belville challenge, we must use a majority of Belville parts to build a vignette—a scene with a backstory that we will explain after we're done building. Although it's not a timed build, we still have to be finished by 3:45 p.m. I put my cell phone down on the table and see that I have fifty-seven minutes. I wipe my hand on my jeans. I haven't sweated this much since the moments before slow dances at Fairfield Woods Middle School.

"Go ahead," Esther encourages us as two men in dark gray suits pass behind her. I catch the eye of the older man and he cocks his head slightly—a dog hearing a sound he can't quite place. I wish I could keep walking.

"Do you have any idea what you're going to build?" I ask Abner Finley at the end of the table. We had lunch together the previous day, and it's nice to see a friendly face. I immediately wonder if I've just violated the cardinal rule of an alternate build: don't ask your fellow builders what they're going to construct.

"No idea. I guess I'll figure something out," says Abner, turning his attention to the three clear plastic bags from the sets he has just opened.

Linda, the only female contestant, is having trouble opening her cardboard boxes on the right. I've already managed that feat, so I move to offer her my open box in a bit of chivalry.

"Oh sorry, there's no sharing of pieces," says Esther quickly, seeing me push a pile of parts in front of Linda.

"I wasn't . . . uh . . . I was just trying to trade boxes," I say weakly. In the three seconds of that conversation, Linda has opened her set, and I begin to slide pieces back in front of me. I leave behind my white LEGO kitten, until Linda and Esther point out that I have missed it.

I pretend to look as if I know what I'm doing as I sort pieces from the three sets. The Belville set has large pink castle pieces, white cones, sparkling pink gems, daisylike flowers, and fairy wings. Aqua Raiders features a treasure chest, water snakes, and the bricks to make a giant yellow submarine. Skeletons battle knights with a catapult in the Castle set.

A pile of just over two hundred parts sits on the white tablecloth. I move them around like a kid trying to stall as his parents wait for him to finish his vegetables. Only seven minutes have elapsed, but everyone else has started building. I can hear the click of bricks snapping together. Since talking to Abner, I haven't looked at or talked to the other builders. I'm afraid that I'll see what they're building and be unable to come up with something original.

I immediately rule out using the large pink tower pieces sitting in front of me. I (correctly) guess that the others will use them in their structures, and I hope that if I can't win through technical strength, at least I can be more creative. But so far, I've failed to show traces of either imagination or design skills.

A teenage attendee of the convention wanders over in a khaki fisherman's vest, the lens of his Nikon pointed directly at me.

"What is this?" he asks.

"Belville," I grunt, pretending to be authoritative in using a word I learned the day before.

"I'm going to check out the Mecha challenge," he says, before wandering over to the adjacent table, where five more AFOLs are busy assembling robotic figures constructed of LEGO—emblematic of the Mecha style of building. The final product will look like Japanese anime superheroes or something out of *The Matrix*. I can see why he doesn't stay very long to watch what I do with my Blossom Fairy set.

My first instinct is to build sea monkeys. As I'm mentally cycling through conversations I've had over the past day in an attempt to find some inspiration, I remember a moment with Joe Meno. Early Friday morning, I found him hovering over a collaborative Belville display, where convention participants were encouraged to bring rooms of a hypothetical castle in predominantly pink and purple. Joe had his hands in a small plastic container and was affixing green tentacle-like plants to a baseplate. I watched him work for a minute, until his hands found a scattered collection of alien minifigs waiting to be posed.

"Joe, those are *Life on Mars* aliens. I have no idea what to do with those," I told him, excited to recognize a piece from my garage sale set. (Which, of course, is called Mars Mission, rather than the title of the canceled ABC drama.)

"Nobody knows what to do with them," he replied. When I gave him a questioning look, he explained.

"The proportions are all wrong. They're longer than regular minifigs and too skinny. Look at these arms," he said as he affixed a sloped piece to the alien.

"So, Felix Greco and I were talking several years back. We decided that they're aliens, aliens which live underwater as a race of sea monkeys and that led to building manta rays and attack crabs." He pulled out his cell phone from the red LEGO brick case it is always inside, showing me a picture of a fierce tan creature with articulated LEGO claws.

He went on to describe the creation myth developed in a series of e-mails with Felix nearly six years ago. The sea monkeys apparently can communicate telepathically, yet they maintain a religion and a ruling caste—the Court of Great Minds. Originally they were discovered by Captain Nemo's *Nautilus*, but their existence remained secret until a diary was discovered in the wreck of the doomed ship. Mixed within the fiction is an account of how LEGO sets might have factored into the evolving culture of the sea monkeys. Greco had focused on obscure kits like the Alpha Team, part of a series known as the Deep Sea Mission, drafting a story that the Alpha Team befriended the sea monkeys to fight the Forsaken—a faction of evil sea monkeys noted by their black helmets.

Recalling my conversation with Joe, I'm excited to have a direction and I think he will appreciate the joke. I have only one slight problem. The Mars Mission aliens aren't included in the parts I have in front of me. So I can build a sea monkey vehicle or environment—it just wouldn't feature sea monkeys. "Under the Sea" from *The Little Mermaid* is stuck on repeat inside my head.

Since I'm facing forward and there's now nobody to talk to, I settle into the process of moving pieces around a small green baseplate. I grab a shiny 1 × 4 brown plate and begin to dance it up and down. I consider building a scene from *The Sorcerer's Apprentice*, but the color palette is wrong and that seems dreadfully complicated. Sebastian the crab is replaced by the classical tune that propels brooms to dance magically. I run my fingers through the front of my hair, twirling an errant curl. When I'm stuck for an idea, this usually helps me. I imagine it jump-starting my brain like the crank on a Model-T Ford. A conversation from two nights before in the hospitality suite pops into my head.

"You should do a 'girls of LEGO' issue," Jeremy Spurgeon teased Joe Meno. Jeremy is the editor of *Railbricks*, an online magazine for LEGO train enthusiasts.

"A *BrickJournal* swimsuit issue," Abner Finley said with a laugh, unaware that he would be in the Belville challenge just two days later.

"We have a female builder's section. I mistakenly thought it had to be pink for the first few issues," said Joe.

"That's what I don't get. Why does it always have to be pink for girls?" said Dave Sterling, the green beaded necklace he was wearing bouncing with his enthusiasm. "My wife, Stacy, would be fine with pink, but she wants pink skulls."

"Really? Pink skulls?" I asked. I tried to picture Stacy, dressed in khakis and a green cardigan, playing with pink skulls.

"Yeah, you wouldn't know it," Dave replied. "But she's a huge power metal and punk fan. She built an entire goth record store in our display."

And that's the spark. *Pink skulls.*

I notice the white skeleton minifig, and the inklings of what I'm going to build begin to form. I grab his torso and wonder if I've got the right pieces to construct a grave. Gray pieces from the Castle and Aqua Raiders fit together to form a tombstone. My 1×4 brown plate becomes the dirt for a burial plot, and slick black plates frame the dirt.

I slide a set of fairy wings onto the skeleton torso and am pleased for the first time with what I'm building. It took me only twenty-two minutes to place the pink fabric wings on the skeleton. I separate out the Belville pieces to try to determine what I'm going to build around the grave of the figure that I am now thinking of as a dead fairy godmother. On some level, I register that people are actively watching us build, but I keep my eyes flashing between the time on my phone and the pieces I want to use.

I settle on a plastic pink girl, the original Blossom Fairy, who has a watering can. She's going to be watering her garden and attempting to bring her fairy godmother back to life. I'm confident that nobody else will be working on this motif.

"Abner's working on the Belville," a voice calls out from a group of three guys, all of whom have cell phones clipped to their belts. Before he responds, they all laugh and keep on walking. It's good-natured, and I half-expect them to high-five one another. I wish for friends who would make fun of me for building with a girl's LEGO set.

The next ten minutes pass quickly as I struggle to build a tree trunk and break apart the flowers that come packaged in fours. Circular pieces don't want to snap down on the green baseplate, and I find myself trying to force them down. My fingers have turned red with the effort. I think of my Grandpa Morty, who once offered a simple piece of home improvement (and life) advice. *Don't force something. If it doesn't want to go in easily, you might not be doing it right. So just take it easy and don't force it.*

I stop pushing hard and slowly turn the white, barrel-shaped brick. It quickly snaps into place. I silently thank my grandfather and realize that I have just experienced what Simba goes through when his ancestors impart wisdom from the clouds. God, I love *The Lion King*. I'm surprised to see that my hands have a slight tremor, and I make a mental note to find some manual dexterity exercises to practice.

"Five minutes to go," Esther announces, and I panic. I quickly erect a white fence and some jewel-topped white sculptures, and I place flowers on the grave site. I can't get a golden crown to sit on the top of the skeleton's head. All LEGO minifigs come with knobs on the top of their heads to allow you to stick on hats or hairpieces. Unfortunately, the skeleton has a tiny thread of plastic running through the center, which prevents me from balancing the crown properly. When I can't find the skeleton's legs in the pile of bricks, I decide that those are still buried beneath the "ground," as the fairy godmother hasn't been brought back to life.

As I attach the green fronds and try to keep the pink girl from tipping over from the weight of a watering can, I hear Esther's voice.

"Bricks down; stop building. The judges are here and they will be judging what you've built based on the intricacy and creativity of what you've built," says Esther.

I nervously fuss to make sure that everything will stay upright and then I step back. *Pencils down, the exam is over.* I look around for the first time at the other creations, and I'm glad to see that what I built at least belongs on the table.

The two entrants to my right are first to explain to the four judges what they've constructed. I feel good that I guessed correctly about people beginning with the oversize pink tower pieces from the Belville set. Both have elaborate pink castles presiding over pitched battles as part of a vignette based on traditional knight warfare. The sound of my heart pumping blood drowns out their explanations. I catch only bits of their explanations—"princess warrior," "heat of the battle," and "snakes attacking."

Then the four judges are standing in front of me. The process is meant to be informal, and they simply ask if I can tell them about what I've built. Esther is joined by Tracy Dale and Chris Petrie, two women who run Brick-a-thon, a LEGO brick store in St. Petersburg, Florida. These are some of the most active women in the female fan community.

I smile, and as I exhale, I begin talking.

"This is essentially a garden scene. It's a story of a girl and her fairy godmother, but with a twist. Sadly, this little girl's fairy godmother has passed away and she is attempting to bring her back to life. You'll notice the fairy godmother's skeleton is half-raised from the grave, her legs are still buried."

I'm proud that I didn't mention that I couldn't locate the skeleton's legs, and that dictated my decision to stop building at the torso. The judges are smiling politely, but I have no idea if it's because I'm talking at such a rapid pace or if they wonder whether I was drinking while building.

"She has fairy wings, a magic wand, and a crown, which unfortunately didn't stay on her head—as she is a skeleton minifig." I kick myself for sharing that detail, until one of them sympathetically chimes in and saves me from revealing more information about my building deficiencies.

"Oh that's right," says Chris, "those minifigs don't have the hollow opening on the top of their heads."

I silently thank her and rattle on for another thirty seconds. "The girl has actually filled her watering can with blood, which has come from this fountain over here." I point to the corner of the vignette, where I have filled a gold-topped fountain with pink jewels meant to represent blood.

"Thank you," says Esther, and we are all glad that I'm done talking. The judges smile, and I step back, running a hand through my hair.

"Dude, you're pretty dark," says Chris from Kentucky.

"I guess I am," I respond.

Linda, the art historian whom I inadvertently tried to cheat with earlier, has constructed an impromptu art museum. She tells me later that she was inspired by the lecture on LEGO as an art medium that we both attended instead of going to lunch.

Meanwhile, Abner is the last to display what he has built. A customized chariot is rolling up to a castle where knights are preparing a feast for the arriving lady. He has managed to turn a barrel into an open oven, and the white kitten is upside down and being prepared for dinner. I laugh, and suddenly don't feel so dark.

But then, realizing I just laughed at a tableau that featured a cat being roasted, I feel even darker.

The judges thank all of us and explain that the results will be announced at the awards ceremony on Sunday night. We're told that we can carry our creations into the ballroom where Brickworld is being held. Esther has written our names on scraps of paper, and each of us puts down our small scene on the table reserved for Belville creations.

My scene takes up five inches of a four-foot table, but I feel genuinely proud. In fifty-seven minutes, I have addressed my biggest regret and answered my biggest question.

I spent the first thirty-six hours at Brickworld upset that I hadn't brought anything to display. A lot of the social scene revolves around talking about what you've built, how you've built it, and what you're going to build. Without something you've created, you can't have those discussions. When you go in empty-handed, it's like walking into the executive washroom as an intern and striking up a conversation. It just feels like you're asking too many questions in a place where you're not quite ready to be just yet.

On the other hand, my biggest question was a simple one: "Can I build?" Not just stack bricks, but build something that would make people want to ask me questions about the choices I made and the pieces I used. In short, I want to become a builder whom other people talk about.

During the two days after the Belville challenge, I find myself lurking near the table where my creation is displayed. I'm hoping to overhear conversations about what I've built, and I'm curious to see if anyone will care.

My ears perk up when a six-year-old girl with blond pigtails pulls her father over late Saturday morning on the first day of the public exhibit.

"Look, Daddy, look," she yells. I'm excited because she's standing right in front of my scene.

"What honey?" he asks. I wait, involuntarily leaning forward.

"Pink. Pink LEGO," she screams happily, and drags him toward the next table, which features hundreds of minifigs.

I haven't won over the critics just yet.

One of the largest space displays anywhere, AFOL Brian Darrow's thirty-four-foot long Blacktron Intelligence Agency is fully assembled only for shows like Brickworld.

8

Everything a Princess Could Wish For

A few hours later, and Saturday evening is getting close to Sunday morning. Kate has returned from visiting friends in Chicago. We're in our hotel room, and I'm going to unveil a surprise. Earlier I bought a LEGO set at a charity auction. I hold it behind my back and tell her I have a present. She holds out her hands and closes her eyes, as is our custom.

"Oh man, we have to wait until Christmas!" she exclaims, quickly explaining to her Jewish husband the rudimentary steps involved in opening the 2007 LEGO City Advent calendar. The set is designed like a traditional Advent calendar, with twenty-four cut-out windows. The idea is to open one window each day, beginning on December 1, to count down the days until December 24, Christmas Eve.

"Nope, it's from 2007." I snatch away the briefcase-size box and begin to open window number 10.

"Wait." She stops me. "You have to open them in order."

"How many numbers are there?"

"Well, dear. How many days are there before Christmas?" asks Kate. I stop asking questions.

She pops a minifigure out of window number 6. "This one looks like he's been eating a lot of chocolate. He might be a policeman or an airport manager."

"This is the municipal set, that's what he would be," I reply.

"Nope, he's a luggage handler. There is a little suitcase." She opens number 8.

"That makes sense. What little kid is going to be like, yeah, I finally got an airport manager?"

"What little kid is going to be like, yeah, I got a luggage handler?" huffs Kate.

"Some kid who has a dad for a luggage handler," I suggest. She is not impressed by this retort.

Another minifigure in overalls appears in window number 10. "This guy looks like a miner or a policeman. At least he doesn't have a scary chocolate mouth. But he does have weird hair," she tells me.

"He's a plumber."

"Oh, look, another airport manager. I have to say, facial hair and LEGO guys—not so much. This one kind of looks like that critic . . ."

"James Lipton?" I suggest.

"Yeah. James Lipton as an airport manager." She moves on to another minifig with a broom. "Oh, this looks like old James Lipton."

"Do you think he's fallen on hard times?"

In box number 22 is the final minifigure. "He's a submarine operator," Kate says confidently.

"How many municipalities own submarines?" I ask my wife, who actually works in city government.

"Oh, that's a bullhorn. He's a police officer. There's the police officer."

We sit there in pajamas, playing with the figures, the fire hydrant, and the trash barrel for the better part of an hour. Small pieces set up for a LEGO city. We're playing like children, and right then it doesn't feel weird that we have no children of our own to share this moment. Kate collected miniatures while growing up—furniture for a micro-size dollhouse and tiny porcelain puppies. I wonder if she is getting hooked, but I'm skeptical, because the odds of my wife turning into an adult fan of LEGO are about as good as her correctly identifying the occupation of a minifig.

The next morning I take Kate on a tour through the convention. We don't have to wait in line to buy tickets. I just show my magnetic attendee badge, appropriately made of LEGO bricks, and her visitor pass.

Across from a re-creation of Jurassic Park, we see Dave and Stacy Sterling's town and train display. They're one of only a handful of couples who not only are attending Brickworld, but who actually build together. In fact, there just aren't many women at Brickworld—only twenty-two attendees this year. LEGO is a boy's club, seemingly from an early age.

"I think there is something that genetically skews us towards boys, but we can do better," LEGO CEO Jørgen Knudstorp told Reuters in March 2008. "There is something about the idea of constructing and deconstructing or destroying which frankly is an important part of Lego play that is a very boys-type of activity."

It is that idea that leads Esther Walner, the moderator and creator of the Belville competition I participated in the previous day, to lead a roundtable discussion, Female Fans of LEGO, on the second day of the convention. The main topic on the floor is how LEGO can attract more girls to the hobby. Esther puts the room at ease, standing with her hands clasped behind her back. She is wearing a simple blue dress, and her brown hair is neatly tied up in a scarf. A castle builder and steampunk fan, she's actually applying her degree in medieval studies to her interest in LEGO.

"I was close to being an empty nester with only one little one left at home. For seven years, I played with LEGOs with him, not knowing that there were adults out there who played with LEGO. I happened to see an ad for Brickworld and was amazed to find a community of adults," says Esther, who is attending the convention for the second year.

She lives in St. Louis Park, Minnesota, a ripe area for adult fans in the well-represented TWINLUG because of their access to the LEGO Imagination Center. The sixty-five-hundred-square-foot display was the first retail store to open in the United States, when it fittingly was built inside the Mall of America in 1992. Her story encourages the women around the room to talk about how they got started as builders.

"Like so many of you, I got involved with LEGO because of a guy," says Virginia Alvarez, a wry smile spreading across her face. "I had to drive my son to meetings because he wasn't old enough. But then, I wanted to build the things that guys build—I just wanted to build them in different colors."

Tracy Dale, one of the judges from my Belville contest, suggests that Virginia might not be that different from the guys after all.

"You wouldn't believe how many guys buy pink bricks from our store. I have no idea what they build with all of those pink bricks," she jokes.

The concept of pink bricks drove LEGO to introduce the Paradisa line in 1991—a line that evoked Miami more than any particular theme. The idea was to create colors that might appeal more to girl builders. Pink, turquoise, and pastel-color bricks and elements were the most salient features of the sets (with names like Sunset Stables and Cabana Beach) that were produced for three years. Lackluster sales suggested that colors were not the way to engage girls, so LEGO moved into the world of role-playing with the introduction of Belville in 1994.

Mention of the name "Belville" brings groans from the ten women in the room, many of whom feel the sets aren't designed to help girls be builders, but are just meant to be pretty.

"There are so many premade pieces and so much pink. Not every girl's favorite color is pink or purple. I didn't want to play with Barbie. She was blond and pink, but I was dying for a brunette doll," says Alice Cook, a fellow member of TWINLUG.

Criticizing the LEGO Group for its color choices seems to be a general trait of adult fans, regardless of gender; the great "bley" debate raged among male and female builders alike. But within the arguments over pink or purple pieces, a bigger complaint seems to be under the surface: LEGO just doesn't get girls. It's a fact that LEGO itself seems close to admitting.

"There is genuine bafflement on their part how to attract female professional builders. I don't know if it is because female builders tend to keep a lower profile or there just aren't as many out there because they didn't play with LEGO growing up," says Joe Meno.

In 1963, Godtfred Kirk Christiansen drew up a list of ten requirements for creating a quality toy. The second on that list was that LEGO be good for both boys and girls. It was always seen as a unisex product, even if marketing or social norms unintentionally turned it into a toy for boys. LEGO's approach didn't change for nearly two decades.

Alice works in the LEGO retail store at the Mall of America. "It's difficult because I'll see a mom with a boy and a girl," she tells the group. "And she'll say to the girl, 'You don't want Star Wars, you want Belville.' Or even worse, 'We're shopping for your brother now and we'll get something for you next.'"

In 1979, LEGO unveiled its first set exclusively for girls: Scala, a line of buildable jewelry. Over two years, LEGO released nine sets that encouraged kids to customize a hand mirror, a bracelet, a necklace, or a ring with printed tiles. LEGO later expanded the Scala line to include dolls. These were figures larger than minifigures, with actual strands of hair, and they came with a range of accessories from hair dryers to puppies.

"Girls had become girls again, after the 1970s and the first half of the 1980s unisex period," Lars Koelbaek, LEGO's international marketing manager at the time, told the Associated Press in July 1995.

The company discovered in the 1980s that sales figures for girls were dropping. The challenge for LEGO remains today: How can the company make products that appeal specifically to girls?

"LEGO was such a big success that we didn't really feel that there was a special need for girls," Koelbaek said. "Recently, we had to admit that we had a wrong conception of it."

Scala evolved into the line known as Clikits in 2003. And here LEGO showed how it had evolved from 1979. Clikits debuted after four years of market research, during which LEGO contracted out to discover that mothers believed arts and crafts led to the promotion of positive values. Suddenly LEGO was a tween toy, aimed at girls between seven and fourteen, and sold in the clothing retailer Limited Too.

LEGO was consciously marketing to girls, offering up marketing-speak to justify the interlocking pieces designed to create friendship bracelets, picture frames, and customized tote bags. The product line existed until 2008, when the trademark Clikits girls Daisy, Heart, and Star were discontinued.

That same year LEGO was accused of gender stereotyping by Sweden's Trade Ethical Council against Sexism in Advertising when a product catalog depicted a girl playing with a castle in a pink-themed room and a boy playing in a blue room with a fire truck and airplane. The captions on the pages read respectively, "Everything a princess could wish for," and "Tons of blocks for slightly older boys." In attempting to change its marketing approach to girls, LEGO may have inadvertently reinforced the very idea that they were seeking to eliminate: that standard bricks are only for boys.

In looking purely at aesthetics, LEGO may have forgotten the value of play for girls. The women gathered suggest that LEGO should instead be focusing on how the bricks will be played with rather than what the bricks look like.

"I think LEGO should look at things that are either historically based or relate to real life. Each construction event is solitary;

you're super in your own element. I wonder if they could reinterpret LEGO as social or interactive, it could allow women to play together," says a woman named Jacque, her voice rising from beneath a mass of black curls.

A large part of me wonders if the boy builders are the ones barring the door to the club. Even at the Female Fans of LEGO roundtable, the three guys in the room contribute a disproportionate amount to the discussion, seemingly telling women what they want. When you combine that with an entirely male atmosphere, it seems that it would be difficult to find acceptance as a female builder.

I know just whom to ask. "Does anybody ever bug you about bringing Stacy along?" I say to Dave as Stacy shows Kate the goth record store she designed and built for their joint display.

"Nope, they're just happy I found somebody who loves LEGO as much as I do," says Dave.

This is a couple we would hang out with on a Friday night, if they lived near us. Dave and Stacy seem to love each other as much as they love whatever they're doing. In 2002, Dave hit the Midwestern rallying circuit in his 1986 Dodge Omni GLH. Stacy was there as his co-driver. But when you blow a part or bust up a car, you can't reuse the pieces. The investment in rallycar racing didn't make sense compared with the cast of the Star Wars and Harry Potter sets they were buying. LEGO can always be dismantled and turned into something else.

Now they create joint displays in the basement of their Trempealeau, Wisconsin, home that has been converted for LEGO storage, building, and photography. Dave's trains run throughout a building layout designed by Stacy. He points to a helicopter that sits on the roof of a brick structure.

"Jamie gave this to me. He was just here. He wanted to know about my building techniques." Dave has a huge smile because he's just been complimented by one of the adult fans who has reached the promised land.

Jamie Berard, from Metheun, Massachusetts, is a bona fide set designer living in Billund, Denmark, and working at LEGO headquarters. He is part of the company's contingent attending

Brickworld. The blue-and-white LEGO helicopter he has given Dave is one of the city sets he has designed.

As Kate and I travel between the two display rooms, I introduce her to Kathie Bonahoom, Bryan's wife. Her red hair pulled back into a ponytail, she is directing people toward the second ballroom of LEGO creations.

"Be careful," Kathie jokingly warns Kate. "It seems like Jonathan is starting to enjoy himself."

Kathie is teasing, but finding a partner who understands their addiction to LEGO is a real concern for adult fans. At best, your partner can see why LEGO is so important—that it is not a child's toy and you are not an overgrown child. Most adult fans would even settle for a girlfriend who is neutral toward the hobby, who just files it into the nebulous category of "man activities."

"My fiancée keeps a tight rein on me. Since we got engaged last year, I've made just four BrickLink orders," joked Adam Tucker near the end of his architecture lecture on the first day of the convention —a comment that drew laughs and commiseration from the married guys in the audience.

LEGO has come between spouses and ended a number of marriages. Some adult fans hide the costs of their habit, and financial struggles can devastate a healthy relationship. In addition, there's the constant reminder of an AFOL's collection, as set boxes and loose bricks begin piling up around the house.

I'm telling Kate about Duane's collection as he and Joe say good-bye to us on our way out the door.

"Make him have a LEGO room," says Duane, when Kate asks for advice.

"Be careful," Joe says to Kate, echoing Kathie's warning. "LEGO has led to a lot of divorces."

Kate laughs, but it is the laugh where I can tell she's not amused. "Well, I'm here . . . right?" she answers.

I'm leaving the convention early and with genuine regret, but a friend has just had a baby and I'm not allowed to leave Chicago without a visit. In the car, I put my newfound LEGO powers to the test. It's not quite *Searching for Bobby Fischer*, but it's close.

As I peruse the passing scenery, LEGO elements stand out like misplaced Tetris bricks.

A mailbox appears blocky or a Toyota Scion rumbles by and you see how it is basically just a rectangle on wheels. Before you know it, you're looking at everything and thinking, "I could build that out of LEGO."

It is an easy thought, one that sneaks in quickly, almost reflexively. It feels like the moment when you begin dreaming in another language—a breakthrough that you're not quite sure you actually had. As my wife and I drive throughout the Chicago suburbs, I continually remark to her on the squat brick row houses and dilapidated warehouses—repeating my new mantra: "I could build that out of LEGO."

She lets that go on for about two hours before finally telling me I have to stop. At least she doesn't threaten me with divorce papers. But if she did, I could build them out of LEGO.

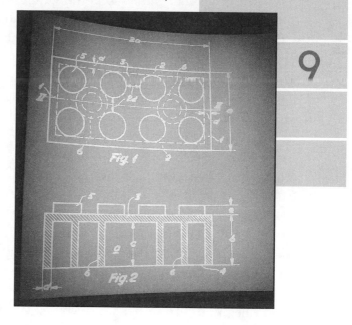

Figures 1 and 2 from the original LEGO patent filed on January 28, 1958, illustrate the interlocking stud-and-tube system.

9

I Go on a Playdate

Traveling with LEGO turns out to be like a day at the beach. Bricks get into everything, and you're not sure exactly how that happened. I'm searching for a pen in my laptop bag to interview a local brewer in Kansas City for a magazine article when I instead pull out two minifigs.

"My kid loves LEGO," he tells me, our feet dangling from bar stools in the taproom of the brewery.

"So do I," I say sheepishly, hunting for that pen.

On the drive home, I feel something digging into the underside of my thigh and discover three 1 × 1 blue headlight (a square brick with a round opening on its face that resembles a car headlight) bricks on the driver's seat. Hiding in the corner of my suitcase are several 2 × 2 red bricks; I will find them four months later when I'm getting ready to head home for Thanksgiving. Maybe this is what it is like to have kids—toys turning up in unexpected places.

When LEGO bricks have fully taken over one half of my L-shaped desk and are piled high in every storage container in our house, I make the decision that I need to start sorting again. I also need to start scheduling my appointments better. In the next few days, I'm slated to meet with a LEGO BrickLink seller and a LEGO consultant, and I still need to find time to build. The challenges of working with people and compartmentalizing my life are becoming as difficult as locating the translucent end of a LEGO light saber I haphazardly dropped into a box of parts.

I'm beginning to understand why LEGO purists hate MEGA Bloks. The popular plastic rival from a Canadian toymaker is generally dismissed by adult fans of LEGO as either of inferior quality or just a poor substitute for their true passion.

I find twenty-six MEGA Bloks in a few hours of sorting and begin hurling them toward the trash. They can't be categorized or sorted; and although they interlock with LEGO elements, the fit isn't quite perfect. And this mixing is exactly what LEGO has always feared.

In the past decade, LEGO has filed suit in Canada and the European Union arguing that MEGA Brands, Inc., is guilty of trademark infringement. LEGO ultimately lost both suits. The studs were deemed a matter of patent law because the functional design meant they weren't eligible for trademark protection.

"Cylinders are the obvious engineering choice for the connecting knobs and are the first shapes that come to mind to a competent engineer," wrote Justice Frederick Gibson of the Canadian Federal Court in the 2002 decision of *Kirkbi Ag and Lego Canada Inc.* v. *Ritvik Holdings Inc.*

LEGO had been seeking damages in the amount of $25 million. With the decision, MEGA Brands was free to continue producing bricks, since LEGO's Canadian patents expired in 1988.

That is not to say MEGA Bloks lack fans. MEGA Brands, Inc., is a powerhouse. They've secured licenses for the Harry Potter series (after LEGO dropped the license and the sets) and Pirates of the Caribbean. The publicly traded company had sales of $79.1 million in the first quarter of 2008.

The MEGA Bloks story is another tale of a family business. Victor and Rita Bertrand founded the company in 1967 as Ritvik Toys, Inc. Today the company is run by the second generation, with COO Vic Bertrand Jr. and CEO Marc Bertrand continually clashing with LEGO.

The Canadian company utilizes a similar stud-and-tube interlocking brick system to LEGO. Its mini size, introduced in 1989, is equivalent to LEGO's DUPLO line. Micro bricks, the same size as the standard LEGO brick, came into production two years later.

Ultimately, this is the Coke-Pepsi debate of the interlocking plastic brick world. It's simply a matter of taste and cost. But when it comes to sorting, there is no place for MEGA Bloks in my collection.

I didn't think I would need inspiration for sorting, but I spend as much time trying to decide on a system as I do actually sorting. I turn to Andreas Stabno, and I ask if I could come visit the BrickLink store he manages, to see how he organizes his five hundred thousand LEGO bricks.

The store happens to be in his basement; so the following Sunday he meets me at the door of his two-story home on a quiet cul-de-sac in nearby Lee's Summit, Missouri. His two daughters stand shyly by his side.

He hands me a small piece of paper with tape on the back. It's my press pass for the day and it reads, "Junulest [journalist], Mr. Jonathan, Press." Our roles established, we head down to the finished basement to see the operations for the store.

"I started with a closet. And then my personal collection grew into a LEGO room. It was my wife who ultimately got me organized. We alphabetized everything by color and size. Each drawer has the type and color. Ziploc baggies are a good idea too," says Andreas as we walk down the carpeted steps.

The basement is split into two main rooms. To the left of the stairs is the play area with a home theater setup and LEGO creations in various stages of completion or deconstruction on three large racks. On the other side of the stairs is the headquarters for BrickScope—his online storefront on BrickLink.

"The sole purpose here is to be able to find everything fast. When we're processing orders, we just want to get everything out the door," says Andreas.

The standard bricks are in a small U-shaped closet off the main room: bricks on the left, slopes in the middle, and plates on the right. Everything is marked with labels delineating the size and the color. Clear tubs are stacked from the floor to the ceiling. Henry Jones Sr. figures sit in plastic bags next to Harry Potter figures.

"The good stuff sells really fast, while some stuff has been sitting here a couple of years. That's the challenge. You can't pick and choose what you want from a set—the good comes with the bad," says Andreas.

He slides out the bottom bin from a freestanding rack to illustrate his point. Hundreds of rubber band holders are piled inside. LEGO makes rubber bands that encircle the gears on Technic wheels. The holders are essentially packaging waste, but because they're made by LEGO, they're kept.

"These are useless," says Andreas, fingering the gray plastic pieces that look like small TIE-fighters and shaking his head, "but all it takes is for someone to figure out a cool use for a part and post it online to change the market."

In other words, dark green bricks weren't always twenty-five cents apiece and white bricks won't always be a nickel. Everything is inventoried in BrickLink. Once you enter a set number into the online store, the parts are entered automatically into your inventory.

"Let's say we buy two hundred Indiana Jones sets. That means we've got two hundred Harrison Fords; but we've also got two hundred coiled whips and messenger pouches," says Andreas.

The true money maker is an L-shaped sorting desk tucked under the stairs. Gray storage cases, the kind designed to hold screws and nails, line the back half of the desk. They are labeled alphabetically: *Axe. Bag. Batarang.* They are filled with minifigure accessories. I have never seen so many Obi-Wan heads.

"People love minifigs, anything Star Wars–related, and female heads. It's like an impulse buy at the grocery store—people just throw a few of those little added extras or fun accessories into their order," says Andreas.

On the desk is a computer printout of the latest orders Andreas has to fill. He asks if I want to pull an order for a customer. He hands me a white tray with sixteen open squares, three bathroom-size paper cups (the kind you used to wash your mouth with after brushing your teeth as a kid), and a $5.11 order destined for a LEGO fan in Arizona. Andreas will later fill a $5.11 order that came in a half hour later, for completely different parts and destined for Australia.

I make several laps of the two-hundred-square-foot room to find thirty-two total pieces—sixteen plant parts and sixteen 1×1 tan tiles.

"I bet he's making a vignette, maybe with a garden?" I guess as I pull parts.

"That's the fun of this job, trying to figure out what exactly somebody is going to build with fifty minifig arms," says Andreas.

It takes only four minutes, but it still seems like a lot of work for $5.11. I'm benefiting from the months that it took Andreas and his wife to set up the store. The parts still need to be packed according to the instructions of the buyer, sealed in a manila envelope, and dropped off at the post office.

The remains of Andreas's train collection are the only LEGO creations on display in the storeroom. The six shelves of parts are likely the few things in the room that he won't sell. But pieces have gone missing, a railing or a corner brick. And that seems to be the true cost of running a BrickLink store: you can't really be so attached to what you're selling—it just doesn't make business sense. Bricks become a commodity, to be bought and sold according to their value in the market.

In contrast to the store, there is no system of organization in the playroom. A replica of the World Cup trophy sits next to clear tubs of loose brick. A massive green and yellow subway layout rests on a table. I see a blue elephant and then notice a Spider Man set, which I'm fairly certain isn't LEGO.

"That isn't MEGA Bloks, is it?" I ask.

"It is. I got it as a birthday gift," says Andreas. He quickly trails off and picks up two Mindstorm bricks, meant to be part of a robot capable of solving the Rubik's Cube.

He jokingly tells me about standing in line at Walmart and a Kansas City Chiefs game to show off his entries in building competitions: the blue elephant and the trophy.

"The other competitors were probably six to nine years old. I didn't care about winning, I just wanted to show what I had built," says Andreas, laughing for the first time since I've been there.

The rooms represent the two sides of Andreas. There is the former collector who wants to stay connected to the hobby he loves by running a small business for fellow collectors. But somewhere in the breakdown of sets and the establishment of a business plan, Andreas the builder has gotten lost. It's hard to appreciate a subway car when you know that it took $50 of your inventory to put it together. Particularly when the condition is so important on BrickLink. Some builders will only use new parts, concerned about crimps or bricks that smell because they come from a smoking household. And those who do buy used parts expect a discount, even for elements in like-new condition.

"So, wait, people can buy bricks online?" asks my father-in-law, Bob, after dinner that night. "Without buying the sets?"

"Sure. They just pay for the elements they want. You just pick tiles or bricks in the color you need."

I can tell he's not quite getting the difference between element types, so I grab four buckets from my office and push aside the dinner plates to show him. It's easier to demonstrate with the actual pieces.

"This is a slope. This is a headlight," I hold up the angled piece and 1×1 brick in quick succession.

Kate grabs a blue 2×4 plate. "And this is a plate, it's one-third as tall as a regular brick. When it's smooth, it's called a tile."

I feel like a proud papa—my wife knows the different LEGO bricks. But I don't compliment her, because I know she'll think I'm patronizing her.

The discussion moves away from LEGO and into the political machinations of the Kansas City government. But a funny thing happens while we're talking. We all start building something. Kate begins constructing a sculpture that consists of interlocking rectangles made of plates and grille tiles in blue and dark gray. I am snapping together a red, white, and blue spaceship, while Bob is stacking bricks into a large square.

"I'm not sure I'm building anything," says Bob, frustration creeping into his voice.

"Sure you are, you're building right now. What did you want to build?" I ask.

"Well, I just was putting bricks together. I didn't think about what I wanted it to look like," he answers.

"Well, that's why it doesn't look like anything."

Unconsciously, Bob and I have been discussing the basic tenets that underlie LEGO Serious Play—the business consulting arm of the LEGO Group—where executives like Bob use LEGO bricks to solve their organizational problems.

In 1996, CEO Kjeld Kirk Kristiansen was searching for a way to improve the strategic planning at LEGO, feeling that the company wasn't being innovative in the face of a new wave of electronic toys. He began talking to Johan Roos and Bart Victor, two professors at the Swiss business school IMD (International Institute for Management Development), about developing a business strategy process for LEGO. Roos and Victor quickly came to believe that LEGO bricks held the answer to solving the organization's difficulties.

The duo worked on various implementation strategies before being teamed with Robert Rasmussen at LEGO. Rasmussen was the leader of the concept team for LEGO Mindstorms and had experience working with academics, having partnered with the MIT Media Lab to develop the robotics kit.

At the core of LEGO Serious Play is Seymour Papert's theory of constructionism. The MIT professor theorized that people learn by building something that helps explain and define relationships. His work, in turn, was in part based on the ideas of the famed Swiss philosopher and psychologist Jean Piaget, who suggested that knowledge is the sum total of our experiences.

The LEGO bricks are what connect those theories in practice. The participants build sculptures and explain their constructions through metaphor and storytelling. Employees who might have difficulty with a face-to-face confrontation can instead express their feelings by placing a minifigure in a particular spot on a baseplate.

Kristiansen established a separate entity from LEGO, entitled Executive Discovery, to fund the new initiative. Rasmussen was named president, and Serious Play launched in 2001 as the first LEGO product designed exclusively for adults.

"The kind of creativity and learning we instinctively accomplished through play, when we were children, is exactly the skill needed in today's business meeting rooms," said Bart Victor in a September 2001 press release from LEGO. "We've turned the LEGO idea of open-ended play into a model for business strategy."

Rasmussen stayed on with Serious Play until 2003, before leaving to start an independent consulting group, Rasmussen and Associates. One of his last trainees was a former Royal Navy lieutenant named Gary Mankellow. I reach out to him because he happens to live just outside of Kansas City, and he knows why LEGO Serious Play hasn't yet caught on in the United States.

But right now Gary is only worried that the battery on his laptop is going to die again. A picture of a LEGO duck is on the screen; and our neighbors in the coffee shop in the Plaza shopping district of Kansas City look on curiously—as likely to be attracted by the image as by Gary's slight British accent and his striking white hair. Before the computer can shut down, he talks as fast as he can

"It's universal and it's tactile, so when you combine that with business communication strategies, I was instantly sold," says Gary.

Gary is not an adult fan of LEGO. The closest he got to LEGO as a kid was Tinker Toys. He is a business consultant, having launched Dynamic Adult Learning in 1996 when he left his sales trainee position at Pfizer. In fact, none of the other people he trained with were AFOLs. They were professionally trained consultants willing to spend $3,000 to learn if LEGO actually had business applications.

"I remember during my training that I was trying to build a model about managing. I'd never built with LEGO before and I couldn't find the cogs I needed to make a moving machine. I got very frustrated because when the time was called, I wasn't done. When it came time to tell my story, I said that I keep building these things, but I never get them finished. That was something I had never realized about my business," says Gary.

He has the smooth polish of a motivational speaker—exactly the type of partner LEGO sought for the launch of Serious Play. The idea was to use established consultants to legitimize a children's toy for use by adult executives to solve real business problems.

"The majority of people who want to do this likely can't have LEGO Serious Play be their only source of income. And LEGO would probably argue that they have always wanted it to be one of the tools in a consultant's bag," says Gary.

Accordingly, LEGO has struggled to identify what it has in Serious Play. So it makes absurd sense that a British expat living in Kansas City would be one of the fifty-three trained partners in twenty-seven countries. While consulting sessions involve LEGO, the point is not necessarily to get corporations to buy more of LEGO's product, but instead to use LEGO's product to transform their business. At the same time, the audience is adults, very serious adults, a decidedly different consumer than five- to nine-year-old boys.

"So the challenge for LEGO Serious Play is that it's still in its infancy, but they're starting to work with some major multinational firms like Shell and BASF. But how does this create business for LEGO? It's the instructors forming the partnerships, and often there's a limited window of contact," says Gary.

Originally a subsidiary, Serious Play was folded under the education division of the company. A year after Rasmussen left in 2003, the training program was put on hold in the United States. It seemed as though LEGO was constantly revising the concept. Although Serious Play has more traction in LEGO's home country of Denmark, companies in the United States still appear wary about using a consulting session that involves a child's toy.

"We did something like that once. I only remember that I wasn't happy with what I built. That's about the extent of what I took away from it," says Bob when I ask if he's ever done any training with LEGO.

Another possible explanation for the lack of buy-in from the corporate sector is the high cost of LEGO itself. Gary estimates that for a typical daylong session with eight to ten people, he's going to need about $2,000 worth of LEGO bricks. That's a heavy investment from a potential client before he's even asked for a consulting fee. Although at that price, his case for presentations is a Castle fan's dream, with forty skeletons designed to represent the skeletons in a corporate closet.

At the same time, LEGO bricks are also how Gary usually makes a sale. He asks potential clients to picture a duck made from LEGO.

"When you ask people to build a duck, you'll get six different ducks. It's like going into a business meeting and saying, 'Okay guys, we want to talk about the budget.' Everybody immediately has their own picture of the budget. People get that right away," says Gary.

Google is arguably the most prominent example of a company that believes the creativity inspired by building with LEGO bricks is tied to business innovation. The first server cases for the technology company were built out of toy bricks because they were cheap and modular. As Google grew, so did the influence of LEGO's values at the company. In attending LEGO-sponsored workshops, Google has come to embody the idea of taking play and design more seriously. The New York City headquarters have a LEGO build room, where clear tubs hold elements, sorted by color and part, on rows of white shelves. LEGO mosaics of co-founders Sergey Brin and Larry Page hang on the wall. But the room isn't just a corporate perk; it's a clear message that creativity can come from building. This is what Gary hopes for every time he approaches a new company, that he can materially impact the culture of the organization.

The relationship between Gary and LEGO is called a partnership, but it now seems to be closer to that of franchiser and franchisee. In addition to the training fee, LEGO instituted an annual licensing fee for LEGO Serious Play and requires that a partner complete five days of training. That licensing fee allows the use of LEGO's logo and access to marketing materials. At the same time, LEGO also began offering an in-house license facilitator training program, where companies could send a human resources person or company trainer for a day of training at a cost of $800. Despite new costs and the potential for competition from the very companies he's trying to attract as clients, Gary continues on as a LEGO Serious Play partner for one reason: he believes in what he is selling.

And although Gary is not an adult fan of LEGO, it would seem that his relationship with the company is not that different from AFOLs'. LEGO has almost all the power, dictating the terms of the relationship as they constantly retool the Serious Play program. At the same time, LEGO Serious Play doesn't seem to offer the promise of a lot of money or even celebrity, but it does have exclusivity. As one of only fifty-three trained partners, Gary has something that adult fans crave, and that is access. But he doesn't want to use LEGO bricks to build the Chrysler building. He wants to use them to rebuild Chrysler.

10

I Give My Wife a Beach House

The mantel in our living room is slowly filling up with my creations, as I try to keep them away from the jaws of my dog and the paws of my cat. A ring of trucks encircles the base of our television, while the biplane I built several months back is starting to get dingy. Unattended LEGO bricks magnetically attract dust.

Kate orders me to clean everything up, but suggests that I turn the top of the bookcase into a rotating LEGO display. It not only is larger than the mantel, but it sits in the corner of the living room. As this is one of the few limitations she's put on my building, I agree without argument. It will still be one of the first things people see when they walk into the house. And I start to think that we need something more impressive to display, which at my building level means buying a large kit as opposed to designing an original creation.

I feel slightly devious when I bring home the LEGO Creator Beach House, a yellow home with a black roof that has tons of architectural details. It's the set that I thought my urban planner wife would pick out as the one she wanted to build.

"Ooh, what's that?" she asks, coming in the door. I have strategically left the Beach House box on the coffee table in our living room.

"Oh, just a new set. I was planning on building it tonight. Want to help?" I ask casually.

"Yes," says Kate enthusiastically, turning over the box and getting lost in the details.

After a week of building by myself, I'm a bit anxious when we start ripping open the plastic bags together. And I quickly get frustrated, as we both search for parts and snap pieces onto the gray baseplate. I stop talking because I don't want to lash out at my wife and grab a piece from her hand. I feel that I see connections faster than she does or notice parts in a bag that she continually stumbles past. She's more deliberate, making sure that she is doing everything right. I'm an impulsive builder, trying to go faster in order to get to the next step. Our LEGO building apparently mirrors our personalities.

Kate stops talking, focusing on the picture-based instructions and building the base of the 522-piece house. The problem is that each step is based on the bricks that were laid in the preceding step. It quickly becomes obvious that this construction site can't run without a competent foreman. To avoid an argument (we only fight over home improvement projects and driving directions), I relinquish the final say to Kate. So I become a brick monkey, grabbing the pieces that Kate needs and laying them out for her to take in rapid succession. This turns out to be effective; it's the same strategy we used when laying a brick paver patio in our backyard over Labor Day weekend. After I leave to attend an evening rehearsal for the improvisational comedy troupe I belong to, she continues building.

I've always seen improv as my secret weapon as a builder. The ability to change directions immediately and find humor in unique situations is helpful when it comes to MOCs. Also, I can still laugh at myself when I have unconsciously built another camel. Perhaps most important, one of the cardinal rules of improv is to accept and build on whatever someone says in a scene. My experience with teamwork onstage makes it a lot easier to take the instructions of a LEGO foreman, find what she needs, and offer support during the building process.

"I finished the first floor. I hope you don't mind," says Kate when I return. She also holds up a tissue box she has cut in half to help her keep bricks close by without losing pieces to the couch. My wife is a builder. We leave the model unfinished and I promise to wait until she comes home the next day to start again. But I'm worse at sharing than I thought, because the next day I sit down in front of the construction site over lunch. *I'll just pop in a few pieces.* And suddenly the roof is done and the Beach House is finished.

The desire for "just one more" has been reawakened. It's that little voice that begs for another minute before bed, one more chapter in a book, or a bit more whipped cream. It's a child's voice, and it's starting to pipe up with LEGO building. There's always one more page in the instruction manual. And the truth is, you're always one step closer to finishing.

When I tell Dave Sterling about the feeling, he sympathizes. "Whether it's putting one more brick on, building one more set, or buying one more copy of a set . . . it's a constant battle between the kid inside and the adult voice of reason. More often than not, the kid wins."

When you become an adult, there is nobody older to tell you that you have to stop. You must be your own voice of reason, offering up a counter-voice—there's work tomorrow or chores to do now. And it's easy to see the voice of reason get drowned out, because it's never offering a fun alternative. That is how you end up with a house full of LEGO, because it's nice to feel like a kid for a while, indulging your wants in place of your needs.

The Beach House is the first larger-size model I've completed, and although I can appreciate the finished product that I built with my wife, my overarching desire is to build something better, something of my own design. Something that people will focus on instead of a store-bought model. I need a signature style. The great LEGO builders, like great artists, are recognizable in what they build. And most of their inspiration seems to come from the theme they love. The space guys build fantastical transport ships. The castle fans have articulated cliffside dwellings, and the Technic builders are all about intricate machines.

I haven't fallen in love with a theme, in part because I didn't build thematically as a child. Well, that, and the fact that LEGO Ninjas lasted only from 1998 to 2000.

"I feel like I need to build something huge that will catch everybody's attention," I tell Joe Meno over the phone. He has recently returned from introducing *BrickJournal* to the crowd at Comic-Con in San Diego.

"You don't need to have a big collection to build well, you just need to use parts in interesting ways and build things you like," says Joe.

The number of bricks and the scale in which people build will give clues to their style. Minifig scale, in which everything is built around the size of a minifig, is approximately 1:48, and is probably the most common for group displays. Some AFOLs are known for constructions in micro scale—tiny re-creations of buildings and objects. Buildings can be scaled down to a ratio as low as 1:1,250. At LEGOLAND, building models are constructed to a scale of 1:20, meaning the real Empire State Building is twenty times larger than its theme park counterpart. A Miniland USA figure, a man or a woman made of bricks, is eighteen times smaller than the average human.

With a collection of maybe a few thousand LEGO bricks, I think I'm probably more suited to building in micro scale. And the idea of making very small re-creations of large objects reminds me of my favorite store as a child: Think Big in New York City, which made micro and mega versions of everyday objects. Unfortunately, Think Big was a failed retail concept. I still covet the overstuffed baseball glove chair. Micro is a theme unto itself, transcending the space-castle continuum.

When I look through my collection, I see lots of small tires. That is not an accident; LEGO is the largest manufacturer of tires in the world, with 306 million produced per year. It's why Andreas Stabno will never be able to sell all of the tires in his BrickLink store. A bag of tires at a LEGO convention is a sucker's buy.

Joe has advised me to look for the most obvious feature of a given model, whether it is Groucho Marx's glasses or the arch of a Volkswagen Beetle. If you can boil down a building or a car or a sculpture to a series of small, recognizable pieces, then you can create something that is dramatically better than you expected when you start.

The wheels I'm looking at are small, no bigger than my thumbnail, so I decide to make a series of micro-scale vehicles, just two studs wide. I start with a yellow construction vehicle. Translucent 1×2 bricks form the cab, and a yellow 2×4 plate serves as the base of the truck. I use only ten pieces total, but it's my favorite construction I've built.

I have a stack of translucent bricks from the Pick A Brick cup I purchased at Brickworld, so I know I'm going to build a line of trucks with the bricks forming the front windshield and windows of the cab. The fun comes from hunting down unique elements to give the impression of what I'm trying to build with just a single piece. A hinged gray 1×2 Technic brick (meaning it has holes for pins rather than studs) and a gray spaceship seat become the back of a dump truck. Building one model always seems to inspire the next. In the course of a search, I start pulling elements that suggest the top of a flatbed truck or the shape of a garbage truck. I'm not building in rainbow mode anymore; instead I'm focusing on getting colors to match actual trucks I've seen or the pictures I pull up for comparison on the Internet.

After four days of building small trucks, I finally find what I would have wanted to build as a kid: a monorail. The boxy nature of the trucks, when combined with a 1×2 element that resembles a toolbox, captures the shape of the coolest kind of train. I also start to think about design elements. The track is just an inverted plate, attached to supports from the Mars Mission set like the kind that I used for my biplane. The plate, studs pointing down, simulates track ties, and the exposed tubes give it a railroad feel. At twelve studs long and two studs wide, this MOC stretches the width of a sticky note.

Dave posts a comment after I put up a picture of the monorail MOC on my blog: "Dude, that MOC is hott. Yeah, you score two 't's' for the monorail. Nice work on this one. I really dig the use of the 'toolboxes' for the front and rear."

It is the first public compliment I've received about something I've built, and it feels good. My self-confidence as a LEGO builder is officially tied to responses from the Internet.

Online is also where I can find a lot of ideas for future projects, including a LEGO vignette, typically a small scene constructed on an 8×8 baseplate.

"The best vignettes capture a slice of life, and tell a small story in a scene, often with a sense of humor. The small size both encourages creativity and makes it possible for people with small collections to be on the same playing field as those with very large collections," wrote AFOL Bruce Hietbrink in his March 2005 post on LUGNET, trying to define the first scenes he had seen from Japanese builders.

The vignette interests me because it is as much about building skill as it is about your ability to use your sense of humor. I find out that BrickCon, an AFOL convention I will be attending in October, will be having a group display around a zombie theme. This will be like the Belville challenge, except I'll have time to prepare.

Although you're free to put a lot of time into planning a vignette, the actual build time is meant to be short. I grab an 8×16 green baseplate and start to think about zombies. I also look at the clock and see that I've been playing with LEGO bricks for the better part of three hours. This means I'm late to pick up our weekly basket of vegetables from a local farmer, which Kate and I do as part of a community supported agriculture program.

And thus, a zombie farmer vignette is born. A skeleton head on a minifig body clutches a hatchet, getting ready to "harvest" from a patch of minifig heads and torsos. I reason that even zombies are getting into the whole "grow local, eat local" movement, with organic brains. The joke, it turns out, takes a bit too much explaining when I try it out on my wife.

The zombie farmer joins the menagerie on top of the living room bookshelf. However, most adult fans don't just display their creations in their homes; they want to show off their MOCs online. It's a way to rank what they've built against other creations and also get some feedback. And so I register for Brickshelf.com, a controversial photo host that is loved by some adult fans of LEGO and reviled by others.

In 1999, Virginia AFOL Kevin Loch was just looking for a place to show off some of the cool LEGO creations that he had discovered. The software engineer launched Brickshelf as a side project, posting notices to LUGNET when he added new MOCs. A year later, he opened up the hosting site to the public, encouraging members to post their own MOCs free of charge.

Over the next seven years, Brickshelf swelled to host 1.7 million photos and 24 million page views a month. Loch's hosting bill began to creep up, and the demands of running the site became too much. In July 2007, the site was shut down without warning for a few days, setting off a firestorm among AFOLs.

"Brickshelf has discontinued operation. We apologize for any inconvenience," was the short explanation on the home page.

The ire of adult fans erupted on LUGNET, attacking Loch and bemoaning the loss of their pictures.

"What was once a great service to the AFOL community has become an embarrassment," Bill Ward wrote a few days after the outage. "Kevin's utter lack of communication with the community is unforgivable. It's time to sell BS to someone who gives a damn."

Brickshelf wasn't sold. Loch agreed to keep it running with the help of heavy users, who would pay a $5 membership fee. But several AFOLs (particularly those who had lost photos during the site's outage) felt it was too little, too late. And Brickshelf was no longer the center of the LEGO fan universe. Many adult fans migrated over to Flickr, the photo sharing service, and to MOCpages.com, a new photo-hosting site launched by the LEGO-certified professional Sean Kenney.

"With so many alternatives suddenly vying to be that second 'something,' I'd urge everyone to exercise caution in the coming months. . . . [B]ear in mind that Flickr probably can't become the single LEGO hub that replaces Brickshelf," wrote AFOL Andrew Becraft in a July 2007 post on Flickr.

Andrew is the voice behind the Brothers Brick, an influential LEGO fan Web site, and a former LEGO ambassador. He was one of the few to seek out compromises in the debate over Brickshelf.

The LEGO Ambassador Program debuted in 2005 after the then community liaison Jake McKee introduced the idea in January of that year.

"LEGO Ambassador's mission is to help provide inspiration for LEGO builders of all ages and from all parts of the world," wrote Jake in a post on LUGNET that invited applications.

The idea was to find builders who were active online and offline in promoting LEGO. In exchange for signing a nondisclosure agreement (NDA), ambassadors would be given access to preproduct launch information and internal e-mails within the company.

"I wanted to help adult consumers understand the realities of the company and help company members understand why adult fans are interested in certain things," was Jake's response when I asked him about the early days of the Ambassador Program.

On one hand, this was an incredibly risky move by the LEGO company. Even with an NDA, they were sharing sensitive product information. They were also asking nonemployees to become involved in the corporate culture. At the same time, the program reinforced the established relationship between adult fans and LEGO. The fans would not be financially compensated for their time or efforts spent promoting the company. They would be rewarded with exclusive information, the product equivalent of spoilers, and an occasional gift of brick. Access was the currency. And many AFOLs, like Andrew

Becraft, saw the Ambassador Program as an olive branch for the uproar caused by the brown and gray color change.

"The LEGO community failed to ask anyone in the adult fan community when that happened. It's about compatibility and people's collections. The color change led directly to the formation of the Ambassador Program. They realized they made a huge mistake," said Andrew when we talked by phone.

The first four cycles were for six months each, and ambassadors had to reapply if they wanted to serve more than a single term. When Andrew submitted his name in 2007, it was with the idea that he could improve LEGO's communication because of his involvement with the AFOL site Classic-Castle.com and the growing general readership of his blog, Brothers Brick.

"Every social group has its own lingo and jargon. In my day job [as a lead technical writer for Microsoft], I have to bring in new people and help them understand what we're talking about. It's something I think about a lot and was trying to bring to the LEGO world," says Andrew.

That year, LEGO was still choosing the applicants, and the selection process was completely internal. It wasn't until the fourth year of the program that the LEGO Company required people to be nominated by fellow adult fans and then selected the nominees with a goal of geographic, gender, and builder diversity. The result was like the United Nations, with forty ambassadors from twenty-two countries. And as in the real United Nations, women continued to be underrepresented, with only three female ambassadors. The idea that fans were controlling their representatives to LEGO also represented a subtle shift in power. It seemed that LEGO finally had figured out that the key to interacting with, and in some cases managing, the adult fan community was to provide exclusive access.

"LEGO understood they needed to court the AFOL community. By having the appearance of transparency and democratic equality, it helps to legitimize the ambassador program," says Andrew.

In addition to being a former ambassador, Andrew has a skill that I need to learn if I'm going to share my MOCs with the online world. He takes beautiful pictures of LEGO minifigs, his most famous being a customized series of LEGO Aztec gods.

Taking photos of LEGO bricks is difficult. The shiny plastic reflects the flash, and more often than not, the final image is blurry or unfocused. White bricks tend to appear yellow, and detail is hard to discern because of shadow.

"Daylight is best, which we don't get a lot of in Seattle," Andrew says. He offers me a few simple tips. "Just grab a large piece of white posterboard and a tripod—you're good to go with a cheap point-and-shoot on a time delay with the macro setting."

I haven't bought posterboard since elementary school, and making a photo box feels like a craft project. LEGO tends to photograph better against monochromatic backgrounds, particularly white. It's hot in the August sun as I line up the small trucks and monorail on my driveway. I lie down in order to set up the shot properly. The tripod is slick in my sweaty hands and the concrete is burning my stomach as I put my eye up to the viewfinder. I mount the digital camera about eight inches from the photo box and set the time delay.

In the few seconds' pause before the shutter clicks, the camera overbalances on the tripod and I end up with a time-release photo of my driveway and car tire. I'm wondering if I've broken my camera, when I look up and see a neighbor walking the dog. I wave from my prone position, a LEGO monorail in my hand. She waves back.

When I started building with LEGO bricks again, I never realized there were so many things you needed to do outside of snapping pieces together. There is sorting and storing and planning and drawing. And now, photographing. At some point, building seems to be the reward for doing all of these other tasks. I have heard adult enthusiasts say that it seems as if they never get to build anymore. I've only just started, and I'm not building nearly as much as I thought I would.

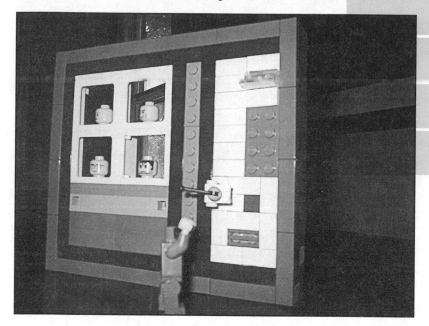

The prototype for my LEGO vending machine, which offers up a variety of head options for those minifigs in need of a new look.

11

The Stranger Side of Building

Early one night after the calendar has turned to September, I head into our third bedroom and grab my suitcase to pack for Brick Show in Bellaire, Ohio. Instead of preparing this room for a baby, I've been stacking more bins of LEGO on the floor. My foot sends a small rectangular box skidding across the room—a World of Mosaics set I picked up for a dollar at the liquidation of a secondhand shop. The slow takeover of the bedroom carpet makes me feel empty. These are supposed to be my kid's toys, not mine.

Out of the corner of my eye, I notice the MTT Trade Federation sitting up against the opposite wall. *Today's the day*, I tell myself. But I don't even crack the box. The Star Wars set is turning me back into a middle school kid, putting off making that phone call to a girl I like. I remember staring at the clock, the phone in my hand as I sat on my beanbag that looked like a soccer ball. *Just five more minutes. I'll call at 7 p.m. Okay, at the end of* Duck Tales. *7:30 p.m. goes by*. I was like a nervous snooze button.

My inaction is not surprising, considering all of the things that remain unsaid between Kate and me. The room is pregnant with all of the topics that we're not talking about: sex and creation chief among them. I mistakenly think the world of adult fans is free of sex, forgetting that sexual intercourse was the most interesting thing to talk about in middle school, and still is to most grown men. So, even when trying to avoid it, I'm stuck focusing on sex and creation.

Time plus a culture of men acting like boys always produce one guaranteed outcome: penis jokes. Some 99.9 percent of the LEGO creations I find online are not adult content, despite the ages of the builders. But out on the fringes, I stumble across a dirty space subtheme, Bonktron, which popped up on LUGNET in 2005.

"The Bonktrons are a hedonistic cult devoted to nothing but the peasures [sic] of the flesh. . . . They were originally part of the Classic Space regime, but found their philosophies too prudish and departed the more populated regions of space to found their own colony," wrote Australian AFOL Allister McLaren in his September 2005 post introducing the fad.

The first Bonktron spacecraft, classified as "a deep penetration recon ship," was called the "Throbtastic Jismatron X3." It was an absurdly phallic spaceship, constructed primarily in tan with a red tulip-shaped nose cone. The idea of turning LEGO bricks into a naughty MOC wasn't a new one—Brickfest 2004 featured a gray Viagra Moonbase with an extendable corridor—this was just the first time that such a theme had been posted online. Over the next two months, a long white rocket—the Long Range Obliteration Vehicle (Experimental), or L.O.V.E. rocket—and the Millennium Phallis were uploaded to LUGNET. The ships tended to feature a disturbing number of minifigs with bare chests and mustaches.

Like all penis jokes, this one gets less funny with repetition. Bonktron creations were quickly banned from Classic-space.com; the Web forum for LEGO space enthusiasts apparently was too prudish. By 2006, "Bonktron" was merely an adjective to describe a spaceship with a form that was a bit too familiar, another way to tease a fellow builder.

But that doesn't mean that crude representations of LEGO pornography don't exist. The pizza delivery guy and sleepover party motif can be found all too easily online. YouTube pulls up 825 videos when you search for "LEGO porn," most of which are stop-motion animation involving LEGO minifigures. Whereas Bonktron is a bit cartoony and involves some actual building skills, watching a minifigure in a simulated sex act is just uncomfortable. It belongs in the category of places we *can* go, but don't *need to* as a society.

In policing itself, the AFOL community has set up standards and often has been the first to criticize creations that could negatively impact the family-friendly image of LEGO. The rules are simple: no booze, no sex, and no drugs. It seems there is an unspoken agreement that AFOLs will build in this kid's version of the real world. But you can find hidden touches and jokes: a roof that reveals beers in a cooler, minifigs in compromising positions behind a castle wall.

Still, adult fans can't control the entire Internet, and despite LEGO's careful control in selecting partners, bricks will sometimes appear in unseemly situations. In fact, the fifty years that the company spent imbuing the plastic bricks with the values of childhood play and imagination were likely the reason that the Polish artist Zbigniew Libera approached LEGO in 1996 seeking a donation of bricks for an undefined art project.

LEGO provided the bricks, and Libera shocked the company, as well as the world, by creating sets that mimicked concentration camps and torture scenes from the Holocaust. One box featured a LEGO skeleton being beaten by a prison guard; another showed five skeletons being marched into a facility surrounded by barbed wire. The boxes for the seven sets included safety warnings and the words: "The work of Zbigniew Libera has been sponsored by LEGO SYSTEM." LEGO responded immediately that it had not sponsored the work, in an effort to defuse the public relations nightmare.

"If we had known before what he was going to do, we never would have given him the bricks. But we talked about it and decided [that] to make a big thing about it now would only draw more attention," said Peter Ambeck-Madsen, LEGO's director of public relations.

The concentration camp sets were part of a series of creations by Libera, which he called "Correcting Devices," designed to show the difference between the world marketed to children and the world that actually exists. Libera, who also modified Barbie dolls to make commentaries on aging and beauty, sought to translate the horrors of the world into a language that children could understand by depicting them through toys. But kids weren't the only ones affected; many adults were horrified by Libera's work, by seeing a toy they associated with their childhood used in such a light.

Our plastic brick creations become reflections of our values or perversions. I don't like LEGO porn because of how it makes me feel, and the Holocaust sets are wrong because they sully the memory of building with my father. Adult fans want to protect LEGO because they want to protect their own childhoods.

LEGO bricks are not cuddly. They're sharp and hard to the touch. But our associations are fragile. Those experiences and memories can be played upon, used to imbue inanimate plastic pieces with deeper meaning. Yet a piece of art doesn't have to be disturbing to have a dramatic impact on our culture. It needs only inspiration—and where better to start than the Old Testament for Brendan Powell Smith, thirty-five, the originator of the Brick Testament, a collection of LEGO vignettes that depict scenes and stories from the Bible.

Brendan is one of the few adult builders who I knew existed before I even started researching the AFOL community. If you've ever seen a LEGO Garden of Eden or Noah's Ark, comic-book panel-style stories with captions under photos of LEGO vignettes, you probably know him, too. He's written three books in his Brick Testament series: *The Story of Christmas, The Ten Commandments, and Stories from the Book of Genesis.*

In the beginning, for Brendan, there was LEGO and religion. The former was his favorite toy while growing up in Boston, and the latter was instilled in him weekly by his mother, who taught Sunday school at their Episcopalian church. But everything changed when Brendan entered the Dark Ages at the age of twelve.

"The LEGO in my house got boxed up and put in basement storage. I also made a conscious decision to try and put aside what seemed to me to be childish ways of thinking. . . . Though I hadn't set out to have this process affect my religious beliefs, in the end it did quite profoundly, and the short version of the story is: I found myself being the only atheist I knew in my family or community," writes Brendan when we exchange e-mails about the Brick Testament.

At Boston College, he studied religion, immersing himself in the Bible. He was searching for an answer to why people were drawn to Christianity.

"Although the Bible is the world's all-time best-selling book, and millions of people would claim to base their lives and their morality upon it, the vast majority of believers and non-believers alike have never actually read it," writes Brendan.

If people weren't going to read the entire Bible, he reasoned, an illustrated work might be a better way to get them to see what was actually inside the pages. In the years after college, Brendan took his childhood LEGO boxes out of storage and began buying sets on eBay.

"As I started constructing a LEGO Garden of Eden, it further occurred to me that this could be the opportunity I'd been looking for to retell the Bible's stories in ways people would find fun and engaging," writes Brendan.

He was working as a Web designer in 2001 when he created the first six stories from Genesis and published them online.

Here he showed off his wicked sense of humor, and thus the
Reverend Brendan Powell Smith was born, a tongue-in-cheek
name he discusses in question 10 on the FAQ page of his Web site.

Is he really a reverend?

Most ministers, priests, or other religious clerics would not
actually use "The Reverend" before their *own* names, for
to do so would be presumptuous and rather vain. The Rev.
Brendan Powell Smith is not an ordained member of any
earthly church, and is widely regarded as being both highly
presumptuous and extremely vain.

The content of the stories was seemingly just as irreverent, with
fantastic tales of beheadings, rape, incest, prostitutes, and wrestling
with God. However, although at times graphic, the stories were all
taken word-for-word from the Bible. The popularity of the site grew
over time, leading to a book-publishing deal and Brendan's decision to work full-time on the Brick Testament. His life in Mountain
View, California, is once again about LEGO and religion.

Listening to someone talk about building with LEGO just makes
me want to build something with LEGO myself. When I spill out
my Pick A Brick cup onto my desk, I notice that I have a lot of 1×4
red, white, and green tiles. And next to those tiles is an assortment
of minifig heads piled on top of 1×2 translucent plates.

I doodle out the rough shape of a vending machine and refine it
based on pictures I find online of snack and soda dispensers. I will
build a vending machine for LEGO minifig heads, with a headless
patron trying to decide on his mood. I want to achieve a smooth
surface, so this will be my first attempt at building with the Studs
Not On Top (SNOT) technique. The idea is that by changing the
orientation of the bricks or plates, you can achieve more detail. In a
typical creation, all of the bricks are facing the same direction, usually pointed up. SNOT uses hinges, specialty LEGO elements, or
Technic bricks to place bricks at an angle to each other. The builder
can then choose whether he wants a studded or a smooth face.

It turns out there are not a lot of studded buildings and cars
in real life, so SNOT techniques are needed to help bring LEGO

elements together without the studs showing. SNOT also offers the chance to offset LEGO bricks, wherein a row or corner might stick out half the width of a plate in order to simulate the ledge of a window. This technique is known as Studs Not In a Row (SNIR).

I build a four-window vending machine, five inches tall and six inches wide. A gearshift doubles as the change-release button, a 1×2 gray grille tile is the coin refund slot, and a 1×2 translucent corner piece is the dollar bill accepter. The end result is too square—more of a vending box than a machine—but I like the idea of using SNOT techniques to build. The face of the machine is tiles, with the exception of a 2×4 gray brick that I have left exposed to simulate the keypad where you would enter your choice. A headless minifig stands before the buttons to complete the vignette.

I'm satisfied with my creation until I search for LEGO vending machines on the Internet and discover that somebody has made a fully functioning model that accepts coins and vends snacks using Mindstorm motors and sensors. Suddenly I'm back in Operation MindStretch, the fourth grade program for gifted students, trying to build a bridge out of spaghetti that will hold a tennis ball. In the meantime, the guy next to me already has a bridge capable of supporting a six-pack of soda.

The vending machine raises conflicting emotions: I badly want one for my office, but on the other hand, it is getting frustrating to continually find a more refined version of what I've just finished building. We all start with the same bricks, so I can't stop comparing myself to others. To blow off some steam, I decide to hop on the exercise bike in our sunroom. I play video games while exercising; it makes me feel as if I'm at least accomplishing something while guiding my virtual self to a Super Bowl win in Madden.

Only this time, I put a copy of LEGO Star Wars into my PlayStation 2. Just as LEGO has been used to redefine the concept of porn or art, the video gaming world is getting a blocky makeover. The transition from blocks to pixels seems easy, especially since the introduction of an iconic protagonist—the minifig—as goofy as Earthworm Jim and as identifiable as the original Karate Champ participants. LEGO quietly has established a rich history of video gaming; but it's really only since 2005 that the gaming community has started paying attention to what LEGO is producing, beginning with the release of the first Star Wars–themed video game.

LEGO initially focused on educational computer games that were blocky, both literally and figuratively. LEGO Island was released in 1997, the main point of the game being that you had to deliver a pizza to a jail. The game was forward thinking in that you could customize the environment, which was constructed of LEGO elements. The next year, LEGO rolled out a few clunkers in LEGO Chess and Creator, a construction simulation game.

But with the release of the Mindstorms line in 1998, the company saw that having a presence in the digital world could be to their advantage. LEGO joined the circuitry circuit, attending the Electronic Entertainment Expo the following year to promote the robotics set. The Bionicle line scored a series of hits with computer games based on the backstories of the action figure–like characters popular with boys. Suddenly it looked as though LEGO might be able to compete with some of the electronic toys that had caused the company's profits to precipitously decline in the late 1990s. The success of three LEGO Star Wars games developed by Traveller's Tales led LEGO to roll out additional themed games based on licenses, including Indiana Jones and Batman in 2008.

The early games were largely ignored by adult fans. Many see them as part of the "juniorization" of LEGO, in which the target audience for products seems to be younger and younger. But AFOL Jim Foulds thinks that LEGO can bridge the gap and connect with adult gamers via LEGO Universe, the massive multiplayer online role-playing game being developed by NetDevil.

"It's going to be a LEGO world where you can control everything, and we want adult builders to have a voice in that world," Jim tells me while setting up LEGO Universe bricks for a display at Brickworld.

With wavy orange hair and a black jacket adorned with the yellow horseshoe-shaped logo of LEGO Universe, he is one of the first people I will see at several conventions this year. Foulds

This oversized LEGO minifig bellhop greets guests in front of the LEGOLAND Hotel in Billund, Denmark. The suitcase he's about to pick up is made of leather.

The torsos for an army of storm troopers roll off the assembly line at LEGO's manufacturing plant in Billund, Denmark. The rebels will be crushed one minifig at a time.

This is the ten-foot motorboat replica created by LEGO artist Nathan Sawaya that I helped move across the docks and streets of Seattle. Despite being glued together, at several hundred pounds it decidedly does not float.

This twenty-two-foot LEGO Titanic, the result of eight months' work by AFOL Scott Fowler, is on display at BrickCon 2008, Seattle. It comes apart in three seven-foot sections.

My entire animal repertoire consisted of a yellow whale and a rainbow camel—everything else looked like something from the island of Dr. Moreau.

Here is the stegosaurus that Kate and I put together in an attempt to avoid talking about the child we wished was there to put it together with us.

This biplane is the first my own creation (MOC) that I was proud to have built. (The next one will include space for the pilot's legs.)

I built this zombie defense vehicle for BrickCon 2008, Seattle. It's been packed carefully in suitcases thrice and, thus, rebuilt twice.

AFOL Adam Reed Tucker managed to complete this to-scale recreation of the Burj Dubai tower for the 2008 BrickWorld convention in Wheeling, Illinois.

The Victorian architecture of San Francisco is recreated in LEGOLAND California's Miniland—where I briefly pretended to be Godzilla as I walked the streets.

The inauguration ceremony for President Barack Obama is recreated in
LEGO bricks at LEGOLAND California.

Some of the world's most elaborate Bionicle creations are by Breann
Sledge, who offered building demonstrations and examples of some
of her larger works at the 2008 BrickShow in Bellaire, Ohio.

is acting as a community liaison for LEGO, helping to promote the game at adult fan conventions and working with beta testers. He's also charged with teaching the game development company NetDevil about how LEGO elements might interact.

Adult fans, and all game players, will have a LEGO minifig avatar—a representative in LEGO Universe. And for a community with so much interaction online through enthusiast forums and e-mail, LEGO Universe offers something that previous video games didn't. This is the chance for AFOLs to overcome geographic limitations and form a real-time virtual community of LEGO builders—basically an evolution from the user groups of the 1990s. Adult fans from Germany could hold a virtual convention with participants from around the globe. It's a strategy that Joe Meno thinks could really work.

"Just imagine a speed build, where everybody would just show up, get instructions, and then build competitively and be judged. People from all over the real world who could never build together could see each other's work," says Joe.

I'm curious about LEGO Universe, but I frankly don't have high expectations for LEGO Star Wars when I start up the PlayStation. But then I hear the Star Wars music accompanying the game's credits, and my heart starts pumping harder. I reason that it is solely because I've begun pedaling. Forty-five minutes later I'm still playing and enjoying myself. I'm a Jedi and I'm fighting for the rebellion. When my LEGO Obi-Wan Kenobi dies, he dissolves into a bunch of LEGO bricks and immediately comes back to the screen. I've noticed I tend to wield my light saber with too much indifference and am as likely to strike my computer-aided Jedi friend as our enemies. I make a mental note to warn Kate if we ever play together. This game is stupid, repetitive, and awesome.

The best part is that it keeps me from having to step foot in that third bedroom and look at the MTT Federation. The mindless killing of LEGO drones is an outstanding way to avoid admitting that I don't have the courage to face a set that isn't really more difficult than the Beach House I built with my wife earlier in the month. So I leave for Bellaire on September 4 without having opened the box.

A LEGO penguin and polar bear, inhabitants of the Zoo Room inside the Toy and Plastic Brick Museum, sit on ice blocks made of cotton balls.

12

A Man and His Museum

I have wanted to talk with Dan Brown, the founder and owner of the Toy and Plastic Brick Museum, since March. He's my white whale of adult fans. I thought we would meet at Brick Bash; he was one of the sponsors of the public display in Ann Arbor. The museum sent T-shirts, but he never arrived.

"He's got a huge brain and heart; sometimes his heart just gets in the way of his brain," Duane Collicott told me at the time when Dan didn't show.

Then there was Brickworld in June in Chicago, which Dan and I both attended. We ended up waiting in line next to each other outside the LEGO retail store in the Northbrook Court Mall. I turned on my digital recorder and we begin discussing professional LEGO builders. But the store opened two minutes later and the interview was over.

Dan looks a bit like Adam Sandler in profile, with short brown hair and a slight bend in his leg when he walks. At forty-two, the electronics recycler has discovered his passion. He has spent the last five years building one of the largest LEGO collections in the world. As a result, he's something of a lightning rod in the AFOL community.

First, there was controversy on BrickLink when he bought an existing storefront. Some users felt it was disingenuous for Dan to use the store's feedback, a system similar to eBay's wherein customers can rate a seller. They reasoned that Dan was a new seller and shouldn't benefit from the store's ratings. And recently Dan has faced pushback from AFOLs at conventions who argue that he is buying in bulk as a reseller, preventing hobbyists from getting the sets they want and taking advantage of the discount offered by LEGO for adult fans.

Underneath the criticism, I usually detect the same jealousy that people exhibit when they talk about Adam Tucker's architectural models. It's like being on the playground as a kid. The other guy has more toys, and that seems unfair. I think most adult fans really just want to know: how exactly did the largest collection of LEGO models outside LEGOLAND and LEGO U.S. headquarters end up in an Ohio town with a population of 4,589 people?

I'm heading to Dan's museum in Bellaire, a three-hour drive south from Cleveland Hopkins International Airport, to find out. It's September 4, the Thursday night before the second annual Brick Show he's organizing. A bridge away from crossing into West Virginia, I take the exit for Bellaire off Route 7. I pass the Eastern Ohio Regional Wastewater Authority's treatment plant and turn right just after a brick sign that welcomes me to "Bellaire: The all AMERICAN TOWN." A white wooden bench with "Toy Museum" painted in red directs me to the left with an arrow. As if in competition, the GPS beeps, saying that the Toy and Plastic Brick Museum is only a half-mile away. All I see are bungalows and Craftsman-style homes packed onto a narrow street.

The street opens up and a two-story brick building, the former Gravel Hill Middle School, stands at the edge of a blacktop parking lot. I pull into the lot, my headlights splashing across a painted mural of a toy train and a LEGO carousel with its frozen-in-motion dancing cows to the right of the open front doors. A two-foot DUPLO figure peers out from one of the primary-color windows. I'm here.

A LEGO gnome sits at the base of the stairs to greet me, but his appearance is unsettling in a Grimm's fairy tale kind of way. *Up these steps,* he seems to say, *you'll never be the same.* A life-size LEGO replica of Darth Vader stands in the middle of the first-floor hallway. The Dark Side is slightly calming.

"Dan?" I call out, my voice echoing off the tan tiled walls.

"In here," a voice rings out to my left. I walk past a Guinness World Record plaque and a LEGO wizard, into a former classroom off the hallway.

"You made it," says Dan, sitting cross-legged on the floor in jeans and a gray T-shirt as he snaps bricks into a yellow LEGO wall that rings the entire room. A large chalkboard dominates the wall where Dan is working. Dan's wife, Carol, sits in a folding chair, her head down, face hidden by long, straight black hair as she rips open bags of LEGO knight minifigures. She looks up briefly to say hello before getting back to the task of sorting through shields and weapons. There are hundreds of plastic bags on the floor, and blue LEGO buckets are stacked haphazardly between Dan and Carol. It looks like a messy playroom on steroids. A wooden ramp extends through the door into the middle of the room. It will be the only way to enter after dozens of LEGO baseplates filled with vignettes are placed on the floor representing the interior of the castle.

"Just twenty more to go," says Dan, gesturing at the yellow LEGO bricks by his feet. The yellow walls, which stretch to the underside of the chalkboard rails, will form the outside of a collective castle display at the convention over the weekend. While he builds, Dan tells me about the beginnings of the museum.

"In 2004, I approached LEGO at the Toy Fair. There I had the good fortune to meet with [LEGO special project manager] Bill Higgins," says Dan.

Higgins was often involved with new partnerships for LEGO, having worked with a retail developer, the Mills Corporation, to design a holiday promotion that including leasing retail space in fifteen mall locations the previous year.

"Bill did it his own way, and I have no kiss-up ability whatsoever. I just can't suck up to anyone, and that's what Bill liked about me," says Dan, gesturing for me to follow him out of the room.

Our informal tour of the museum has begun. It's a weird feeling, having unfettered access to an adult fan's entire collection. My relationship with Dan is starting out on the opposite foot from relationships I've had with other AFOLs. He's showing me his bricks and building rooms before I earn his trust, before we've spent any real time together. It's a bit like entering a cheat code in Mike Tyson's Punch-Out!! video game.

We enter the Space Room across the hall. In the center of the room, two LEGO children sit inside the framed-out cockpit of the Millennium Falcon. A Yoda mosaic and an R2-D2 model are off to the right, along with a historical collection of space theme sets sitting on shelves. Dan directs me to an eight-foot table that is covered with Bionicle robots, each about the size of a large cat. They are all the work of Alaskan AFOL Breann Sledge, a rare builder in that she's female and loves to build almost exclusively with Bionicle.

"Those are Breann's models. She's amazing. She's been building for hours over at the LEGO Crack House. I have to go get her soon," says Dan, looking at his watch.

The LEGO Crack House is the nickname for the second school building that Dan purchased at auction in 2004, where he stores the inventory for his BrickLink store. Breann is one of several adult fans he has invited to come display their work, using a government tourism grant of $2,500 to help defray some of their travel costs.

In the hallway, we come across Tom Erickson bobbing his head to the *Kill Bill* sound track, his skinny frame hunched over a series of custom Star Wars landspeeders. He is an adult fan and vendor in town for Brick Show. Across from him, hundreds of sets are stacked on the floor. They partially block the door to the gift shop—the first room that was completed in the museum (proving Dan is an entrepreneur if nothing else). An adjacent room at the head of the hallway has a Dutch door, with the top half open. This is the master builder's room, where small models are carefully displayed on wooden shelves stacked nearly to the ceiling. Dan points to a yellow figure sitting at the computer. The model has salt-and-pepper hair and glasses.

"That's Bill [Higgins]. We couldn't have done this without him; a lot of the models here are because of him sharing my vision," says Dan.

We begin to climb the steps behind the Darth Vader to the second floor, and I ask where Dan finds all the models.

"I'm tracking nine models in the United States and three in Germany. We got a new referee from England, and I'm mad because I just lost out on a Tigger on eBay," says Dan.

When he bought the two school buildings, Dan had a vision for a LEGO museum, one that would celebrate LEGO as art and display the works of the artists who worked to build LEGO models. And he wanted to fill it with all of the models that the LEGO Group didn't want or need—those that had been created for limited-time promotions or partnerships and were destined to be recycled or destroyed. In some ways, he was taking his computer recycling business model and applying it to LEGO. He would pick up anything they didn't want; they just had to tell him where to go. People wouldn't come to Bellaire to see old monitors or hard drives, but they would want to see the incredible LEGO models he would collect.

"I try to spend money on things that are one-of-a-kind, very neat, or tough to get. I know I ticked off a lot of people on eBay because I picked up a lot of displays that other people wanted to put in their basements. But I want all of it out there for people to enjoy," says Dan, gesturing to a pair of life-size LEGO men in shiny silver protective suits stirring a metal bucket of red plastic bottle caps in the center of the second-floor hallway.

The museum is essentially one of the world's largest private collections turned into a display for the public. This is Dan's escape— an escape from all the jobs that he had to do to get to this point.

Here, he can forget about his time working for Microsoft as an IT guy installing Novell 3.12, or running a flea-market food truck. At the top of the stairs is Duane's white bridge, encased in glass. It's like seeing an old friend. Behind the bridge, a four-foot-tall Dora the Explorer is posed to look like she's talking to a similar-size Diego beside a bank of old red school lockers.

"LEGO made Dora the Explorer sets? How did she end up here?" I ask.

"Yeah, back in 2004, I think. I'm not sure how exactly they ended up here. We just got two large wooden crates on our front doorstep one day addressed to us," says Dan.

He walks through the nearest door, and I follow. We're in the Zoo Room, where LEGO animal models have been placed in a series of wooden-frame cages wrapped in chicken wire. Across from a LEGO Winnie the Pooh, a LEGO polar bear peers out from beneath a cave built out of cubes covered in fluffy white material, as two penguins stand on ice floes. A large white cow, the kind featured in art series in Chicago and Kansas City, is against a bank of windows, the ceramic covered in Scala and LEGO accessories.

"Basically, we try to create a theme in each room, and I think it kind of worked out. This one turned out great," says Dan, putting his hand on the side of the cow.

The exhibits are a bit like oversize dioramas. It's difficult to reconcile thousands of dollars' worth of models inside obviously hand-built displays. But how do you judge the quality of somebody else's dream? I don't want to be callous, and the organization feels right—a loose homage to the themes of LEGO sets.

"What do you say to people who just think this is about you?" I ask him, noticing a blue Chupacabra LEGO model in the corner on a bale of hay.

"I don't want this to be just my opinion. That's the one problem I have with the museum—right now you're just seeing me. I don't want it to just be me, I want everybody else to come and build and make this a community," says Dan.

I believe that he wants to share the models with as many people as possible; but I get the distinct impression that he also wants to be known as the guy who achieved that feat.

On the same side of the hallway as the stairs we walked up are three classrooms also organized by LEGO theme: History, Western, and Mars rooms. The lights are off in the Mars Room, and Dan pauses before we enter.

"Walk in," he says, a big grin on his face. I step through the doorway and hear Dan smack the wall. "Now, look up."

A scaled-up two-foot minifig from the Mars Mission theme pops out from the ceiling, the hydraulics behind it making a whooshing noise.

"That's great." I laugh, my heart racing from the alien a few feet from my face. We walk into a space-themed room that is lit by blacklights. It's like being in a dorm room at a fraternity house. Across from a robotic version of the alien minifig is a rectangular glass tank that could be the largest aquarium I've ever seen. It's a traveling display built for Space sets.

"How on earth did you get this?" I ask Dan.

"I wasn't just getting things from LEGO, I was getting contacts from people that did things for LEGO and were working with the company to make wild stuff. I even made it a point to meet the guys that pack boxes," says Dan.

This is the side of his personality that likely drove a wedge between him and LEGO. He is opportunistic—a side effect of being a serial entrepreneur. In his drive to acquire models, Dan has worked with LEGO vendors and subcontractors, not all of whom are happy with LEGO. And I'm sure he understands how to play off those feelings.

"I don't lie," Dan tells me. A moment later he amends, "I would only lie for something important, like to save somebody's life." I believe Dan, but I wonder about his definition of important. The ultimate goal of acquiring more models means that Dan is constantly in deal mode. He always wants more, and he's not afraid to ask for it.

Yet when he is being earnest, Dan is charming. I can see why people would want to help him. He talks quickly, the words tripping from his lips.

Dan's drive is what launched the museum; it's also what made it difficult for him to work within a corporate framework like that of LEGO. Things began to change in the beginning of 2005. Dan was supposed to get surplus brick from the LEGO Outlet store in Dawsonville, Georgia. LEGO's first retail outlet in the United States, open since 1999, closed on January 22, 2005, but the bricks never arrived. LEGO was still restructuring, trying to manage costs. That July, a 70 percent controlling interest in the four LEGOLAND parks was sold to the Blackstone Group for $460 million. The parks are now run by the Blackstone subsidiary Merlin Entertainments, the same group that operates the Madame Tussauds wax museums.

"I had a ten-year plan, and then Bill retired in 2005 and it was like I never existed," says Dan.

As LEGO reorganized in order to focus on its core products, it seemed that nobody was really sure what to do with Dan. His contract with LEGO was nonstandard. He's an authorized LEGO retailer who has never signed a nondisclosure agreement. He was a stud that stuck out a bit too far, and without a mentor like Bill to advocate for him, Dan's aggressiveness was seen as abrasive by some in the organization.

LEGO's position is understandable. It's difficult for a multinational corporation to deal with a single person. With his own ventures, Dan can approve or disapprove everything immediately, while decisions at LEGO need to pass through the proper channels. And even if that process happens relatively quickly, I sense that Dan's impatience would leave him feeling unsatisfied. It's not just that Dan is nonstandard, it's that he believes he should be exempted from the standard rules.

Dan was no longer allowed to use the LEGO name in promotions, and the future of the museum seemed uncertain. The opening date got pushed back to 2006. Dan began unpacking models on February 11, wearing three layers to keep out the chill in the unheated school. However, he still had a relationship with LEGO. On the way back home from his twentieth high school reunion in upstate New York, he stopped at LEGO's U.S. headquarters in Enfield, Connecticut. He and his son Conrad drove back to Ohio with a rented Penske truck full of new models for the museum, including a scaled-up minifigure in a helicopter and a Mars Mission spacecraft.

The carpet leading to the museum basement is dark blue with a repeating pattern of LEGO bricks—old carpet from LEGO corporate headquarters. As the lights flicker on, I think I see another person. But it's actually a life-size replica of NBA player Dirk Nowitzki wearing a Big Red jersey, the local nickname for the Bellaire High School sports program. Next to Dirk, a LEGO goat wearing a red "Lifeguard" shirt sits atop a lifeguard's tower with a whistle in his mouth.

"At one point, LEGO knew where every model was. They had serial numbers on plates, but not since they've started to be mass-produced. They're scared of it ending up in a porn shop or things like that. But the lifeguard, I just got it from a topless club down in Georgia. So, it was already happening. The worst-case scenarios were already happening where liability could be an issue," says Dan.

The goat model is a perfect illustration of the complicated relationship between Dan and the company. Dan rescued the goat lifeguard from a non-family-friendly environment in order to display it in his museum. It's the kind of move that LEGO has historically done, taking a model out of public circulation to protect its corporate image. Yet the defender of the brand has trouble getting a meeting.

"We're half a world apart and they won't talk to me," says Dan as we sit on the school's bleachers, "but as someone at LEGO has told me, just because they like you, doesn't mean you have all the levels of approval for what you're trying to do."

It also doesn't help that Dan can't keep himself from testing the boundaries. In August 2007, as he was getting ready to unveil his museum to the world, LEGO approached.

"They called and said not only can you not use our name, but you can't be open. It's four years later and we're dealing with this stuff all over again," says Dan.

He removed the words "LEGO® Store" from the planned sign out front, and the museum was allowed to open.

Dan wanted something that he felt would immediately put the museum on the map. He has saved his favorite part of the tour for last. In the former gymnasium, a massive forty-four-foot LEGO mosaic of a semitrailer covers the former basketball court. He's not sure exactly how many bricks are in the construction that covers the length of the gym floor, but it's at least 1.2 million studs. More than 250 children each contributed a square to the mosaic during the first Brick Show.

"LEGO didn't like the idea that I had a Guinness World Record, but if they ever try and do better, I'll just move the tractor trailer over and add more to the trailer," says Dan.

Guinness certified the mosaic build from the first Brick Show as the largest LEGO image in the world, measuring 80.84 square meters (870.15 square feet).

"Now I've got my claim to fame, but where do I go from breaking the world record? I have always wanted to do Yellow Castle," says Dan, flexing his fingers, which have tightened up from building.

Guinness will not be coming to Bellaire to verify the build, because it is not an official LEGO category. But for Dan, the idea of gathering people together is what is important. In the middle of discussing the mosaic, he remembers why he walked me down to the basement. He goes behind the bleachers to a control panel that is next to a wheelchair lift. The stage lights suddenly begin flashing in primary colors. On the stage is a three-piece robotic LEGO band, Plastica, that used to be a showpiece at FAO Schwarz in New York City. When Dan tracked it down, it was in a ceiling storage space at the Yankee Candle headquarters in South Deerfield, Massachusetts. One robot mimics playing the drums while another moves his guitar. The lead robot singer begins singing in a futuristic voice their signature song, "Just Imagine."

In the basement of the former Gravel Hill School, I'm watching $62,000 worth of robotics play a made-up song just for me. This is the real LEGO museum. I forget about the paint peeling in the corners and the fact that I feel as if I'm inside someone else's dream. I am stunningly happy. I can't find the words, but Dan does.

"It just"— he pauses—"it's just really fun. I went from this lifestyle where everyone was pissed off all the time. I was a cubicle technician, running into people that were at the end of the world."

The robots abruptly cut off in the middle; a circuit breaker has been tripped. Dan adds it to the list of things he will need to fix before the convention on Saturday—another item in the long list of adult responsibilities. The quiet is jarring and the moment is over. Dan has to leave to pick up Breann, but he checks in with his wife, Carol, before leaving. She's still sorting minifig castle weapons.

"I didn't know she could build until two weeks ago, and I've known her for twenty years," says Dan, grabbing his jacket by the door.

"So it's got you hooked too?" I ask Carol. I'm curious to find out what the woman married to Dan thinks of the museum.

"What I told him then and I told him now, I don't have to like LEGO to like you," says Carol.

She tells me the story of meeting Dan over two decades ago, when her sister invited him to their house for a game of Dungeons & Dragons.

"He came to the door with his cute kind of duck walk, and I wondered, who is that?" says Carol.

Theirs is a love story, not a LEGO love story. The game started, and it was then that Carol truly noticed Dan.

"When we were playing, he was always looking for a way to have fun inside the game. He didn't play like anyone I had ever met," says Carol.

I agree with her. Dan doesn't play like anyone I've ever met either.

Dan Brown (left) and I pose with a maxifig—an eight-foot, scaled-up version of a minifig—in the stairwell at the Toy and Plastic Brick Museum.

13

It's Okay, I Work Here

The last time I was in Ohio, Kate and I were halfway through a cross-country drive from Brooklyn to Kansas City in March 2007. The twenty-two-hour drive was going by slowly, as I struggled to adjust to Kate's blue Volkswagen Beetle.

It was only the second time I'd driven a stick shift, a fact that didn't escape my fellow drivers on the road. But I'd avoided drawing their anger until we came to a toll near West Virginia with a line snaking a dozen cars long. I managed to coast toward the toll window, and I thought we'd be fine until the driver in front of us took an inordinate amount of time to pay the toll.

In stopping suddenly, I failed to engage the clutch, and the car came to a shuddering, groaning halt. And then the horns began. A horn blared, flat and loud, as I fumbled to shift the stick and restart the car.

"It's my fault," I told Kate.

The horn sounded again. I started the car, but released the gas too quickly and we stalled again.

"It's not your fault, they're being jerks. God, why can't people just learn to wait, like, a minute," replied Kate.

I stalled another three times as I began to feel the cars lining up behind us. The air conditioning cycled on and off and it started to get hot in the car.

"It's my fault," I repeated over the sound of the horn.

We rolled past the booth, alternating between coasting and a jerky, uncoordinated tapping of the clutch, brake, and gas. I threw the coins in the basket and skipped a gear in my rush to get moving. The car caught for a second and then bucked forward.

"Honey, it's not your fault. You're doing the best you can," said Kate as we mercifully sped away from the tollbooth.

"No . . . it was my fault. I was leaning on the horn with my arm each time I had to restart the ignition. I was the one honking at myself to go," I explained.

Kate was still giggling when we pulled over less than an hour later in Zanesville, Ohio, to stop for the night. A Fairfield Inn promised free Internet and had the same name as my hometown. It won the road-trip game of motel roulette. When we went to bed that night, we had no way of knowing that hundreds of LEGO models were less than ten minutes away.

The LEGO bricks are calling eighteen months later. Dan's phone call wakes me, and I roll over in the Zanesville Super 8 motel, opening my eyes to see the glowing clock numbers: 8 a.m. It's

Friday morning, the day before the convention. I get myself up and awake and head over to the museum, saying a silent prayer of thanks that my rental car is an automatic.

No one is around outside the building except the motionless carousel cows, but the front door is unlocked. I go inside and wander into the Space Room. Breann Sledge looks up tiredly, busy weaving thin rigid tubing through the holes of elements, making a quick repair on something that looks like a cross between *Alien* and a Komodo dragon. The "Baerwyrm" is a twisting mass of gray and black plastic as large as Breann's torso, extending slightly longer than her straight black hair parted in the middle. She's spent the last five days building the articulated tail and bony midsection of this intimidating monster from LEGO and Bionicle parts.

"I've always been a collector of action figures. If you want to build your own action figures out of Bionicle, all you have to do is measure the toys and then turn that into bricks," says Breann when I ask her about a collection of smaller figures that seem poised for combat. She picks two up and stages a mock fight, making explosion sounds and noises that mimic robot commands.

Breann is well known in the AFOL community as one of the preeminent Bionicle builders—as much for the fact that there are not many adults who build large-scale constructions with Bionicle as for her creativity and skill. At a time when most were building robots or warriors, she was building a fridge out of Bionicle, intertwining the bioorganism's body parts to create a kitchen appliance. Online, she's been called everything from "Breanicle" to "Bioniclina" to a "nerd-babe."

"It's always been boys, so I guess I never really noticed," says Breann when I ask if it's hard to be a female builder in a world dominated by guys. She lifts up the Baerwyrm, getting ready to move her MOC out to the hallway. I don't offer to help, having learned my lesson that you never move anybody else's creation unless you're ready to rebuild it. I haven't even seen half the parts that Breann has used, let alone know where they would go.

I've got the morning to myself in the museum, and I decide to explore some of the rooms that I didn't see the day before. The History Room is first on my list; it's Dan's tribute to LEGO. A six-foot yellow LEGO man in a NASA suit stands in front of the chalkboard, where a signed wooden mosaic of Kjeld Kirk Kristiansen rests on the rail. I recognize it from Brickworld as the work of brick engraver Tommy Armstrong, a silver-haired adult fan from North Carolina whom I have never seen sans suspenders. It's as if Dan has assembled artifacts from my trip into the AFOL world. I can't decide if this means that I'm more connected than I think or simply that Dan has accumulated a truly massive collection.

I glimpse the museum's former life as a school from the teacher's pose of the NASA man and from the two students facing him, hunched over actual school desks that have individual bricks glued to their wooden surfaces. In the back of the room, wooden cars and ducks as well as plastic bricks from the 1950s and 1960s sit inside square glass cases. The condition of what's in this room matters; these are some of the only models in the museum that the public can't touch. The tone of this room is different as well; it feels the closest to a traditional museum.

The collection of dozens of pieces is impressive, because LEGO wasn't introduced in the United States until 1961, which means that most of these toys originated in Denmark or other parts of Europe. Interestingly, Dan often approaches the LEGO company with his finds to confirm that what he has purchased—for example, an over-size white plastic cross imprinted with the LEGO logo—is genuine.

"I guess there just needs to be a happy medium," Dan said when we talked about it the day before. "You're dealing with Americans, and the company is coming from a culture in Denmark that is more reserved."

A common respect for the company's history seems to be that "happy medium" where Dan's aggressiveness in acquiring models is recognized by LEGO because he unearths pieces that likely wouldn't be found otherwise.

Immediately down the hall from the History Room is the Western Room. Here I see Dan's sense of humor on display. LEGO Bart Simpson and Milhouse wait outside a saloon door next to a table of poker players, all scaled-up minifigures originally built at LEGOLAND California. Inside an old mailroom window is a LEGO clown—a slightly creepy, but funny, surprise.

Dan pops his head into the room; he's gathering everyone together to talk about getting ready for the convention. A crowd of a dozen volunteers and vendors gathers in the first floor hallway in front of the LEGO Darth Vader. Dan clears his throat, wipes his hands on his jeans, and addresses his convention staff.

"I want it [the convention] to deal with something that no one has done before. At BrickFair and everywhere else, it's—okay, here is the crowd, let's charge them ten bucks and cover the cost of what we're doing. I'm charging two dollars. It just basically pays the general employees' cost of being here," says Dan.

AFOL convention organizers often see public display days as a kind of necessary evil, since in essence, the families that come are helping to subsidize the cost of the event. Many convention organizers are basically volunteers, donating their time and in some cases money to rent a meeting room or event space.

"If AFOL events end up putting their organizers in debt, then there won't be any AFOL events," wrote Duane Collicott on LUGNET in October 2007, in a discussion over the money raised during conventions.

Some fans also see public days as a part of giving back, showcasing the talents of adult builders and helping to promote LEGO. There is also pride in knowing that thousands of people are coming to admire and take pictures of what you have built. But the visitors who pony up the admission fee are only temporary attendees of the convention; they're not there to make friends or attend classes to discuss building techniques. They are only connecting with the LEGO. And they never see what's behind the scenes at the carnival.

For Dan, it's different. The attendees of Brick Show are likely to come back to the museum, which is in essence a permanent public display. The convention might last only a weekend, but the museum is still open fifty-one other weekends a year. So he looks at his convention from a customer service experience perspective, trying to offer kids and parents a reason to return. And that approach extends to adult fans, whom Dan is trying to sell on augmenting or helping to build the museum's collection.

"Erickson Bricks is making custom bricks for [name badges]. We're doing a trade. It's not like you have to make me five hundred dollars' worth of stuff, it's whatever you feel is appropriate," says Dan. It's a pay-what-you-want approach to an AFOL convention—which is decidedly unconventional. Vendors usually have to pay per table, such as the $25 fee charged by BrickFair held in Washington, D.C., the previous week.

Dan's anti-establishment ethos seems to attract adult fans who share his worldview—fans like Tom Erickson.

"I'm a LEGO rock star, living on beer and Funions," jokes Tom. "But I also need gas money," he says over lunch at a nearby Pizza Hut that day.

If you saw him get out of his Toyota EFI microbus, you might think he was a member of Phish. With a dirty-blond goatee, red LEGO T-shirt with a yellow brick graphic on the front, and leather choker on his right wrist, Tom, thirty-two, has perfected the style-conscious look of someone who just doesn't care how he looks. Yet the whirling mind of an economist and opportunist is what drives Tom around the convention circuit.

"Buy low and sell dear," he says, paraphrasing one of the early axioms of Wall Street.

It was Civil War reenactors who initially got Tom back into LEGO. In 2006, a close friend passed away, and he took over the friend's small toy soldier shop in Moline, Illinois. It was a time-intensive business—each toy soldier had to be hand-painted. "The customers demanded perfection, and it helped me realize that I want my toys to be durable," says Tom.

To help defray the costs of running such an expensive enterprise, he put in a few LEGO displays and opened a BrickLink store. Over time, the focus of the store began to shift from toy soldiers to LEGO. Tom's online BrickLink store was paying the rent of the brick-and-mortar shop. When his friend's son decided to take over the toy soldier business in March 2008, Tom switched to selling LEGO full-time. By then, he was already known in the AFOL community as the "other brick engraver," after creating custom brick badges for BrickFair.

"Tommy [Armstrong] is the original brick engraver. But I can make this work; it's two years before any new business takes off," says Tom.

It's strange to think of anyone as an upstart in the adult fan community, but Tom Erickson is the new kid on the block in comparison to Tommy Armstrong, who debuted engraved bricks at BrickFest in 2004. Custom magnetic name badges made of bricks with names and hometowns burned into the side have since become the standard at conventions. And while Tom sees two brick engravers as a case of competition in a free market, some feel that he has just taken Tommy's idea. And of course, LEGO purists shudder at either of them searing or altering a brick to make a key chain.

When we return from lunch, Tom gets back to his engraving setup, laying out the design for Brick Show bricks on a computer. Dan grabs me when I walk in and asks if I want to help out during the convention. He tells me to pick out a white T-shirt from the gift shop and leaves to make sure the A-frame signs have begun going up around Bellaire directing people to the convention tomorrow. In under a minute, I've gone from attendee to convention staff.

Later that night, in the middle of building the Yellow Castle wall, I take a break to act as a judge in the fourth-grade coloring contest—the entries are being taped to the wall for visitors to admire. My status rises the longer I stay at the Toy and Plastic Brick Museum. I go back to stacking bricks, absentmindedly holding them in my mouth like nails. I do the same thing at home while cooking raw chicken, licking grease or sauce off my fingers. Neither tastes particularly good or is a smart idea.

The next morning I walk in the front door of the museum, sporting my official staff T-shirt with its graphic of gold LEGO bricks and the words "Bellaire Ohio Toy Museum: Solid Gold!" Dan places me in charge of the building room on the second floor, where kids and parents are going to be constructing battle scenes for the interior of the Yellow Castle build. I get a staff brick badge from Tom. Dan has prebuilt white, blue, and red "houses" out of LEGO to provide some consistency to what everybody builds. Each builder—adult or child—gets an 8×10 stud "house" after picking a color and an oversize gray baseplate, forty-eight studs wide by forty-eight studs long (fifteen inches by fifteen inches).

By the door, I notice four cases of unopened baseplates that retail for $14.99 per baseplate at LEGO's shop. And scattered all around the room are loose bricks and LEGO elements, including various plastic tubs filled with the knight minifigs that Carol was sorting the other night.

"Dan, there are thousands of dollars of bricks in this room," I tell him, holding up a few unopened boxes of NBA minifigs.

"Sure, but I never want to get to the point where I say this is a two-dollar part and you can't use it. It's LEGO, you're supposed to play with it," says Dan.

And so he opens up his collection. It's a generous streak that I think few adult fans would share. But I understand what Dan means when I meet his twelve-year-old son, Conrad. He's helping me to organize the room and make sure kids have the parts they need to build. I watch him move around from group to group, offering them different pieces, and I see flashes of Dan the salesman.

My thoughts about the museum and its founder are interrupted momentarily. "Do you know when the food truck is getting here?" a woman asks me.

"I think the local fire department is coming; but they're a bit late," I tell her, realizing that there are a lot of community people participating in the convention. It's not just adult fans who want to see this weekend succeed. As a result, Brick Show has the same vibe as a fair or a block party where local people are chatting about life as much as about the LEGO creations.

Later I help this woman's son figure out how to connect two houses with an arched LEGO piece. "You must be a great builder, you're great with kids," she says. *Is this single mother flirting with me? Wait, she called me a great builder.* The building compliment is a bigger ego boost than her overly friendly tone. But I'm brought back to earth quickly. Another mother is asking me something from the front of the room.

"Can you help my daughter find a horse? She can't find a horse anywhere." In the piles of jumbled brick, it's difficult to find a specific piece, but I discover that I'm able to remember where I've seen various parts from earlier in the day. I squat down next to a storage tub that a brown-haired boy in a Yankees T-shirt is riffling through. He holds his hand up in victory—he finds the horse before I do, but he needs it for his creation. So I don't have a horse for the little girl.

Feeling confident, I decide to build her a horse myself. After all, this is LEGO, it's supposed to be turned into something else. A few minutes later, I hand the mother a creation made from tan slopes and brown bricks.

"Oh, what's this?" she asks.

"It's a horse," I respond.

"Oh," she says uncertainly. "Of course it is. Thank you, that was very nice."

I find a reason to explore the museum soon after, because I feel my face growing flushed. I have made the little girl a camel—a cousin to the camel that sits on the bookshelf in my living room—definitely not a horse. Although it has been said that a camel is merely a horse made by committee, I have no idea how history will judge a lone man who continually issues faulty horse designs. It seems my LEGO animal skills are not that far along after all.

The camel incident aside, I find myself enjoying the day. I spent three summers of my college career as a camp counselor, and this is proving to be not that different. When each kid has finished working on their baseplate, I ask them to tell me the story of what is happening: "a robot attacking an alien," "a monster trapped inside the castle wall," and "bad guys fighting good guys." The castle theme has been dwarfed by the children's imaginations.

I hear my knees pop later that night as I sit down across from Brian Korte, the convention's first day having drawn to a close. A few adult fans are gathered around a foldable dining table with attached benches—the kind found in every school cafeteria when I was growing up. We're all eating pizza that Dan bought, with the exception of Brian, who is busy putting together panels for a dragon mosaic.

"Dan, last night I was pretty freaked out when I was walking out of the LEGO Crack House with a bag of grass," says an adult fan wearing a New York Mets baseball cap.

I look up sharply, wondering if I have missed a double meaning in the nickname for the second school building. But the man is smiling as he points to a ziplock bag filled with LEGO grass elements.

I laugh, and Brian smiles back, but he's got headphones in, so he hasn't heard the joke. His brown hair is as neatly parted as the brick piles he has sorted in order to finish the light blue patterned layout—the background of the dragon mosaic he's building during this year's convention. I ask Brian what drew him to mosaics.

"I enjoy this style of art, it's making something that is bigger than the sum of its parts," he says, sliding off his headphones and running his palm across the bridge of his nose.

Brian, thirty, is not alone. Mosaics are a growing category for LEGO builders because the cost is predictable, the design is scalable, and custom software exists to help turn photographs into pixelated mosaics. Besides color, the main variations among mosaics concern the orientation of the bricks: they can be either studs-up or studs-out. It's easiest to think of those terms by how you view the model. With studs out, you would see and feel the bumpy studs if you touched the mosaic. Studs up, you see the sides of the LEGO bricks, allowing for more detail; and you can use either plates (one-third the height of bricks) or bricks. But using more bricks increases your expense, and studs-up mosaics usually need to be glued to keep the pieces together.

In 2004, Brian was a Web designer looking for a unique wedding present for two friends. Relying on his experience as a cross-stitcher, he designed and built a gray-scale LEGO mosaic of the couple. The response convinced him that there might be a business in building custom mosaics. He launched Brickworkz that year in Richmond, Virginia. Portraits of couples turned into corporate commissions. A mosaic of Yoda he built during that time now hangs here in the museum, in the Space Room.

"They're expensive and tedious, but they're worthwhile," says Brian. "But I don't glue them; otherwise, I could have never turned my ex-girlfriend's head into Yoda."

Brian came to Brick Show in 2007 to design and help build the image that garnered the museum a Guinness World Record. He brought with him 525 pages of instructions, which had taken him more than a month to map out. Together with Dan and his staff, Brian built for thirty-six hours to complete the outline of the semitrailer, a minifig sun, and landscape. The children who came to the convention then put together their own baseplates to fill in the trailer of the truck.

Brian still has a few hundred 1 × 1s to snap in place before stopping for the night, but I head back to the Super 8 motel in Zanesville, Ohio.

It's early Sunday morning when I walk up to the back door of the museum and find Breann and Tom outside, sipping coffee, waiting for Dan to come unlock the building. I take a seat on the stone steps, my back achy from squatting beside kids the day before.

"This is really adult fan heaven," says Tom. "It's just an amazing collection of LEGO."

"I know, it feels strange, like the townspeople are living in the same town as Charlie and Willy Wonka—only they have no idea that Willy Wonka's factory is all that special," I reply.

And yet, that's the strangest part of the Toy and Plastic Brick Museum. The town of Bellaire doesn't understand the financial and sentimental value of the collection inside the former school. But adult fans don't get what Dan is doing either—they don't trust that he is willing to share. This is in part because adult fans' collections are so personal. It's rare that anyone gets to see where someone else builds, because showing off a work in progress opens you up to criticism. The idea that someone would have an entire museum constantly in progress is unfathomable. So adult fans hang back to wait and see if Dan will succeed, preferring to spend their money traveling to established conventions or to LEGOLAND.

Dan arrives slightly out of breath, flips open the door, and announces that he's headed to the LEGO Crack House. I ask to tag along and hop in the car alongside Thomas Mueller, whom I bonded with while building the Yellow Castle wall on Friday night.

Less than five minutes later, we pull up to the back of a school building that looks much like the old middle school that houses the museum.

"Welcome to the LEGO Crack House," Dan says with a spooky laugh, opening the door. Pallets are stacked haphazardly, boxes marked with "preschool" are lying around, and there are containers of Bionicle still shrink-wrapped in plastic. We go up to the second floor of the school, where the rooms are in various stages of organization. Pick A Brick boxes line the hallway. The "Chaos Room," as Dan calls it, has plastic bags of bricks waiting to be parted out and sorted. There's another room filled with just DUPLO bricks; and a third classroom shows signs of Dan's previous life, with boxy computer monitors sitting ten deep.

The paint is cracked and peeling in places, but this building, like the museum, is a gold mine, with more than 2.3 million bricks stacked on tan metal shelves. I have never seen so much LEGO in one place. Dan surprises me with a gift.

"This is wild," he says as he hands me a dark blue Bionicle set with blank white paper on the box where the product normally would be advertised. The lack of graphics is intriguing; it feels as if anything could be inside. When I turn it over, I can see through the unwrapped portion of the clamshell case that blue LEGO system bricks are bagged inside the book-size box. It's a bizarre packaging mistake—LEGO bricks and Bionicle are separate licenses—one that likely never should have shipped from the packing plant in Tennessee. Yet it's here in Bellaire, Ohio, and frankly, I'm not surprised.

This is a 13,824-piece mosaic of the Star Wars icon Yoda—forty-five by thirty inches of LEGO art by Brickworkz's Brian Korte.

14

Becoming a Brickmaster

I return from my trip to Bellaire with a renewed sense of purpose as a builder. After being surrounded by intricate models for four days, I feel compelled to improve my skill set and try to learn to build like the master model builders. It's a bit egotistical, but I want Dan Brown one day to covet something that I've built. However, I remind myself that Daniel LaRusso didn't just show up at the All-Valley Karate Championships ready to rumble; there was a whole series of skills he needed to master.

I also have a more immediate goal. In the wake of failing to build a horse at Brick Show, I need to expand my repertoire of LEGO animal constructions beyond the camel. I grab a bucket of yellow parts and spill them onto the dining room table. The bricks form a loose shape, like tea leaves, and in them I see the beginnings of a project. A rudder piece from the Aqua Raiders set that I used in the Belville challenge approximates a whale's tail, and a small pile of inverted 2×2 slopes could be the creature's bottom jaw. A window becomes an oversize eye, and I use a SNOT (Studs Not On Top) technique to add fins at ninety-degree angles to the whale's body. This is not a model built to scale, but it is instantly recognizable. I think that's because I nailed something simple: the whale's mouth. An inverted 2×3 slope rests below an inverted 2×2 slope, leaving a slight indent, which suggests the trademark half-smile that all cartoon whales seem to share.

I inform Kate that I am now a BrickMaster. She likes the whale, but she's skeptical about the honorific until I show her the *BrickMaster* magazine and Bionicle set that have arrived in the mail. *LEGO Club* is the free product magazine that anyone can receive; but if you are willing to pay $39.99 a year, you will receive six *BrickMaster* magazines, six exclusive sets to build, and the right to be called a BrickMaster—"the ultimate LEGO fan."

"LEGO segments their customer base with different types of content," wrote Joe Pulizzi in a June 2008 entry on his blog. "While *LEGO* magazine is great for many of their customers, a good portion of their customer base, which I would consider the 'high-spenders,' need more attention and have more advanced content needs. Thus, *BrickMaster* was born."

Joe is an adult fan. He also happens to be one of the Web's leading thinkers on content marketing. The consultant started analyzing his attraction to LEGO once he started building again with his two adolescent boys. Joe remembers getting the original *Brick Kicks* magazine in the 1980s. Just like *BrickMaster*, it was a bimonthly publication that focused on LEGO builders talking about innovative models and wacky uses of LEGO. The Spring 1989 edition featured a profile of thirty-eight-year-old "Tricky

Dick," a tortoise in Britain that had a set of LEGO wheels attached to compensate for a right hind leg lost to a dog bite.

"Getting kids and adults involved in being a LEGO fan is all about imagination. They give you the sets, of course, to start, but LEGO cultivates that through all of their contests. It's about creating, thinking outside the instruction manual," says Joe when I reach him by phone in his Cleveland office.

The spirit of creative competition celebrated in *Brick Kicks* is still on display at AFOL conventions, with builders pushing one another to find more imaginative uses for parts. White and translucent bricks look like smoke floating up from a chimney, gearshifts become bunny ears on a television, and radio dishes are patio umbrellas. The scale of creations at those conventions could be lifted directly from the pages of the magazines—models that seemingly were being built only by master builders in the 1980s.

"Anybody who likes LEGO wants to share their creation. You want to take pictures of it, put it online, get comments, and make friends," says Joe.

With *BrickMaster*, LEGO appears to be developing the next wave of adult fans in the same manner as the generation that grew up reading *Brick Kicks*. Inside the magazine, kids are celebrated as builders with the "cool creations" section; but today the company is taking advantage of technology to connect fans with one another. MyLEGO Network is a social networking site that lets kids show one another their MOCs and play LEGO-themed video games. It stands to reason that kids with large LEGO collections are more likely to keep building through the Dark Ages and become adult fans.

This might be the chicken-egg question of AFOLs. Do adult fans exist because LEGO has encouraged friendly competition and developed builders since childhood? Or is LEGO merely responding to the wants of a group of adults who dreamed of becoming master builders as children? It reminds me of a discussion at Brickworld that spontaneously arose during a talk about why adult fans go through a Dark Ages.

"How much is LEGO doing to support online communities?" asked Scott, an AFOL from Alabama.

"We were supporting Brickshelf for a time; but we stopped that and decided we needed to step back. We're here to experience your community. But as soon as we take ownership, it's not the AFOL community anymore. We need this community to be self-sufficient," responded Steve Witt, a LEGO community relations coordinator.

Steve is in a unique position to comment on LEGO's policies because he's one of the adult fans whom the company has hired to try to define its relationship with the AFOL community. Only twenty-six, he's arguably the most powerful adult fan in the United States. He also has instant credibility because not only does he have historic knowledge of sets, but he also still builds regularly. With bushy black hair and a thick goatee, Steve could be any young guy just out of college, eating lunch at Chipotle, still attached to Nerf guns, and playing World of Warcraft for hours after his day job.

The difference is that his day job is working for LEGO. After graduating from Texas Christian University, Steve wasn't sure what he wanted to do with his degree in education. An avid space builder, Steve met Jake McKee, then LEGO community relations coordinator, through TEXLUG in Dallas. Jake agreed to take him on in 2003 as an intern, because LEGO had a hiring freeze at the time. After Jake left LEGO to launch his own consulting business, their two-man department had shrunk to one. In May 2005, Steve was promoted to head community relations coordinator just six months into the LEGO Ambassador Program.

After Brickworld, Steve and I play phone tag, and I don't know what to expect from a conversation with him. At AFOL conventions, Steve has something of a split personality. There are the glib one-liners that shut down hecklers during Q&As and I think help him navigate the tricky position of knowing more information than he can share. But there is also an earnest side indicative of a person who wants you to like him, and there are the hints he can't help dropping about upcoming releases.

"I like to think that I'm basically the same; although I do sometimes put up a bit of a front at conventions," Steve says when I ask him what it's like to be a LEGO fan inside the company.

"You can see the difference between the two worlds in something simple: the fan community and the company even have different names for colors."

But he's not just a liaison at conventions. Steve is also the adult fans' voice within the company, explaining how adult consumers might perceive or react to production decisions. He tries to reach out to employees to let them understand why AFOLs connect with their product. To do that means discovering what his coworkers are passionate about, be it action figures or fonts.

"My dad collects stamps. I see no point, but I appreciate that he loves it. Passion for anything doesn't mean you're crazy," says Steve.

Toward the end of our conversation, I ask Steve about Dan Brown, telling him I just got back from the Toy and Plastic Brick Museum a few weeks ago.

"I don't have that much interaction with Dan," says Steve. It's the only truly corporate answer I've received from a very noncorporate person. What he doesn't say tells me a bit more about where Dan stands with the company. He's outside, and LEGO is still deciding if they're going to let him look in.

While talking to Steve, I've put together most of a World of LEGO Mosaics set. It's the box I snagged at a thrift store for a dollar the previous month—a blue–and–white shark with flowing green seaweed on a clear baseplate. At sixteen studs by sixteen studs, it's not much bigger than a bread plate, only taking the edge off my desire to build. I need something more.

I have a grand plan to build a monster black-and-white mosaic of Kate and me. I credit Brian Korte's portfolio with the inspiration, having seen the black-and-white mosaic he made from a photograph to give his fiancée, Molly. Since then I've wanted to build something I could give Kate as a gift, and I have settled on a ninety-six-stud-square mosaic.

The picture I have in mind is from a vacation to Normandy, France, taken in our time-honored tradition of holding the camera out in front of us with one hand and getting a shot of our heads smushed together.

"Step 1 is reducing the pic to 96 pixels [by 96 pixels—so that each pixel is a Lego stud]. Then you'll see what you're dealing with. It won't be pretty any more. This is what separates the programs from the artist," writes Brian when I e-mail him for advice.

I open the vacation photo in Photoshop and set to tweaking it so it will make a good mosaic. I change the contrast on the photo to black-and-white and reduce the size of the picture. The image quickly morphs into an arrangement of blocks; it's not even clear to me what each of the blocks represents. I begin to play with the levels and curves, hoping I remember enough from a one-day impromptu lesson from a newspaper editor in Revere, Massachusetts, about six years ago. I also adjust the portrait into five colors to match the LEGO color spectrum: three grays, white, and black.

"You have to capture them as a portrait, not mimic the photo," Brian told me earlier when I asked how important it is to match the mosaic to the photo.

I print out four guides, each of which represents a quarter of the mosaic. I'm ready to build.

When he gets to this point, Brian told me, he often brings in friends to help him finish his large-scale models, buying them pizza in exchange for an evening of snapping the studs into place, following his printouts where one pixel equals one stud. He tells me that he occasionally hazes new builders by telling them that the LEGO logo (featured on each stud) needs to be facing the same direction on every brick of a studs-out mosaic. The positioning of the LEGO logo doesn't matter; but I'm glad I'm not that naive.

I don't have nearly enough bricks to even start my mosaic, so I get ready to place my first big BrickLink order. I spend two hours on the site comparison shopping before I realize that the cost of having bricks shipped from four different sellers negates any real cost savings. I'm disappointed that 1×1 white plates will cost me nearly six cents apiece, because I need 180 of them; but I'm ecstatic that 1×1 black plates are only three cents. I buy 7,790 bricks, doubling my collection with a click of my mouse. In one week, $224.76 worth of LEGO elements are slated to arrive at my house from Yorba Linda, California.

I get impatient waiting for the bricks to arrive, so I go to a local source for the green baseplates that will form the base of the mosaic. The rain falls softly as my car idles in front of a generic gray office building ten minutes from my house. The digital clock reads 12:15 p.m. It's time to make the exchange. Andreas Stabno appears in the revolving door and motions for me to come inside.

"You got the stuff?" I joke. He's brought six green baseplates, thirty-two studs wide and long. I hand him a check for $29. Andreas is glad to see that I'm working on a big project. I finally understand how he felt picking up the monorail set in the parking lot of a St. Louis train station.

I think about surprising Kate, but the dining room table will be my main workstation for the next few months, and I think she'll figure out something is up.

"I bought six baseplates from Andreas today. I'm building a ninety-six-by-ninety-six mosaic for you," I tell her. It's easier to start with $29 and then work my way up to the BrickLink purchase.

"That's great; but don't you mean nine baseplates?" says Kate.

I pause; my master building project already has a pretty big problem. I've done my math wrong on an art piece that is basically a creative use of math. Six baseplates would leave me with a ninety-six by sixty-four mosaic.

"Right, that's what I said, nine baseplates."

But that's the beauty of BrickLink, because five minutes later I've sent $15.33 electronically to Cincinnati, Ohio, for three green baseplates.

I get excited each day the mail comes, hoping it is the large box of bricks for my mosaic. Instead, my second LEGO BrickMaster set arrives, a nifty green army jeep with an Indiana Jones minifig. It's one of the few sets I put together that I immediately decide I will not be cannibalizing for parts, because it's Indy and you can't disrespect Dr. Jones.

Building with LEGO has opened me up to my other fan ten-
dencies, through both the sets and the other adult fans. The
creative element of LEGO allows the fan experience to be more
interactive. I've been exposed to a lot of different fanboys (and a
few fangirls): the AFOL universe overlaps with comic books, Star
Wars, and Harry Potter—all strong subcultures in their own right.
In some cases, it seems that there is a direct correlation between
geek attraction and building with LEGO as an adult; Indiana
Jones and Star Wars fans often find themselves picking up plastic
bricks after a long hiatus because of specially released sets.

But beyond a direct connection, part of me feels that adults
who are willing to embrace LEGO and redefine a children's toy
are simply more confident in letting their geek flag fly. They're
willing to embrace their fandom in other areas and risk ridicule,
because after all, what's more geeky than playing with LEGO?

I've had only one interview in my career when I felt like a
fan. In my first few weeks as a staff reporter for the *Lynn Journal,*
I learned that Marshmallow Fluff was made in the paper's
hometown of Lynn, Massachusetts. I called and arranged a tour
of the factory and was taken around by a member of the second
generation to run the privately held business. Don Durkee spent
a half hour showing me the manufacturing plant and the process
behind making the iconic marshmallow spread of my childhood.
I failed to ask a single question.

And now I'm about to embark on a second trip as a fan. I'll
be spending three days inside LEGO headquarters: touring the
factory, the set vault, and the Idea House—the former home of
Ole Kirk Christiansen that has been turned into an employee
museum. I hope I can think to ask a few questions.

The 1.5-million-piece LEGO Mount Rushmore sits above Legoredo—the Old West reincarnated—at LEGOLAND in Billund, Denmark.

15

Danish Rocky and a Real Star Wars Expert

The C Terminal at the airport in Amsterdam has the least con-fusing duty-free stores of all time. Kate and I roll our bags past LEATHER, DIAMONDS, and SHOES. None interest me.

"Toys," reads Kate aloud. "Want to go see if they have any LEGO?" But I'm already inside the shop. I buy a small catapult set explicitly for the dwarf and troll minifigs. I have no intention of building the kit, but I think I can use the green heads for a zombie build.

It's late Saturday morning in the third week of September and we're taking the commuter flight to Billund, Denmark, the head-quarters of LEGO. I'm envisioning the plane filled with happy children—like the pre-island scene in *The Lord of the Flies*. But once we board, with the exception of a single ten-year-old, the rest of the passengers look like the businessman sitting next to me in designer jeans and a collared shirt.

After the plane has taken off, I pull out a binder of articles concerning LEGO to prepare myself for my arrival at company headquarters. I stack these on top of *The Unofficial LEGO Builder's Guide* and start taking notes. I look up from reading and see that Kate is working on the Trebuchet set, having just snapped together a dwarf minifig.

"Poor guy can't bend his legs," says Kate, noting that the dwarf's legs aren't hinged, making him shorter than a traditional minifig. A few minutes later, I hear an evil-sounding *rawrrr*. Kate is walking a troll waving a black flag emblazoned with a white skull toward me. I burst out laughing, and the guy next to me looks up from his leather portfolio to give a polite smile.

My wife is a bit punchy after the overnight flight to Amsterdam, and we're seated in an exit row—not a good combination. "Weapons test," says Kate as she launches the 2×2 round brown projectile from the trebuchet and it shoots forward into the row ahead of us. Kate has to unbuckle her seat belt to retrieve the piece. We are relatively well-behaved for the rest of the hour-long flight. On touchdown, the man to my right gets up to grab his lap-top bag from the overhead bin. It's black with four primary-color LEGO bricks on the side and a red LEGO luggage tag.

"Enjoy your stay here," he says, smiling before deplaning.

"Thank you," I mumble, my cheeks reddening with the certainty that fate will make him one of the LEGO executives I'm destined to meet in the next few days.

There is no doubt that Billund is a company town. Any traveler landing at Billund Airport in 1964 would have disembarked in the hangar built for LEGO, just off the grass airfield owned by the company. An actual terminal wouldn't be constructed for another two years. Today the airport is owned by the eight surrounding municipalities and sits just a half-mile from LEGO corporate headquarters.

The children I expected to be on the plane are apparently all in the lobby of the LEGOLAND Hotel. As we approach the front desk to check in, I notice a few kids begging their parents to buy the sets that are piled in displays around the desk, while others are busy playing around the circular pits filled with DUPLO bricks.

LEGOLAND is only open for another hour, but I'm too excited to wait until tomorrow, and Kate agrees to use the first day of our two-day pass to go into the park. The hotel is connected to the park by an elevated walkway, and thus less than an hour after we've arrived in Denmark, we're walking through the turnstiles of the amusement park just as 1.4 million people do every year.

LEGOLAND Billund initially was conceived of as a promotional tool in 1968.

"Legoland was created when growing throngs of tourists began to interfere with work at the LEGO factory," wrote Robert D. Hershey Jr. in a 1977 *New York Times* profile of the burgeoning company in Denmark.

The first shot at franchising LEGOLAND was not successful. A second park opened in 1973 in Sierksdorf, Germany, LEGO's largest toy market. It closed only three years later due to a lack of attendance, and twenty years passed before the second LEGOLAND theme park was introduced in Windsor, England. Its success led to LEGOLAND California opening in 1999, and another attempt at the German market in 2002 with LEGOLAND Deutschland in Gunzburg. The parks have been run by Merlin Entertainments since 2005. The amusement park operator intends to open a fifth location in Dubai in 2011; a sixth, named LEGOLAND Florida, in Winter Haven, the same year; and LEGOLAND Malaysia in Iskandar in 2013.

Kate and I are slightly older than the target demographic of two to twelve.

"I wonder if we're the only ones here without kids," says Kate. I think we are. In fact, it seems that there a lot of kids who simply haven't brought their parents. It hurts a bit because we're still trying to have a baby, but the combination of excitement at being inside LEGOLAND and sleep deprivation morph those feelings into euphoria. We have enough time to walk around the park once, noting the location of Miniland and the rides we have to go on in the morning. Before I want to leave, we're being hustled out by polite but firm park employees.

Plastic lamps filled with monochromatic LEGO bricks hang over the stairs that lead back to the hotel walkway from the park. I make Kate take several pictures, convinced we can recreate the effect in our house.

"We have to get LEGO everything," I tell her, jumping from LEGO brick to brick on the patterned rug in the hotel lobby. She would rather have a copy of the LEGO mosaic Mona Lisa that hangs there. The hotel is actually under construction, but it's still slightly strange to see eighteen-inch-tall LEGO figures mock-painting or repairing the building's entrance. The scaled-up minifigures are cheerfully posed near the front door and front desk, leaving no doubt about the theme of the hotel. As we struggle to stay awake so we'll adjust to the time change, children run up and down the hall eager to get to the free video-game kiosks with LEGO Indiana Jones.

Kate and I are expecting a bit more luxury for $400, but our room is spartanly Ikea. I try to convince her that our bed frame is made of LEGO, but she quickly figures out it's more likely to be particleboard. I lend her my pajamas after she opens her suitcase and discovers that her contact lens solution has leaked onto her clothes. That night, we've been asleep for a few hours when I hear the click of the door opening. I open my eyes. The light from the hallway spills into the entryway, and I see a large shadow cut across the light. An intruder is in our room, and I'm not wearing pants.

"Get out!" I yell. The man's response is an incoherent mumble, possibly in German. Who could get that drunk in the most family-friendly hotel I've ever stayed at? I debate getting out of bed, trying to decide if it would be more or less intimidating to the stranger to be confronted with a pantless adversary.

"Get out," I repeat, dropping my tone an octave to use my camp counselor voice, but staying underneath the covers. I see the shadow begin to retreat. Kate wakes up and yells, "Get out!"

"Shut the door," I command. The drunk mumbles—a decent impression of a Danish Rocky—and the door snicks closed.

In the morning, we go back to LEGOLAND. I keep looking around to see if any large guys pushing strollers are hungover, but nobody seems to be weaving. I hold hands with Kate as we walk toward the center of the park to get a look at LEGO Mount Rushmore, the first on my list of models I want to see. It's built at a 1:12 scale, it is composed of 1.5 million bricks, and it sits outside the entrance of the Old West town known as Legoredo. With shipping, it would cost a cool $100,000 to buy that many bricks online. There is surreal, and then there is walking through a theme park in western Denmark while Kenny Roger's "The Gambler" plays over the loudspeaker. We buy lunch at Billy's Western.

I had asked Joe Meno for food recommendations in Billund. "Danish hamburgers are really odd," he warned me via e-mail. "Pizza is different too, but not quite as bad as the burgers."

If Danish hamburgers are odd, I wonder what Joe would think of what we do choose. A Fransk dog is a hot dog shoved inside a cored-out baguette filled with mustard or mayonnaise. They're perfect for eating while walking. Unfortunately, they also fall prey to the law of diminishing returns, bringing a bit less satisfaction and a bit more indigestion with each subsequent one purchased.

We stop briefly at the Indian Trading Post, where a tall, fit white man wearing a Native American longshirt and headdress tries to sell tomahawks to the park guests while greeting them with a "How, How!" This is the America of 1855 as imagined by the America of 1955.

At times, it's easy to forget that LEGO is a Danish company. Most of my friends are surprised to learn that LEGO bricks didn't originate in the United States. But here at LEGOLAND, Kate and I notice some differences from the typical American theme park.

The most obvious is the Traffic School, where good behavior is the rule of the road. Kids earn a mock "driver's license" for operating a small electric LEGO car according to the laws of the ride. The kids must obey traffic signs and fill their cars up at gas pumps at certain points. It's unclear why this ride is fun; the whole thing seems designed for the children of uptight accountants.

A number of rides are also human-powered. Children hoist themselves up a rope to the top of a tower. Kate and I are both dangerously winded after a fire truck ride where we have to operate a hand pump, something like a seesaw device on a rail car.

The pirate boats evoke the atmosphere of Pirates of the Caribbean, except the six-passenger faux-wooden boat travels past scenes made entirely out of LEGO. Our knees touch the front of the safari cars as they wind on a track between LEGO giraffes and flamingos. The rides are very tame, meant for small children to enjoy. As a result, Kate convinces me to ride the Dragon, a mini roller coaster that screams around a single loop after a LEGO wizard utters a magic spell. It's only the second roller coaster I've been on in my thirty years on earth. A week after I rode the first, a car flew off the track of that particular coaster, and that sealed the deal for me. Until now. Our photo from the Dragon at Billund shows me grimacing with my eyes shut. Thankfully the camera doesn't have enough resolution to catch the few tears that streamed from my eyes. However, they might be captured nicely in a mosaic with 1×1 translucent tiles.

But we didn't come to LEGOLAND for the rides; we're here to see Miniland, the brick re-creation of famous cities and landmarks. This is where adult fans come first because it's usually the best work of master model builders in the park. We spend three hours among the twenty million bricks.

"They have working locks," says Kate, marveling at the canals and harbors of LEGO European cities. The boats and cars run on electric circuits or pulley systems. I love the details. It's like a continuous game of *Where's Waldo?* A top-hatted chimney sweep cleans out the chimney of a Victorian building, and a LEGO father stops to buy his daughter an ice cream in the park. The buildings are brought to life by these tiny scenes that capture moments in time with figures that don't have faces. The bonsai-scale landscaping is nearly as impressive. A LEGO Miniland figure pushes a brick lawnmower among real flowers and trees that are proportionally correct.

It's also exciting to discover parts and buildings in colors that have not been commercially available. Although the idea of Miniland and most large-scale models is that the model builders attempt to use the parts available to the public, sometimes they have access to parts in unique colors or batches that are no longer on the market. There are flesh- and brown-colored buildings in shades I wish I could buy. I settle for purchasing several pounds of minifigure accessories and translucent 1 × 2 pieces in the Pick A Brick section of the nearby gift shop.

After spending the entire day at LEGOLAND yesterday, I can't wait to see where LEGO bricks are made. I've got a few loose mini-fig heads in my pocket as I walk from the hotel up Systemvej road toward LEGO headquarters. "Systemvej road" roughly translates to "System Road," another sign that the town and company are as interlocked as the bricks they make.

"I'm here to see Jan Christiansen," I tell the receptionist, pronouncing it "yan," rather than my first instinct to try it like the second Brady Bunch sister. Thankfully, nearly everyone we encounter speaks almost flawless English.

"There are a number of Jan Christiansens," she says. "Are you looking for the one in accounting?" Of course there are a lot of Jan Christiansens—both the first and last name are common in Denmark. This is quickly beginning to resemble a bad job interview.

"No, I'm a journalist and he's part of media relations . . ."

"Oh, you mean *Jan* Christiansen, there's only one of him," says the receptionist, rhyming his first name with "pen."

Jan comes out to greet me, and thankfully he is taller and skinnier than my seatmate on the plane. He introduces me to Aksel Krabbe Nielsen, the visitor manager, who will be guiding us around the production plant attached to the corporate headquarters. Aksel has a flat-top haircut and the glasses of a NASA employee from *Apollo 13*. Jan also explains that a photographer and a reporter from a newspaper in Hamburg, Germany, will be joining us on the tour. The factory is connected to the headquarters building via a short hallway that is just long enough to build anticipation.

"This is, um . . . you have seen it before, Darth Vader's space-ship, the Millennium Falcon?" asks Aksel at the beginning of our tour, pointing out LEGO's most expensive model to date.

"That's Han Solo's ship, actually," I can't help but correct him.

"Oh, I see we have a real Star Wars expert here today," he replies, laughing with the German newspaper employees.

I'm not an expert, I want to say, *that's something that everybody in the United States knows.* But instead, I just smile and laugh along with them. They are making Star Wars minifigures in the plant today—clone troopers—at a rate the Kaminoans could only dream of: thirty-six thousand per minute.

"Do you have the Amy Winehouse LEGO people here?" asks the German reporter. LEGO recently has created graphics of pop culture figures for publicity, but never actually produced the mini-figs. It was briefly a strong topic of debate on the adult fan forums. I'm about to correct her, when Jan explains that the minifigs were never really made.

"So, do you have them here?" the reporter asks again. Behind her a row of LEGO minifig heads are rolling down a conveyor belt into a box. I can't believe she's worried about Amy Winehouse when we're in the middle of the place that makes LEGO minifigures.

I find myself initially stumped for questions, too stunned by my surroundings to interrupt Aksel's standard patter. So I take pictures and awkwardly work the buttons on my handheld video camera. I keep waiting for somebody to stop me from capturing the inner workings of the factory, but nobody does. I inadvertently appear in a lot of the German photographer's shots, but I feel rewarded when I give him a tip on how to avoid getting glare from LEGO pieces.

Minifigures are among the most complicated and expensive pieces made by LEGO, requiring up to six passes through a stamper to imprint faces or designs on torsos. The torsos are spun around a slightly vibrating circular container and weighed for the correct tolerances before a machine inserts the arms. The hands are then added to the arms.

"We don't mix bricks and minifigs," says Aksel as we walk from the production side of the plant to where they assemble the sets. He's a LEGO diehard, having worked at the company for twenty-five years and four months, according to his calculations. He started as a cowboy in LEGOLAND.

It is Aksel who introduces new employees to the culture of LEGO. I can see why as he is proud of the toys they make, but I'm willing to bet he doesn't build at home (he doesn't). He has the perfect mix of investment and detachment that makes for a lifelong employee. It also means that he is nonchalant about the vast size of the factory that produces tiny bricks.

Steam issues from giant pipes running along the ceiling designed to keep the humidity at a proper level in the factory. Black LEGO shovels fall into black bins. Bricks are put into red and blue bins. And everything runs on bar codes. LEGO produces 19 billion elements a year, 2.16 million elements per hour (about fifty pieces in the time it took you to read that sentence).

The parts become sets on the packaging lines. The pieces are separated and then counted with an optical sensor as they are inserted into small boxes. The boxes are continually weighed, and an alarm sounds if the weight isn't correct. That alarm alerts an employee, who does a visual inspection to figure out what parts are missing or need to be added according to the instructions for a given set.

The box then continues down the conveyor belt, where the pieces drop into a plastic wrapping machine. Once all the bags for a given set are collected, they are then inserted into the set box, which has just been folded by another employee. I keep wondering if some of the people I'm watching have put together any of the sets I have bought.

To meet the rising demand, LEGO opened a second production facility in 1988. Jan drives me over to the large warehouse and manufacturing plant, Kornmarken, which roughly translates to "rye fields." The industrial area is named for fields and grains in homage to Billund's beginnings as an agricultural village. Most of the sixteen hundred people who work at LEGO commute from other cities.

Three oversize bricks in primary colors lie at the entrance as if dropped by a giant child. I thought the first assembly plant was large, but Kornmarken is five hundred meters long, about a third of a mile. The floor of the fifty-two-thousand-square-meter facility is scuffed from feet and forklifts. The plastic granulate that will become LEGO bricks is stored in silos. Sixty tons are processed every twenty-four hours. A sound like faraway boulders tumbling in an avalanche accompanies the granulate as it travels along an intricate system of tubes to the molding machines.

Before I left for Denmark, I called Dave Sterling—it helps to know a plastics engineer. Dave's first job was working in plastic product development, trying to find more efficient or heat-resistant plastic. His company has actually supplied LEGO with the glow-in-the-dark granules for specialty elements such as the castle ghost.

Dave dreams of working at LEGO as an engineer, dabbling in LEGO-ometry—short for LEGO geometry—the name given to the study of the production and tolerance of LEGO. The basic idea is to figure out how many parts you might be able to make from a batch of plastic granulate. In his mind, it is how LEGO approaches the plastic and molds that defines the company.

"What makes LEGO special is the quality—the combination of materials, properties, knowledge of mold design, and how they machine their own tools," Dave told me.

All of the molds and machines have been built and maintained in Denmark. On average, LEGO discards only eighteen out of every million elements produced in Billund for failure to meet quality standards.

The material used to make LEGO pieces—acrylonitrile butadiene styrene—also is used to make everything from golf club heads to the plastic recorders you played in grade school. Each of the three chemical components lends a property that is associated with the little LEGO bricks. Acrylonitrile increases the surface hardness of plastic, helping to prevent scratches. Butadiene is a rubber, providing shape to the plastic. Styrene melts at a fairly low temperature, making the granules easier to process.

As Dave explained, "ABS has everything LEGO would want. It has good dimensional stability and can be molded to tight tolerances. It also has good fatigue and creep resistance, which is important because every time you flex a brick, it's like stretching a rubber band. Eventually it breaks."

The plastic granulate is heated to 235°C (455°F) until it melts inside a container that resembles an espresso machine. The heated mixture then drops via gravity to compress in the mold. Water is used to cool the plastic in eight to twelve seconds. The mold opens and the elements are pushed out onto a conveyor belt. The runners, the extra plastic outside the molded element, are cut into small pieces and recycled. Everything is automated to make sure the molds are completely filled and emptied at the right time.

"Tolerances are critical," Dave told me, "because when you stack bricks up, your tolerance stacks with it. LEGO wants precision because otherwise the bricks from 1979 won't work with the bricks from 1999."

Technic pins and dwarf legs are being made side by side. The mold releases with a satisfying *pop*, punching out LEGO pieces by the dozen with the sound of an air rifle at the carnival. White and orange 1 × 4s fall into boxes. Endless numbers of dark green 2 × 4s roll down the conveyor belt.

"Do you know how much these are worth?" I ask Jan. He looks at me blankly. I resist the urge to run my fingers through the bin or fill my pockets. Dark green 2 × 4s go for as much as twenty-five cents apiece on BrickLink and, in front of my eyes, six hundred of them are pouring into a box per minute. It's like watching the inner workings of a diamond cartel. Here are dark green bricks in abundance—a bin-full that no adult fan will ever possess. They will just be broken up according to the parts requirements of sets, meaning the secondary market will always be adjusting to what LEGO decides to produce.

I see only two employees working alongside the sixty-five machines here. One is pushing a broom to pick up the loose elements that have fallen to the floor, while another is doing quality testing of the bricks. The lack of people seems emblematic, as LEGO continues to move more manufacturing to the Czech Republic and Mexico to lower costs and to be closer to growing markets. In the beginning of the decade, LEGO employed four thousand people, roughly half the working population of Billund. That number dropped to sixteen hundred in 2009.

Robots circle the floor until summoned by sensors, exchanging an empty box for a full box of parts. The boxes then travel on conveyors to one of four storage towers. The number of red and yellow crates filled with LEGO is staggering.

The last stop on the tour is the mold warehouse. Molds are stacked on orange and steel shelves; Aksel estimates that LEGO has between six thousand and seven thousand molds, of which four thousand are currently active. Molds can potentially be filled five million times, and some have been in use for more than thirty years. Since it takes twelve weeks and up to $50,000 to make one mold, LEGO wants to get the most use out of each.

"What happens when a mold is done?" I ask Jan.

"We put them under the concrete in front to make sure that nobody will steal the molds," says Jan. He's smiling, but he's not kidding.

I immediately think of Dan Brown, who has several prototype LEGO Darth Vader helmets—the test shots that never should have left the factory. Things have a way of sneaking out of factories, particularly as more manufacturing is outsourced to places that are less connected to LEGO than Billund. There's clearly a market for rare LEGO ephemera. The last thing that LEGO needs is a competitor building from the same molds. It would be like the Treasury losing their bill plates.

After the two factory tours, I have a few more meetings and interviews with LEGO employees. As I depart corporate headquarters, I stamp my feet on my way out of the building. I'm testing for a hollow sound, hoping to locate a cache of buried molds. But the concrete is too thick. I can't make out any difference in the sound of my stomps, and I walk away quickly before I get caught. It will be one of the few things I don't confess to my wife. Searching for buried treasure is not as cool as I was led to believe in *The Goonies*.

Inside the vault beneath the LEGO Idea House in Billund is Set 1082, the first set I ever owned—pieces of which are still in my collection.

16

A Guest in LEGO's House

I never expected to come face-to-face with my worst nightmare at LEGO headquarters, but there it is: a snarling red dragon—the namesake of the roller coaster at LEGOLAND. A 3-D model of the LEGO dragon is dissected into parts on the designer Jette Skovgaard Jensen's computer monitor.

"That's only the second roller coaster I've been on in my life. I'm a chicken," I tell Jette as she walks me through how the model was built.

"I'm chicken too. I can't look. But the challenge of something when it's for LEGOLAND—we have to think about the whole family, like how to make it cool for a twelve-year-old and not too scary for a three-year-old," says Jette. I ignore that I'm more than ten times the age she is trying not to scare.

She has the trendy glasses and spiky red hair of a designer in the 3-D Model Center. We're at her desk inside Havremarken, the LEGO offices adjacent to the manufacturing plant. The building immediately makes me think of a Google campus, with employees on scooters whizzing by basketball hoops and table tennis tables in the hallways. The environment is certainly creative. A massively over-scaled red LEGO fire truck sits between cubicles, and nearly every employee's workspace is decorated with a LEGO set or minifig.

I'm trying to get a sense of who the people are behind the brick creations I've been surrounded with for the past several days. Jette is a second-generation LEGO employee. She grew up in Billund, while her dad worked as a technician on the electronics and structural supports for the models that her mom glued.

"When I was a kid, I remember coming in the doors, it was very open. I thought I might leave Billund, but I was afraid. And here it was also easy to get a job once you are inside the company," says Jette.

Today, her three children come with her on occasion to LEGO, eager to see her workspace, just as she wanted to follow her parents to work. Hearing about her family makes me think that working for LEGO is not that different from working for an American factory that comes to be synonymous with a small town. I could be in Elkhart, Indiana, finding out how recreational vehicles are made. LEGO just happens to have landed in Billund, defining the life of Jette's family and thousands like her.

Jette began her career with LEGO as a window dresser in the exhibition department. For the past fifteen years, she has worked as a model designer. When she started designing models, the company was using "brick paper," its own version of graph paper. In 1997, the company began to experiment with software programs for design, creating polygon models that could be morphed into bricks. Today she designs everything from park models to store displays. I mention that I've been bugging Kate about having some LEGO-filled lights in our house at home, threatening to build my own lamp.

"Well, it takes a couple of years to get the feeling of how it should look. Because it's not just an artistic sense, but also a mathematical sense," says Jette. This is her letting me down gently.

LEGO architectural drawing programs are readily available to the public. LEGO Digital Designer (LDD) is the 3-D modeling software that allows people to build creations on top of a piece of virtual graph paper. Through LEGO Factory, builders can even order the creations they have just designed, with all of the parts being shipped from LEGO. An open-source architectural program, LDraw, is also popular. The free computer-aided design software allows adult fans to render 3-D models and create building instructions for virtual sets. Many fans prefer LDraw because there are no limits to colors or bricks available, as opposed to LDD.

Jette walks me through the color palette she can choose from, noting that she has access to nearly every color of brick—although some are obviously more rare than others. Only a few elements have been done in gold, for instance, and the cost of a model made entirely from gold elements is not only exorbitant, it's impractical.

Besides being paid to build, this is the perk of the job that most adult fans covet—a massive supply of LEGO. The designer is the kid on the playground with the most toys. Jette remembers the last time adult fans got a chance to visit the storeroom where bricks are kept.

"It was great to see because we are so used to that stuff that we could just go and pick whatever we want. And yet [adult fans] were just so happy to have a little bag of bricks. They grabbed the transparent bricks like they were gold," she says.

Because my days here have been filled with interviews, I don't have time to visit the storeroom and get my little bag of bricks. I'm more disappointed than I would have thought when it's time to head back to the original LEGO campus on Systemvej. There I meet up again with Jan Christiansen, who leads me inside a stunningly white hallway, where stacks of white LEGO bricks sit beneath signs that proclaim THE JOY OF BUILDING and

THE PRIDE OF CREATION. It feels like an Apple store, but it's the entry-way to the Idea House—the former home of Ole Kirk Christiansen, which has been transformed into a LEGO museum.

This is the second stop on my personal version of the LEGO Inside Tour. Since 2005, adult fans (and children with well-off parents) can pay $1,700 to tour the factory and the Idea House, as well as meet the designers. The Inside Tour is where you go on your honeymoon or for your fortieth birthday—the kind of trip that inspires the stories that your kids get sick of hearing. And I get to go for free.

Still, I didn't expect my palms to be as sweaty as they are when I meet Jette Orduna, the director of the Idea House and the driving force behind the Inside Tour. Jette has the calm manners of a tour guide, gesturing gracefully with her arms to direct my attention to an object, and readily stopping her speech to address any of my questions.

"Are you a fan?" asks Jette.

"Yes," I answer. It's the first time I haven't paused to consider my answer or immediately replied in the negative.

Stark Danish modernity gives way to the brightness of LEGO when we step inside the doors of the Idea House and experience a color explosion. The walls are covered in primary-color panels, lit from behind and detailing the recent history of the LEGO Group. One of the first panels I see explains about adult fans becoming involved with the company through Mindstorms.

"Working with adult fans is very rewarding because of their passion. They love this company," says Jette, who often interacts with adult fans working on exhibitions. As a way to thank them, LEGO often allows AFOLs who are partnering with the company inside the Idea House, which is typically closed to the public.

"So many times this feels like home to them. But we have to work together in the right way; this is a business and they are fans. I just have to make sure fans understand they're still a guest in order to keep that integrity between us," says Jette.

Her sentiment is clear. I am a guest in LEGO's house. She is not admonishing me, only setting up the rules of the tour. In that moment, she makes me think of Jane Goodall explaining how she remains objective: Jette walks among the fans, but she is not one of them.

I like Jette because I get the feeling she has taken the time to understand the AFOL community and found a way to work them into the living history of the exhibit. The Idea House is where LEGO employees learn about the creation of play themes and how the company has evolved.

"It was important to the family that everybody in the company understands why we're here and what we're about. While we're looking to the future, why don't we see what we can learn from the past?" says Jette.

Ole Kirk built this brick house with its pair of concrete lions sitting outside the entrance in 1924. His home became the Idea House in 1990 with a multiroom display that covered LEGO's history. The further I get from the entrance, the more I start to feel that I'm literally a guest in Ole Kirk's house. Between two sets of doors, a fish tank gurgles unexpectedly. His grandson was responsible for feeding the fish. He also happened to be the third generation to take over the company.

"Kjeld is like his grandfather. His connection with the company is emotional; he never wanted to be called CEO," says Jette, as we pass by the fish tank and back toward the early days of LEGO.

Jette shows me a stairway that leads to the administrative offices on the second floor. "I'll be up there if you need me," she says, leaving me to explore on my own.

Inside this house, Ole Kirk Christiansen becomes a real person. There's the desk where he sat and probably reviewed the models designed by his seventeen-year-old son, Godtfred, in 1937. Ole Kirk was a serial entrepreneur and a regular churchgoer with a weird sense of humor. One of his favorite jokes was to dump a bucket of water on an unsuspecting victim. He doesn't seem that different from my dad, who tells nonsensical wordplay jokes and who was overjoyed that my brother was willing to be a part of the family copier sales business.

I will spend six hours inside the Idea House—alone for at least half that time—before I leave for the day. Every surface of the museum is covered with exhibits in the primary colors of LEGO and back-lit panels that explain the company's past, present, and future. At any given moment, I'm filming, snapping photos, or just standing in a slack-jawed way that suggests I'm not all there. LEGO is like no other company I've ever approached to interview. I've never been allowed on my own inside a corporate building, and I've rarely been left to draw my own conclusions without a public relations representative by my side to supply the company's point of view. At LEGO, my public relations representative, Jan, brings a laptop to do work during interviews, never interjects an answer when I'm questioning an employee, and makes it a point to take me to lunch every day. The only thing I can figure is that it's fundamentally a nice company.

I've been alone inside the Idea House for close to three hours when I hear footsteps softly approaching on the wooden floors.

"I didn't know if you were still here," says Jette.

"I'm thinking about sleeping over." She laughs and motions for me to follow her.

Jette pushes on one of the brightly colored wall panels in the middle of the exhibit, and a narrow staircase is revealed. Heading down the stairs, I notice that the white ceiling tiles are the same as in any finished basement in the suburbs. There's nothing to suggest we're walking toward a priceless collection of LEGO bricks.

Below the Idea House is the temperature-controlled, sparkling white room known as the vault, or archives. Inside an unmarked door, a series of rolling white metal bookcases lie on a track, the sets spanning from left to right ascending by decade. This is a near complete collection of all of the sets ever released—even LEGO has yet to determine exactly what sets still need to be found.

"We just need to keep these for legal purposes, maintaining the sets on file in case we have to refer to them," says Jette.

LEGO sees this room as patent or copyright protection; I see it as a path back to my childhood. She winds a black handle, and the entire row of white bookcases slides easily to the right. We walk down the narrow opening to the early sets. Each step literally takes us back in time. Jette holds up some of the early bricks, sold by the piece in barbershops. The earlier sets have a slightly rounder logo, and give off the earthy smell of my grandparents' house in Connecticut.

I ask how the sets have been accumulated over time. "It's not like we go out on eBay and bid on these things." Jette says. "We find sets in Denmark sometimes, and some have even been returned over the years."

I keep reminding myself that LEGO isn't a collector. There isn't an emotional attachment to the product; the amassing of sets has been closer to completing an administrative checklist than following an obsessive quest. While the Idea House chronicles the history of the company, it does so in the context of the Kristiansen family. The bricks are the result of a set of values; they are not necessarily valued sets.

"That was a train that started and stopped via a whistle," says Jette, pointing to a 1968 set. It's two simple railcars, a 4.5-volt electronic train that responds to sound, and box art that portrays a cartoon conductor with a musical note emanating from a black whistle. Jette doesn't have time to be nostalgic; she continues to pull boxes and sets, giving me a running commentary on the vault. Before I realize what's happening, she is lifting the cover of Set 375, showing me the pieces of the Yellow Castle inside the original blister packaging. I hold the box gingerly because I know what it means to collectors like Dan Brown.

"Could we see the sets from the early 1980s?" I ask, my voice cracking slightly.

"Sure," says Jette, twisting the handle. I walk halfway down the aisle and see a familiar box. I grab it without asking for permission. Set 1082, a jumbled collection of red and blue roof tiles that came out in 1982, is the first set I can remember getting as a child. The pieces were mostly slopes and inverted slopes. I think that's why it stuck out—there's not a single rectangle in the box.

"Do you want a picture?" asks Jette. I don't want a picture; I want to tear open the plastic shrink-wrapping. Whether it is an endorphin rush or just the power of a happy memory, I'm elated at finding this set haphazardly stacked among puzzles and DUPLO boxes. This is my LEGO. This is what I wanted when I started building again—the chance to think that I could build anything and the need to use my imagination to turn a bunch of random bricks into something recognizable and complete.

"It's always surprising to me to see how people will react, because they feel so strongly attached to the sets. I never know if someone is going to cry or laugh," says Jette. I smile in response, because I kind of feel like doing both.

The past few days in Denmark have been marked by several moments like this one, when I found myself getting lost in what I was experiencing. And most of them have been unexpected. When Kate and I entered the Mindstorms Discovery Center at LEGOLAND two days before, I didn't think we would end up staying for the better part of two hours. I've been intimidated by Mindstorms since I attended Brickworld, considering that my only computer skill is the ability to type seventy-plus words a minute.

But in a strange way, it is as if we have practiced on the couch in Kansas City in order to get ready to build in public. We now build together seamlessly, with me pulling the pieces according to the instructions and Kate snapping them together. When a motorized car finally runs after we switch outlets, we laugh like we did when we first started dating.

In connecting with each other over Mindstorms, I saw what it would be like to play with LEGO with my children, and I want that badly. I want Kate and me to be sitting at a table, helping our kid to work through his frustrations and feel the joy of making a tiny carousel spin. I get it now. We are missing something from our life without a baby.

I'm not the first adult to be profoundly transformed by messing around with Mindstorms. In fact, the robotic line has changed LEGO's relationship with adult fans more than any single product in the company's history. The typical product cycle for a LEGO line is two years. The first iteration of Mindstorms, the Robotics Invention System kit, launched in 1998 and is still selling strongly today. It wasn't until 2004 that LEGO began to seriously develop the second version of the robotics kit.

"We found after a couple of years that 50 percent of our users were adults. We had dubbed this group the shadow market," says

Steven Canvin, the marketing manager who oversees Mindstorms. Steven has the hair and posture of Chuck Woolery from the *Love Connection* game show, but Steven's glasses and deliberate manner of speech show that he has a lot more depth.

"If we ask children what they want, they would be very pleased to say whatever you want, or they might not have the expression level to give us new input. But instead we have an active recognized target group in adults. They have so much passion that we can ask users to get more involved because they're also pushing for it," says Steven.

LEGO initially identified four adult fans to work with Mindstorms: electronics engineer John Barnes from New York, software engineer Steve Hassenplug from Indiana, engineer Ralph Hempel from Ontario, Canada, and homeschool teacher David Schiling from Washington. They were brought together *Oceans 11*–style, with the company relying on their expertise in construction, hardware, software, and firmware (the operating system for Mindstorms suppliers). The four men were invited to participate in a closed Web forum if they were willing to sign a nondisclosure agreement. Less than an hour later, all four were on board.

"The LEGO Group is known to be a close-knit company that holds its secrets close to its chest. To be trusted with this much product knowledge for as long as we have makes us feel good," wrote Hempel in a testimonial on LEGO's Web site.

This was the Mindstorms User Panel (MUP)—four AFOLs who were invited into the research and development department, agreeing to pay their own airfare to Billund so they would have the chance to influence the second generation of Mindstorms products. It was in those discussions that the Hassenpin was introduced, after Steve Hassenplug talked about the need for a Technic pin that could connect two Technic beams at a right angle. The guy whom I met at Brickworld as he worked a pneumatic centipede has a LEGO piece unofficially named after him.

In November 2005, the MUP was expanded to fourteen people. The following January, a test group of one hundred people received prototypes of Mindstorms NXT as part of the Mindstorms Developer Program. Those one hundred were selected from among ten thousand who applied. The new sets were met with a bit of criticism early, having moved completely to studless building. But the Hassenpin enabled people to build lighter, stronger connections and mimic many of the angles afforded by studded bricks. And LEGO suddenly had an active group of program testers, finding and in some cases even solving bugs with the software.

Mindstorms NXT was released in July 2006, but the original MUP group is still involved.

"They are part-time vigilantes and part-time contributors to innovation cycles," says Steven Canvin. "They find things online that we would never see and point us in the right direction."

But as Jette mentioned in the Idea House, the relationship between AFOLs and LEGO is not usually based on a contract. And in that flexibility lies a gray area, which means that LEGO can benefit from the passion of LEGO fans, but has to trust them to act in a continually altruistic manner.

"I imagine that fans are constantly pushing or pulling, trying to get you to stretch," I say, fishing to see if there is any tension underlying that relationship.

"That challenge is to make sure we are both aligned in terms of our expectations. In some cases, confidentiality gets blurred because they're seeing our product development a year out, and that means the whole system is based on a lot of trust," replies Steven.

We're talking in the all-white conference room attached to the Idea House.

"It's better to have them on your side than against you. Because their knowledge turned to the Dark Side could be quite devastating," I suggest. I don't know if it's nerves, but I suddenly can't stop using Star Wars references. *Maybe I am a huge Star Wars nerd.* I jot down in my notebook to lay off the metaphors from the pantheon of George Lucas.

"I trust them because this is their passion," says Steven. But he's also careful. The initial group working with Mindstorms was handpicked and limited to four people. By the time the MUP was in place with one hundred beta testers, the NXT sets were scheduled for release in six months—not really enough time for a competitor to rip off LEGO if there was a leak.

The slight risk is ultimately worth the reward. The adult fans who have expertise in Mindstorms are like FBI agents who speak Arabic: they're a rare commodity. Mindstorms is a departure from the low-tech plastic bricks that LEGO has been known for over the first forty years of its existence. Even inside the company, the people assigned to market or sell Mindstorms might not have as much understanding as AFOLs of the robotic kits with a $249.99 price tag.

Steven breaks it down simply by saying, "Our products were there; we weren't there yet." Adult fans can serve as that bridge—helping to give product demonstrations at toy fairs and stores, acting as de facto salesmen for the company.

"If we gave them money for their services, it would be like an employer/employee relationship and we would lose their passion. We try to compensate these guys with the best commodity we have, which is LEGO," says Steven.

LEGO had discovered how to turn the passion of adult fans into a tangible benefit for their company. And suddenly executives at LEGO were wondering just what else adult fans could do.

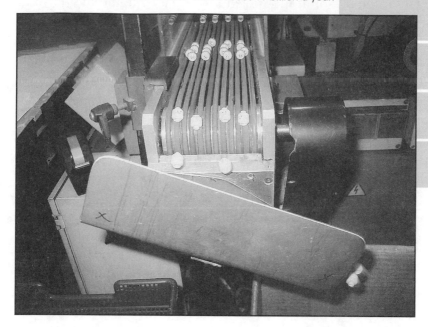

Minifig heads roll off the assembly line at the factory in Billund—just some of the approximately 36,000 LEGO elements made each minute. That's about 19 billion a year.

17

Protectors of the Brand

M y late grandfather was convinced that he could solve the energy crisis. He theorized that if we installed a pinwheel-type device on top of every car, we could harness the power of wind energy while driving. He submitted his idea to every major automaker, and every single one responded with a polite letter explaining that they could not even acknowledge receipt of his idea.

My grandfather just needed someone like Helle Friberg to believe in his ideas. The director of the New Business Group at

177

LEGO is the person responsible for translating adult fans' passion into a viable business model for the company. From Darth Vader cuff links to LEGO block–based Transformers—there's a never-ending list of ideas submitted by people who are certain about what is the next big thing for LEGO. Helle gets to hear them all, because the LEGO Group thinks the future of its business could be in that slush pile. Somehow she is still smiling when we sit down with Tormod Askildsen around a white conference table in the back of the Havremarken building on my third and final day of meetings.

"Everything big turns small, so rather than try to single out a single business opportunity that will give us a billion dollars, we preferred to start up a lot of small initiatives, see them grow, and learn and experiment," says Helle.

She runs a division where AFOLs are central to the business model envisioned by LEGO. The New Business Group has become a de facto venture capital arm for adult fans, acting as a business incubator designed to let LEGO and its partners experiment with micro businesses. The LEGO Group is trying to capitalize on the implicit trust among its existing brand ambassadors—the AFOL community.

"LEGO has one dominating business model. It's the way we invent and bring new things to the market. It's what LEGO has become after fifty years of business. So the idea is now to let people develop their own business on our LEGO platform. As a result, the person might just be more important than the idea," says Helle.

In 2006, LEGO launched a pilot program under the New Business Group that tapped adult fans to design commercially available sets. It was an extension of LEGO Factory, which allowed users to virtually create and order a custom set using 3-D software on LEGO's Web site.

"The idea was, wouldn't it be neat if you could make your own LEGO set? So, we brought in some of the most talented fans to develop their own sets. They develop it and we publish it," says Helle.

The New Business Group creative director Paal Smith-Meyer approached adult fans Chris Giddens and Mark Sandlin about designing two space sets. Star Justice and Space Skulls were released in April 2008.

The same year that LEGO began pursuing fan sets, the first third-party licensing agreement was signed. HiTechnic is a company that produces aftermarket sensors that are compatible with Mindstorms NXT. Then, in August 2007, LEGO agreed to provide a year's worth of funding to *BrickJournal*. The adult fan magazine was able to transition from digital to print issues with the influx of capital.

"*BrickJournal* makes a lot of things happen, but it's like any entrepreneur building a business. We want to get to the point that Joe [Meno] can develop *BrickJournal* as a medium to support himself," says Tormod.

The goal was to limit the financial risk for Joe, letting him focus on community outreach and regularly travel to fan events. *BrickJournal* features information on new product lines, interviews set designers, and profiles prolific adult fans.

"It was cool when they were interested. It was cooler when they said, 'It's your magazine,'" Joe tells me when I ask him about the contract.

The latest business to launch with the aid of the New Business Group is Brickstructures, which produces to-scale architectural models of famous landmarks. The principal is architect Adam Reed Tucker, the co-organizer of Brickworld.

"It's a project that isn't necessarily generating a huge amount of income for us, but it is an experiment in how to work with external partners," says Helle.

LEGO leveraged the custom supply chain established through LEGO Factory to set up the back end of Brickstructures. With the limited release of the Sears Tower and the Empire State Building, LEGO can discover if batch production is efficient while establishing new distribution channels—Brickstructures will be sold in museum gift shops and at the landmarks as well.

Despite early partnerships for the New Business Group that focus on sets, Helle makes it clear that LEGO doesn't see the entrepreneurship arm as a designer incubator. "It's not our end goal to develop LEGO set builders out of great community builders," says Helle.

That might not be the goal of the New Business Group, but the talent of some builders compels them to be noticed by LEGO. And some of those AFOLs end up working for LEGO, like Jamie Berard, thirty-three, an adult fan currently working in Billund as a set designer.

I almost get caught walking a minifigure across the white desk of a meeting room adjacent to the Idea House when Jamie walks in and shakes my hand, a smile on his face. It's strange to see his hands punctuate his points in person; I'm used to watching them from LEGO's Web site, where Jamie narrates a series of instructional videos on how to build simple shapes like columns. He has close-cropped black hair and the skinny build of somebody who seems to be constantly in motion.

Jamie was an avid LEGO fan growing up, spending hours building in the basement of his childhood home in Methuen, Massachusetts.

"Quite often, it would be three or four in the morning and then I would realize, oh, I'm supposed to be sleeping. I think it is part of the reason I don't see myself getting bored or tired, because it's not different from what I was doing," says Jamie.

He always thought he would design amusement park rides, because as a child he didn't know that LEGO hired designers. In 1985, LEGO released the Yellow Airport, and Jamie, at the age of ten, was already building like an adult fan. Despite receiving the airport set the previous Christmas, Jamie asked for it again the following year.

"I started asking for duplicates, because I saw there were some models that I never wanted to take apart because I loved playing with them and loved the themes," says Jamie.

As his friends outgrew their LEGO sets, Jamie inherited their collections and before long had five Yellow Airports. Since LEGO was never a childish hobby for Jamie, he never went through the Dark Ages that stops the progress of a lot of adult builders. In 2000, a year after graduating from Merrimack University, Jamie began to chart the sales cycles in order to figure out when LEGO sets would be cheaper.

"I heard two adults talking in the toy store about buying sets for themselves and what they were building, which was definitely unusual. I was interested, so I asked the guy at the register if that was normal," says Jamie.

He had just seen some of the members of the New England LEGO Users Group (NELUG). Jamie went to a meeting the next month and realized that he wasn't the only adult building with bricks. Jamie had never given up on LEGO, but he also never stopped thinking about theme parks. He tinkered with motors to create LEGO amusement rides and got a job at Disney World as a monorail driver. There he discovered that adults will act like kids if you just take them out of their everyday routine.

"People expect that everything at Walt Disney World is going to be magical. That lets you tap into the idea that anything is possible, and suddenly you've convinced a whole train full of people that they have to lean around the curves in order for you to steer the monorail," says Jamie.

But it's difficult to earn a living at Disney, and Jamie returned to the Northeast, finding work as a carpenter. A new dream job opened up in 2003 when LEGO announced a nationwide Master Model Builder Search for candidates to join the six master model builders at LEGOLAND California.

Jamie made the finals, flying out to California to build at LEGOLAND. He constructed an airplane amusement ride where the planes rotated up, down, and around with the help of the wind. But after a day of building, Jamie's was not one of the three names called. He would not be a master model builder. The loss crushed him.

But it didn't stop his determination to work for LEGO. Jamie drove down to Enfield, Connecticut, to ask if there were any openings in the warehouse department—anything to get his foot in the door. In October 2004, he got his first opportunity, working as a volunteer on the LEGO Millyard Project, the largest permanent minifigure exhibit outside LEGOLAND. LEGO master model designers Steve Gerling and Erik Varszegi led the design and build team of volunteers like Jamie in six phases over two years.

"LEGO has a policy of not paying fans to help, but instead giving them free product, and that to me was sustenance. I would have worked day and night for the company, only expecting LEGO in payment," says Jamie.

The three-million-brick exhibit, located at the SEE Science Center, is a historical imagining of the Amoskeag Manufacturing Company, a former textile manufacturer, in Manchester, New Hampshire. Over eight thousand minifigures were used in staging the downtown Manchester scene as it might have appeared in 1900.

"I think most fans see building as their alone time, and bricks are so valuable to them, either on a sentimental or monetary level. To build in a group setting is a very different dynamic. For the first time I was being asked to build something—it wasn't just what I wanted to build," says Jamie.

He was one of a half-dozen foreman from NELUG who worked with fellow LUG members, but also with volunteers who weren't necessarily adult fans. Steve and Erik would walk around, blueprints in hand, building a level of gray plates one stud high to lay the foundation for the project. That's when Jamie had to help teach people to build, or at least to understand the blueprints.

"You have to translate it to somebody in a language they understand through bricks. And they have to have a good time contributing, but not be doing something we would just have to take down later," says Jamie.

Although he was working alongside LEGO employees, he had no idea he was about to become one. In August 2005, Jamie attended BrickFest, an AFOL convention in Washington, D.C., to sit on a discussion panel with two master model builders and talk about the Millyard Project. He made the fortuitous decision to bring his LEGO Ferris Wheel. His skill as a builder, plus the work he had done on the Millyard Project, convinced LEGO executives that he had the ability to be a set designer. As part of the fan outreach program, they were looking to bring somebody into the company who understood the world of adult fans but also could learn to build sets for an audience of children. To put it in perspective, it's like a movie executive showing up at Comic-Con, viewing a film made by one of the convention attendees, and offering him a development deal on the spot.

By 2006, Jamie was a production designer in Denmark designing new LEGO sets. He remembers packing a cargo container in preparation for moving to a one-bedroom apartment in Billund. When he looked at his lack of furniture and the fact that his clothes were five to ten years old, Jamie saw what LEGO had come to mean to him.

"I was packing up my life and taking stock of just how much LEGO I had. It made me realize my priorities and that the hobby was that important to me. There's something about this medium that lets you get to know yourself better. The LEGO you have is really a reflection on you, and that's pretty powerful," says Jamie.

Set designers must continually work creatively around a series of constraints. New sets have to be built on time, under budget, and even in the right color. It might be time for a blue product, because the town line already has a yellow, red, and green set. When I learn this, I realize that not all fans would want Jamie's job.

"I'm often building something that someone else wants. In fact, most of the time building things that a six-year-old wants. I haven't been six for at least ten years," jokes Jamie.

He works primarily on the Creator line, which tries to teach kids how to build cars, buildings, and sculptures. The first set he designed came out in 2007, a Fast Flyers kit that looked like a red-and-white F-14 jet. As part of the creation process, Jamie also had to adjust to model reviews—the last step before a product is considered ready for building instructions. Here, a set designer has to sit down with more experienced designers, who build his set to see if it needs any changes based on the building experience.

"Building for many fans is a very personal thing or it's tied into experiences with their family. If you are a true fan, you really have to sacrifice a bit of what you are comfortable with in order to explore a whole new side of the hobby," says Jamie.

It's not easy to learn how to build collaboratively. I have a hard time just working on sets with Kate; I can't imagine how it would be if we were trying to free build together.

"My wife makes fun of me because I tell her when I see something that I can build it out of LEGO," I say to Jamie.

I tell him about building my micro-monorails and the decision to use my favorite part, a 1 × 2 element that I have nicknamed the "lunch box." Not surprisingly, he's never heard the name, but he does think the part fits what I'm trying to do.

"People don't need a lot of bricks to build something amazing. They just need to capture the essence of things—which it sounds like you did," says Jamie.

It's the first time I've talked about my part choices, and a set designer has just given me approval on the piece I picked. The near compliment leaves me feeling content with my progress as a builder.

Jamie is content as well, finally getting the access he's wanted since running his fingers through three million bricks on the Millyard Project. He's usually working on sets that use prototype elements at least two years in the future, with some platform projects that are at least five years out.

When Jamie was designing the Café Corner set, a modular building designed for advanced builders, he realized that LEGO didn't make windows that would work for a modular building. The windows for the city theme were larger and boxy.

"Let's make a system again and recapture what made LEGO special for so many fans. I was able to talk to the design lab about the value of having small windows that could be used over and over," says Jamie.

AFOLs have raved about the Café Corner, Green Grocer, and Market Street sets. Despite the high price point, over $100 each, the sets have been well received because of their specialty elements. The recommended building age is sixteen-plus, and the detail on the modular buildings has inspired a new theme and standard for group displays.

"There is always tension because the desires and wishes of the fan community are often quite at odds with what the kids want. But I just try to get them to understand the company's priorities and try to get them little gems once in a while," says Jamie.

Those gems include the choice to build the Green Grocer in sand green, a prized rare color because it more closely mirrors actual building colors. But Jamie couldn't include the LEGO equivalent of Easter Eggs found in DVDs—little surprises in the form of rare pieces or colors—if his coworkers didn't understand the passion of adult fans. It's not uncommon to see employees on a carpet, testing the durability of a car by pushing it around while making engine-revving noises.

"The fans are very protective of the brand, and it's not just a company for them," says Jamie. "But I genuinely feel that this is the one company where I've worked that has the consumer at heart."

Other LEGO employees often approach Jamie to ask his opinion of how a set or product decision might be received.

"I've become kind of the in-house expert on adult fans. I'm not an expert, but at least I've got roots in the community, and if there's a particular theme, I know who they should talk to," says Jamie.

Besides Jamie, designers and the marketing department often turn to the Community Development team at LEGO—the group responsible for managing the company's interaction with adult fans. Tormod Askildsen sits at the head of the group, and under him is Steve Witt in Enfield, Connecticut, and Jan Beyer, also based out of Billund. Jan (pronounced "yan") is a Brooklyn hipster who just happened to be born in Germany. He is the main liaison for AFOLs in Europe and Asia, while Steve covers North America, Australia, and New Zealand.

"We've seen a real change over the past six or seven years. In the beginning there was just LUGNET, but now the whole landscape is filled with user groups online and has totally changed," says Jan, his fingers adjusting his glasses.

I'm sitting across from Jan and Tormod back in the conference room by the offices of the New Business Group. They've been working to piece the adult community together the past five years, with Tormod being promoted to head the team in early 2008. They've managed to work adult fans into nearly every aspect of the sales process from production to presenting the final product.

"Designers find it inspirational to talk to fans, it's like having a sparring partner," says Jan.

The success of Mindstorms has provided a blueprint for how AFOLs can help launch and support products. Adult fans have also presented at trade shows and given holiday demonstrations in toy stores. Their knowledge and enthusiasm are effective marketing tools. It's often Tormod or Jan who will introduce adult fans in an area to the local sales office, to establish a working relationship between the two groups.

"It can be frightening for LEGO employees because [adult fans] sometimes know more—both sides can be wary about the other," says Jan.

I confess to Jan and Tormod that I don't know very much about the adult community in Europe. I've taken a U.S.-centric look at the international toy, focusing on the world of the American AFOL based on my experiences growing up.

"European fans would say people in the United States build big, while American fans tell us that Europeans build small," jokes Jan.

The Community Development group estimates there are approximately twenty thousand adult fans who belong to a hundred user groups, people they think of as "one e-mail away." The LEGO Ambassador Program helps LEGO stay in front of those groups, with forty ambassadors representing hundreds of LUGs.

Many of the differences in how adult fans interact are, ironically, dictated by one of the defining aspects of LEGO's instructions: groups in Europe and Asia aren't as collaborative simply because of language barriers.

"They're both building, but there's a different style to events. The convention style is the dominant style in the United States, while in Europe, it's more about exhibitions," says Tormod.

At the close of the day, Jan Christiansen, my media representative, drives me back to LEGO headquarters on Systemvej, where I'm meeting Kate to begin the sightseeing portion of our trip to Denmark.

"One more thing," says Jan when we arrive, pulling the Dwarves' Mine set from his trunk. It's a $100 set, as big as a briefcase. He moves to hand me the box.

"I can't," I tell him, putting my hands behind my back like a waiter asking if he can take your plate.

"C'mon. Nobody comes to LEGO and leaves without some LEGO," says Jan.

"I don't mean to be disrespectful, but I can't accept the gift, because I'm a journalist," I tell Jan.

"But you're not a journalist; you're a writer," says Jan. I can't argue with his logic.

"That's true," I reply, finally reaching out to take the box. We shake hands, and Jan heads home for the day. I take a seat on a concrete ledge somewhere near the buried molds and contemplate the first gift I've accepted as a journalist. I feel torn because of how badly I wanted to accept the set. Kate pulls up in our rental car.

She respects my ethics, but Kate always gets the wounded look of a child denied a promised trip when I tell her I refused an offer from an interviewee. She has chided me for turning down free beer, sports tickets, and vacations over the years.

"I took a gift," I say, telling her the story.

"It's so cool," she says, turning the set over to look at the pieces, "Besides, Jan is right, you're not a journalist, you're an adult fan."

On the car ride to Copenhagen, I'm glad that she knows what I am.

My LEGO bus sits smack in the middle of the Zombie Apocafest group display at BrickCon 2008 in Seattle, Washington.

18

Good Luck, Boys, That Thing Is Heavy

The need to build grows like an itch. I'm starting to think that somebody with no impulse control couldn't be an adult fan. I have a bucket of yellow and black bricks, the detritus that once was the Beach House set, in front of me. I told myself I wouldn't take it apart; but when I needed a piece to complete the yellow whale, I didn't hesitate to grab it off the house. Then, I said it would just be one piece. I could stop anytime I wanted. In two days, nearly the entire Beach House had been picked cleaner than a car left in Hollywood's version of the bad part of town. I'm a parts junkie.

The Beach House is set to become a zombie defense vehicle, a rolling school bus that either runs over the undead or takes them prisoner. I've had zombies on the brain ever since Andrew Becraft announced on his Web site, the Brothers Brick, a collaborative display—the LEGO Zombie Apocafest—to be held at BrickCon 2008 in Seattle. Think *Shaun of the Dead* meets *Pleasantville.* I already told Andrew I'm bringing something. The only problem is that I haven't built it yet, and the convention weekend is two days away—and we've just gotten back from Denmark.

I take building inspiration from my conversation with Jamie Berard in Billund and am determined to be a participant in this adult fan convention.

"It's a very nurturing culture, the community is good at encouraging your ideas especially when you are a fellow fan. So even if you didn't have that as a kid, the community almost becomes like a surrogate parent cheering you on and patting you on the back," said Jamie.

It's like Little League: everybody plays, and some players are exceptional. Only, I didn't play Little League. And I'm starting to doubt that I'll ever be exceptional. But if Jamie's right, that won't matter, because ultimately it will be about participating.

I find a set of old oversize tires with white rims that dictate the size of the bus I'll build. It's going to be six studs wide. The largest vehicles I've built so far—the micro-scale trucks—are just two studs wide. A six-stud vehicle is minifig size and will need a minifig driver.

I had asked Jamie where he starts when he has to build a car for a set. "Start with something recognizable," he told me. "Think of the front of the car as a face."

I think of the windshield of the bus as eyes, and the grille as a mouth. I create the familiar arch of the front using sloped bricks, which resemble eyebrows, over the square translucent window elements. The hood is just a flat yellow plate, supported by a Technic brick. I draw out the sides, laying out alternating black and yellow plates to create the familiar striped pattern. Once I've got the basic shape of the bus, I begin to transform it into a zombie defense vehicle.

The details are what will make people stop and look at my MOC. It's easy to attach a LEGO skeleton with a troll head to the Technic brick to create the illusion of a zombie speared by the grille. I also use several 1 × 1 plates with clips so that I can attach weapons to the side of the bus. I find a chainsaw and an oversize wrench that I clip along the side. An inverted 2 × 2 red plate gives the idea of a stop sign by the driver's window. I steal chains from a medieval LEGO coinbank that Kate bought me to crisscross around the open roof. At this rate, my office is beginning to have sets that look like they came from the Island of Misfit Toys.

The banisters from the Beach House make the perfect bars of a zombie prison. To finish the bus, I add touches that make me laugh. A street sweeper minifig sits inside a trash can on the roof of the bus, guns at the ready. The final piece I build is a small shelf on the undercarriage, just big enough to hold a LEGO alligator.

This MOC means something more to me because it consists of bricks from my entire collection. There are tires from my brother-in-law Ben's bricks, yellow pieces from sets I've bought, wind-shields from a Pick A Brick cup, and skeletons from Brickworld. The zombies are troll heads repurposed from the Castle set I picked up in Denmark. It is a physical representation of how much my part knowledge has increased.

When I'm finished, I roll the bus along my desk and find myself inventing a back story for the minifigs. It's an unlikely friendship struck up by two city employees, the last vestiges of a government literally torn apart by zombies. But if Frank the street sweeper and Tomas the airport manager (which Kate thinks is the job for every LEGO city minifig) have anything to say about it, the city will survive the Apocafest.

"A lot of adults might say they don't play," said Jamie during our conversation, "but perhaps they do play. It's a little bit of a dirty secret, that almost all adults like the idea of being able to play even if they don't have the time or don't actually play with what they've built."

Kate walks into my office and finds me playing.

"I'm just making sure it rolls right," I tell her, instead of admitting that I was envisioning Frank and Tomas battling hordes of zombies.

"Whoa, cool bus," says Kate. It's the first time she has recognized what I've built immediately. It is awesome. She picks it up, and her fingers brush against the alligator.

"What is this? A crocodile?" She laughs.

"Man's last line of defense," I say solemnly before I start laughing.

I'm not laughing thirty-six hours later when I open my suitcase at a friend's house in Seattle. If I thought the TSA tore apart Joe Meno's ray gun at Brick Bash, it's nothing compared to the carnage that's inside my luggage. Despite wrapping the bus in bubble tape and a few T-shirts, it's been broken into three large parts, and one of the tires appears to be gone entirely. I freak out in silence, not wanting Sean to hear me get upset that my LEGO creation is ruined. That turns out to be a good decision. The bus is back together inside of fifteen minutes.

"This is sweet. We didn't have parts like this when I was a kid. Is this a set?" asks Sean.

"No, I built it from scratch."

Sean hasn't seen a set in twenty years, but it feels good that he might think something I built came out of an official LEGO box. It makes me feel a lot less awkward when I'm standing in line to register for the seventh annual BrickCon. I still clutch the bus with an iron grip, accidentally snapping off a window because I'm certain I will drop it. I anonymously place it on the torn-up streets of the Zombie Apocafest display, next to a jeep filled with two murderous minifigs and a LEGO gun shop.

I notice a teenager in a black LEGO Universe jacket across the aisle. He's fiddling with a NXT motor inside a LEGO baseball stadium, trying to sync the actions of a swinging batter, the crack of a bat, and then a crowd rising and falling to simulate cheering. The motor is buried under the pitcher's mound, and John Langrish is getting frustrated that he can't get the scoreboard to light up. I'm amazed that he's built a scoreboard, let alone one that lights up.

I recognize the youngest of the forty LEGO ambassadors from pictures. John is very much the next generation of adult fans. He's got a patchy black beard to match messy hair above glasses. I see a few interesting pieces that I know are in the LEGO Mars Mission box I found at a garage sale. I tell John about unearthing the box in the attic at an estate sale. I've discovered that every AFOL has a story of a big find. For John it was a standing rack of five drawers for $50, the top filled with rare elements including a whole turkey. The earth-orange turkey alone, which resembles a traditional Thanksgiving bird, goes for as much as $30 on BrickLink. It's been out of production for close to a decade.

"I feel bad sometimes. I ask, 'Are you sure your kids don't want this?' And they say, 'Yeah, my kids are eighteen now.'" John pauses, beginning to laugh. "Well, I'm eighteen now, and I want it."

"Is it ever hard to be the youngest in the room?" I ask him.

"These are people you meet once and you feel like you already know each other. There are forty-year-olds that I would otherwise never come into contact with, but we know each other because of LEGO," says John.

Age is just a number when it comes to spring-autumn romances and playing with LEGO bricks. John gets the scoreboard to light up and tells me to lean in a little closer. Before he replaces the mound, I put my ear by the NXT brick. I hear the faint crack of a bat and the roar of a crowd, meant to accompany the base-ball scene.

"We need to get a speaker," says Aaron Dayman, a fellow member of the Victoria LEGO Users Group.

VICLUG has brought a bunch of Canadian builders to Seattle, the ease of a three-hour ferry ride lending the convention an international flair. Aaron has a baseball hat cocked slightly to the side and the raw enthusiasm of somebody new to the hobby.

"What do you like to build?" I ask Aaron, lobbing up the equivalent of an AFOL softball question, knowing how hesitant I was when attending my first convention.

"I build six-wide vehicles. Is that what you like to build?" says Aaron.

"I built a bus, but I didn't think about it—this one just built itself," I reply.

"So did I. Let's go see them," says Aaron.

He leans over the display, and I point him to the yellow bus.

"Can I?" he asks before picking it up. "The alligator is awesome—it scoops up the zombies, that's the best."

Aaron has built a sleek black bus filled with the kind of special operatives called in to deal with zombies in horror movies. Whereas my bus has exaggerated features and is built for comic effect, Aaron's is streamlined to mimic a government vehicle. We built in the same category but with fantastically different results.

"Nice use of cheese wedges," I tell him.

"I love those. I use as many as I can," says Aaron.

This is what I envisioned when I sat building the school bus at my desk. It's fun to chat with another adult fan about how they figured out an angle or why they chose a particular piece. We're two guys talking shop.

I've been inside the Seattle Center Exhibition Hall for less than an hour when Tom Erickson waves in greeting.

"Hey, Jon the journalist. Want to come move a fourteen-foot LEGO boat?" asks Tom.

"Yes, I do."

There is only one answer to a question like that. Tom walks me out to a red pickup truck. Dan Brown is driving, and my Yellow Castle wall building partner Thomas Mueller is in the backseat. Brett, a friend of Tom's, rides shotgun. On the short drive to Sundance Yacht Sales, Dan tells me about the LEGO boat he has agreed to purchase for $5,500.

"I had to have this boat. You have to get anything made by Nathan," says Dan. It's as if Dan sniffs out models wherever he goes.

"Nathan" is Nathan Sawaya, one of only six LEGO certified professionals in the world. The certified professionals program basically allows talented builders to get access to discounts on bulk brick in exchange for agreeing to build within a set of standards established by LEGO.

Nathan was also one of the winners of the 2004 Master Model Builder Search at LEGOLAND. He became an instant media sensation; nobody leaves his job as a corporate lawyer to get paid $13 an hour to build with LEGO bricks. He left LEGOLAND less than a year later to explore a career as a LEGO artist, and the ten-foot boat we're about to move is one of the models he built on commission in 2005. (Tom was off by four feet when he asked me to help, but it's no less impressive.)

We pull up at Sundance Yacht Sales, where the blue-and-white LEGO boat sits on a blue table in the lobby of the office, which is down a narrow flight of stairs. It's a LEGO-ized model of a nineteen-foot Chris-Craft Speedster. The boat has a propeller, rotating tan seats, and a steering wheel that turns. But the beauty of the boat is in the curved hull created from approximately 250,000 rectangular LEGO bricks. Nathan built it over the course of fourteen-hour days at the ten-day Seattle Boat Show; that's how it ended up at Sundance.

"Good luck, boys, that thing is heavy," says the owner. Nathan estimated it weighed close to a thousand pounds when he was finished.

Brett and Tom begin to unscrew a pair of sliding glass doors. The boat is too wide to carry up the narrow stairs, so that means we'll be taking it out on this floor and wheeling it across the rickety wooden dock. The Sundance Yacht Sales office is, naturally, on the water.

Dan lays out a series of tools and asks me to grab an industrial roll of plastic wrap. He pries off pieces of the sculpture that he thinks could break off in transit. He slides out two windshield panes made from translucent bricks, the front seats of the speedboat, and a LEGO flag attached only by 1×1 cylinders.

After the boat is wrapped in plastic, the five of us together gently lift it and rest it on a four-wheel wooden dolly. I'm glad we're only holding it for a few seconds. Not only is a ten-foot LEGO boat heavy, the bricks dig painfully into my fingers.

"Slow, slow," says Dan as we wheel the dolly over the dock. The sides of the boat hang over the edges of the dock. He's leaning out over the water at the first of three ninety-degree turns. Thomas and I are in front of the boat, while Brett and Tom push from behind. Water laps against the dock, which seems to be bowing a bit with the weight. A single LEGO brick will float, but if this boat goes in the water, Dan's $5,500 investment will sink before we can go in after it.

Two concrete ramps connect the dock to the parking lot. The ramps are normally used for launching boats. The boat's weight is staggering on the incline. I've worked up a good sweat in the thirty minutes it took us to go about six hundred feet. The rudder has snapped off, but the boat is mostly intact because it's been glued. Thomas and Dan secure the boat to the truck with several layers of plastic wrap in order to keep it right side up, but a good two feet still hang out the back of the F150's truck bed.

Seattle is not a flat city, and as we make our way through the hilly streets, I keep envisioning the boat rolling out the back, smashing on the concrete.

"Boy, I wonder what the police are thinking. It would not be easy to steal a LEGO model," says Dan as we drive by two cops on traffic duty.

It's not easy to do anything with a large-scale LEGO model. It's so heavy and simultaneously fragile. And this isn't like my bus; it can't be rebuilt in just a few minutes. I have a greater appreciation for the effort it took for Dan to haul everything he has collected to Bellaire, Ohio, considering the challenges of moving a single piece just 1.6 miles.

The atmosphere is relaxed at BrickCon when we get back. LEGO community relations coordinator Steve Witt is launching Nerf gun projectiles from a raised balcony, attempting to hit LEGO skyscrapers. I see Breann Sledge, the Bionicle builder, camped out at the LEGO Group's booth, piecing together an oversize Star Wars General Grievous set.

Each convention I've attended has had a different feel. Brick Bash was all about learning and playing with LEGO. Brickworld felt more serious, a place to develop building techniques from expert demonstrations. Brick Show was really an open invitation into Dan Brown's collection. And BrickCon seems like a bunch of hobbyists who rented out a convention hall for the weekend. And for the first time, I'm one of those hobbyists. I'm not just observing, I'm one of the 235 people attending. This isn't the first day of school, it's coming back from summer vacation. It's comfortable.

"I've been a LEGO addict for thirty years. I'm here to welcome you other addicts. I'm not here to get you away from LEGO, I'm here to get you more into it," says BrickCon organizer Wayne Hussey during the opening ceremonies.

Wayne pauses when the crowd erupts in spontaneous applause. The opening speeches are interrupted as often as a State of the Union Address.

"This year we're going to do the store differently," says Wayne. "We want to make sure everyone has a chance to buy sets, and the numbered brick you have will determine when you get in the store. Also, guys, no reselling."

Everyone is always anxious to go shopping at a nearby LEGO store, which is being kept open late with discounted sets as a bonus for adult fans.

"In the early days of LEGO conventions, like at the Potomac [Mills Mall] Store near BrickFair, LEGO stores had no idea how to handle adult fans. The scratch-and-dent were still in cardboard boxes. You would stand by the item you wanted most and when they blew the whistle, you could go for it. You would just rip and throw cardboard behind you. It was like hungry bears being taunted by a piece of meat on a stick. It's hanging in front of them and then suddenly you give them a taste—it's a feeding frenzy," says Jim Foulds, the AFOL who is working on LEGO Universe.

LEGO has been working with convention organizers to figure out a method that will leave fans happy and spare the employees from having to clean up the carnage.

The speeches end soon and the convention attendees break up to figure out carpools and compare numbers. Until now, I never thought reselling was wrong. Tom Erickson has told me that the sets he sells at conventions often help him cover his travel costs.

"This is directed toward me," says Dan on the way out to his truck, "but I'll still get what I want."

I'm sure he will, but it makes me wonder if I'm getting comfortable with the bad boys of the convention. Have I inadvertently sat in the back of the AFOL bus?

This retro LEGO bowling alley built by AFOL Nathan Proudlove was named one of the best buildings at BrickCon 2008.

19

Building Blind and the Dirty Brickster

I don't feel the anxiety of the previous morning when I walk into the public display day at BrickCon on Saturday. This is where I belong. But with thirty-two hundred people waiting to see the LEGO creations inside, I start to get uneasy very quickly. *Who are you people?* This is the public, but I'm not part of them anymore. And when a man taking a picture of the thirty-foot LEGO *Titanic* elbows me out of the way, I want to get away from the crush of humanity as fast as possible. I look for the first door that says FOR CONVENTION ATTENDEES ONLY and rush inside. The door to Classroom A whisks closed, and I understand the fear of small spaces that sometimes overwhelms my mother.

"You here for the blind build?" asks a skinny guy with a pony-tail, looking up from a clipboard.

"Yes," I lie as I turn around to see a room of twenty people staring at me. I usually answer questions I'm not ready for with a positive response. It's not based on some life-affirming creed, but instead is a residual effect of a decade of improvisational comedy performances. The fundamental rule of improv is acceptance, the idea of building a scene through "yes and . . ." This is one instance where I will regret that my instincts guided me offstage. The guy glances briefly at my convention name tag before nodding to a folding table on his right.

"Well sit down, we're getting ready to start." The organizer goes on to explain the rules. Each of the fifteen competitors has been given a LEGO Racers set, number 8152. We will be making one of the three vehicles inside the set—the four-stud-wide police car. I look at the box. It's a neat little car, maybe fifty pieces, with lots of translucent red and blue. This is the last time I'll see the pieces: they'll be hidden underneath a black cloth-covered triangle during the building competition.

"On my count, you will open the box and take out the bags for the police car. You'll build the set, and the shortest time with the fewest errors wins. Each error will count ten seconds against your time," says the organizer.

I feel better going into this competition than I did with the Belville challenge, confident enough to wish my neighbor good luck. My hands are steady when I grab the box. In front of me is a wooden triangle covered with black felt. It's open in the front because "[the contest] is being filmed and will be used by LEGO," according to the organizer. This is as close as I'll ever get to *The Real World.*

We all rip cardboard on the organizer's cue. The blind build has started. I glance briefly at the three plastic bags before shoving the one containing the parts for the police car underneath the black curtain. I rip the bag open with too much force and I hear the pieces scatter, a wheel careening off my finger.

I open the first page of the instructions. Thankfully the rules don't mean that you have to invent your own steps for putting together an existing set. The front of the cruiser comes together quickly; it's a 2 × 8 plate attached to a 4 × 4 plate. I mistakenly think this is easy. I roll parts between my thumb and forefinger, feeling for the bumpiness of studs.

The true challenge is that there are a number of similar pieces—1 × 4 tiles and cheese wedges—in different colors.

"How do you know which is which?" I ask a guy sitting in a chair facing my box. He could be the twin of Notre Dame University's football coach Charlie Weis.

"The blue feels different from the red," he says, laughing. I try to decide if he's serious before laughing as well.

At this point, the first competitor, Ryan, has finished. In fifteen minutes, he's put together his police car with just thirteen errors. Ryan will win easily. I wish I were Ryan.

I'm snapping together pieces of the fender and dying a bit inside. The space inside the black triangle is only a foot wide, and yet I still can't find parts. I didn't understand how much I rely on sight when building. I may know the vernacular and can imagine uses for parts, but I have no touch memory. I'm halfway through the instructions when I notice that the police racer has a glow-in-the-dark hood. The irony is not lost on me.

"If you don't make any mistakes, you could win. You just have to get them all right," says Charlie Weis' twin when he notices I'm getting frustrated. I know he's just being nice, but the support is welcome.

After forty minutes, the blind build is called. I'm the only competitor who has failed to finish. They have to get the room ready for the build in a bag, where AFOLs will put a set together without taking it out of the plastic bag. I walk over to the table with fourteen police cars and put down my mangled creation. I place the remaining pieces next to it. The base is off line and the axles are not attached properly. In the first few steps, I attached a plate one stud further than the instructions specified, and everything

I built after that was incorrect. But the LEGO gods are not without a sense of humor; all of my colors are right.

I commiserate with Joe Meno afterward, who has just finished a creative build challenge where he's turned a blue coast guard set into a beautiful bird.

"Blind builds are tough," says Joe. "You have to stay on track or you don't have a chance."

I confess that I hadn't entered my name for the blind build, but just went into the room to escape the public.

"You needed a break, huh?" asks Joe. "These days can be stressful."

Joe would know. At conventions he is constantly in motion, taking pictures and talking to builders about what they've brought. He's also doing his best to promote *BrickJournal*, leading seminars to find out what people want him to include or what they think of the magazine.

"Tonight should be fun," says Joe, smiling.

He knows about the new set that LEGO is planning to unveil at BrickCon. He's known for months, and now he'll finally be able talk about it. Later that night, the crowd of adult fans is buzzing over the unveiling of the Medieval Market Village, which includes two female peasants, two cows, and a whole turkey among its 1,601 pieces. There are as many whistles for the rare whole turkey as for the bar wench when they are shown on a slide.

Female minifigures are always in high demand because they are a scarce resource. They have been since the hospital nurse minifig debuted in 1978. Adult fans often complain that female minifigures have been disproportionately included in big-ticket sets.

"So many of the 'cool' female figs are in rare or expensive sets. The result has been that budget-concerned buyers only end up with the male or generic figs in their collection," wrote AFOL John Henderson in July 2007 on LUGNET.

When you combine scarcity with the demands of a male-dominated secondary market, the prices for female minifigs can skyrocket after the sets have been taken out of production. The Ice Planet babe, a female minifig with a pink space helmet from a 2002 set, goes for $10 in new condition. The female islander, a tourist with a blue flowered shirt (from the ill-fated Paradisa line for girls), and Astrobot Sandy Moondust both regularly sell for over $15 apiece.

And that might explain what's happening at the front of the room. Matthew Ashton, the lead designer for LEGO Playthemes, has just finished talking about how a set moves from development into production, when he announces that LEGO has one more surprise for the adult fans at BrickCon. Matthew is British and has the habit of holding his hands together like a choir singer when he speaks at the microphone. He asks the women attending the convention to come to the front of the room.

"It's time for the first ever Little Miss LEGO Beauty Pageant 2008," says Matthew. "I know you've wanted more female minifigs, well here they are . . . the mermaid, Willie Scott, the queen . . ."

As he calls out each of the names that appear on the projector, a female convention attendee walks in front of the crowd carrying the actual minifig. The crowd hoots and hollers, not for the women, but for the minifigs. The troll hag sorceress is crowned the winner.

The contest is simultaneously sweet and slightly chauvinistic. The female minifigs are what is being objectified, but I can't stop thinking that LEGO will never really understand female builders.

The next event is gender neutral. The Dirty Brickster—the AFOL equivalent of the White Elephant, Dirty Santa, or Yankee Swap—is a game held at most fan conventions. To participate you have to contribute a wrapped present worth $10 to $20, which is placed on a table inside a circle of chairs where the players sit. If you are the first player, you pick a present from the table. There's no shaking or rattling a wrapped gift. You have to take what you pick up. The second player may then choose a new present to unwrap, or he may "steal" your gift. After a present is unwrapped, it can be stolen up to three times by any player whose turn hasn't come yet.

AFOLs root for boxes to be stolen because then they get to launch into a monotone chant of "Dir-tee Brick-stur." Some adults even take particular joy in stealing a box from a child, believing that he or she won't appreciate a rare set or a piece of LEGO ephemera. "Some people bring lame sets, others bring really cool surprises," wrote Joe Meno when I asked him in an e-mail what is a typical gift for the Dirty Brickster.

Forty-nine people have gathered for the Dirty Brickster, and Wayne divides us into two circles. I sit down on a chair in the circle next to Abner Finley, my fellow Belville competitor from Minnesota.

I'm a bit worried about what I ended up putting on the table. Before I left for Seattle, I wrapped the pair of Ewoks and the Chewbacca that I had picked up at a yard sale, certain that the minifigs would be a hit with the Star Wars crowd. But they're still on top of my bureau in Kansas City, forgotten in the packing process, when I join the game.

The first bag to be unwrapped has a collection of LEGO pens. By the appreciative murmuring of the crowd, I can tell it will be stolen. As with any white elephant, the size of the wrapped gift has nothing to do with its value. A LEGO Racers set is unveiled, and a box of classic space parts is admired.

It's quickly my turn, and I know the LEGO pens have been stolen twice. While it would be nice to have something I could use in my profession, I can tell Abner wants them, so instead I walk up to the table filled with yellow LEGO bags and gifts that clearly have been wrapped by men.

My Dirty Brickster gift turns out to be a ziplock bag filled with hundreds of fill parts from SpongeBob SquarePants and Star Wars sets. Nobody wants to steal it from me. Abner walks around the circle, scratching under his chin. "Hmmm . . . ," he says before stealing the pens. The crowd chants, "Dir-tee Brick-stur."

The unwrapping seems to drag on, and I get more anxious for my gift to be opened. I see someone finally pick up the bag and take out the two minifigures I purchased at Tom Erickson's booth for $20 right before the Dirty Brickster.

He takes out the Princess Leia and classic spaceman minifigs, turning the bag upside down to see if there is something else inside.

"That's it?" asks someone to his right.

"Yup," he replies, and a little of the enthusiasm goes out of the circle.

"See, that's too bad," says Abner, and I wince. "Probably some kid, has no idea what something is really worth, just going off the prices off BrickLink."

I don't tell him that I'm the kid who ruined it. I am really embarrassed.

Afterward a guy in a Mets cap walks up to me. It's Alan Bernstein, the guy who bought grass from the LEGO Crack House in Bellaire, Ohio.

"I just wanted to make sure you're happy with what you got," says Alan.

"It's great. What I need most right now is bricks, so a random assortment is perfect."

"Cool, I just wasn't sure. Glad you like them," says Alan.

At least you didn't just put in two minifigs, I want to tell him. I don't walk up to the guy who got my bag. I already know whether he liked what he got.

I wonder if by getting too comfortable, I'm revealing myself as some sort of poser. Just a day after feeling at home at the convention, it seems I can't really do anything right. This is the LEGO epic fail. Am I a guy who shows up to all of the events but doesn't really get what everything is about? I never want to be the fifty-year-old executive who congratulates himself for beating out a grounder off a washed-up former major leaguer at a fantasy baseball camp.

But then I see Joe across the room. He smiles and waves. Aaron Dayman offers me a beer. Dan Brown comes over and brags about the sets he ended up purchasing before the store closed. Thomas Mueller invites me to go out for a beer down the street. None of them cares about my performance in the blind build or my poor taste in gifts for the Dirty Brickster; they just don't want to stop enjoying the convention and talking about LEGO.

And the next thing I know, it's close to two in the morning and I've been sitting next to Lino Martins for the better part of two hours. He's clad in a red and black bowling shirt that says

LUGNUTS, the LEGO car club he helped launch in 2007. With a black circle beard and a pirate-skull cap, Lino should be a tough guy. But he's an artist with a sweet, self-deprecating sense of humor. Lino builds jaw-dropping Miniland-scale cars like perfect El Dorados. My favorite of his creations is a version of his brassy girlfriend, Sue, who is at the convention not out of a love for LEGO, but out of love for Lino. Her Miniland doppelgänger stands in a gothlike black outfit next to her dream car: a '57 Pontiac Safari.

"I love these things. It's all about building," says Lino when I ask him why he's at BrickCon.

I call it a night shortly thereafter and head back to my hotel room in downtown Seattle. When I get there, I lie down on my bed and the bag of bricks from the Dirty Brickster pokes into my side through my jacket pocket. When I wake up the next morning, I find a half-formed car there. It's a terrible idea, as most are after a few drinks, but it's mine. I put it in my pocket and head out for the last day of the convention.

The completed Stegosaurus set looms on our living room bookshelf, behind the finest example of a LEGO camel you'll ever see.

20

Children Not Included

I come home from Seattle with a LEGO recycling truck for Kate. I've taken to buying her sets when I'm traveling. I am as bad as any father in a cell phone commercial. Only I'm not buying things for my kid—they're for my wife. I hand her the orange-and-white LEGO recycling truck; it's roughly the size and shape of my LEGO bus.

"This is sweet," says Kate, using eighties lingo for approval.

"I thought you would like the recycling truck; this one seemed like it was for eco-conscious adults like you," I reply.

Kids are the primary audience for LEGO sets, but I wonder about the kid who really wants a LEGO recycling truck for Christmas. You feel like that kid is due for a beating at school. I guess children would like putting the 1 × 1 rounds into the included trash can or the back of the recycling truck. Kate certainly seems to be getting a kick out of it after she's finished putting together the set. The 206-piece recycling truck isn't really a challenge, though; her building skills are advancing too quickly.

"Look at the back. This is amazing," says Kate, opening and shutting the rear storage compartment of the recycling truck.

She hands me the empty cardboard box, and it joins the handful of other LEGO boxes inside the recycling bin on our side porch. Over the past few weeks, I've been filling the bin. I wonder what the men who pick up our recycling think about the contents. Do they believe we have a child celebrating a four-week-long birthday party? Or perhaps I'm an extremely specific toy reviewer who happens to live in Kansas City. In reality, I'm the guy who overstuffs his recycling bin and is learning how to share his toys with his wife.

It's a weird thing to feel proud of your spouse, but I'm glad that she can knock out sets with the same single-minded intensity of a Chinese gold farmer earning virtual tokens for somebody in the World of Warcraft. It's a good feeling to come home and find her on the couch, the dog sleeping on her blanket-covered legs, with a set of LEGO instructions and storage tubs spread around her in a fan. It makes me think she'll build LEGO creations with our kids, something that many spouses of AFOLs seem reluctant to do. I can understand if they're worried that the obsession of their husbands will be transferred to their progeny.

"I have a gift for you," says Kate. Our fourth anniversary is coming up, and I've had a feeling I was getting something LEGO-related since accidentally stumbling upon a package from their distribution facility in Tennessee.

Neither Kate nor I is very good at waiting to give gifts. I often buy her more than one thing at a time, just so I can give one gift early and hold the other back for the actual occasion. I'm not surprised that I'm getting a LEGO product; it's possible I might have received it even if I had never picked up the hobby. We have a history of giving presents that are meant primarily for children. It goes back to the first gift of our relationship a decade ago. We were apart for the first time; it was winter break from Brown University. Without knowing the other person had bought anything, we sent each other a package. Kate and I had bought each other Marvin's Magic Drawing Board, a black board that when pressure was applied revealed colors underneath. She had seen an infomercial; I had made an impulse purchase in the airport. It was the opposite of the "Gift of the Magi," and it was one of the reasons I knew I would marry her.

Kate hands me a LEGO Yoda pen. The Connect & Build pen has a Yoda minifig at the top, along with several colored beads and bricks that can be interchanged. It is not, however, part of the LEGO system—the beads and bricks aren't uniform. I'm so excited by Yoda that I don't notice this at first.

"Awesome you are," I say in the scratchy voice of the tiny green Jedi master. "This is going to be the only pen I take on interviews from now on. And as long as everybody I interview is between six and nine years old, I should have no problems."

I talk in the Yoda voice until Kate stops laughing. She probably has been humoring me for the last forty-five minutes or so. The Yoda Pen also makes us realize that we both were too attached to oversize or comic pens and pencils in our childhood. I had a large plastic yellow Crayola from the Think Big! store in New York City. Kate, a banker's daughter, treasured her pen filled with shredded money. So we would have been the kind of kids who were excited to receive a LEGO recycling truck.

As I doodle with the pen, I tell Kate I'm glad she didn't end up buying me a set of LEGO cuff links, relaying a conversation I had in Billund with Jai Mukherjee, a director with the New Business Group, who works primarily on licensing for LEGO.

"I don't think everything we do from a licensing perspective has to have a buildable element. Think about it, if you started building in bricks to clothes, it would make it very painful for kids when they play," he joked.

With his shaved head and glasses, I could have mistaken him for the American tennis player James Blake until I heard his slight British accent and the patter of a brand consultant.

"I think the things we are absolutely rigid on are the values of quality, creativity, and fun. We'll never compromise LEGO's quality standards and policy," said Jai.

To illustrate his point, he grabbed a manila bubble mailer. He shook it, and two cuff links fell into his palm—Darth Vader minifigures glued to silver-colored aluminum backings. I've seen the cuff links before on Etsy, an online marketplace for homemade goods. Apparently part of Jai's job is to keep tabs on the unlicensed products being made from LEGO bricks.

"Would you ever wear this?" asked Jai.

"No, but I'm not a giant Star Wars nerd, contrary to what Jan thinks," I replied, nodding at Jan Christiansen, who was busy sending a text message.

"Even if you weren't a giant Star Wars nerd," said Jai.

"It's too much. No, I don't think I could heft those around."

"I get the basic concept. It's just the execution. Has anyone ever really tried wearing these?" asked Jai rhetorically.

According to Jai, LEGO licensees sold approximately $400 million worth of LEGO-related goods in 2007. In addition to the popular series of video games, the company has developed a robust clothing and backpack line. There are LEGO-branded school cones in Germany (that function like the pencil case you got on your first day of school in the United States), LEGO interlocking furniture in Europe, and a series of clickable, customizable watches.

"It seems that there are so many different applications of LEGO now, and there are a lot of different opportunities for people to reconnect. How much are you working with adult fans?" I asked Jai.

"We aren't doing much around adult collectibles. It's a relatively niche market. For right now, we've looked at publishing, starting with the two books released this year," he replied.

One of those books, *Fifty Years of the LEGO Brick*, is sitting on my desk. With a red cover imprinted with dots to resemble studs, the book covers the history of the company and the development of product lines at LEGO. It has webbed pockets with old advertisements and even a replica of the original LEGO patent filed in Denmark.

The other book is the *LEGO Collector's Guide,* which details almost every set created since 1958. Each set is ranked on a scale of one to six yellow bricks, based on scarcity. It's published in German and English, in deference to the two largest markets for the company. The dense eight-hundred-page book, filled with pictures and set descriptions, reminds me of the dog-eared pulp magazines that baseball card dealers would flip through at baseball card shows. The *Collector's Guide* was even meant to be a collectible in itself, with a premium hardcover edition produced in a limited batch.

Reading about LEGO has the intended side effect: it makes me want to buy more LEGO sets. It's a typical Friday night in the suburbs at Home Depot when I ask Kate if we can swing by Kmart, ostensibly to look at storage options for my collection. I've outgrown the right half of my desk, and the floor in the third bedroom is beginning to look like a storage unit.

But when I'm in anyplace that sells LEGO sets, I'm drawn to that aisle first. And there it is, the LEGO Creator Stegosaurus—an articulated dinosaur with green and yellow plates and glowing red eyes. I've loved dinosaurs basically since birth, and here is a 731-piece set that has alternate builds of a Tyrannosaurus Rex and a Pterodactyl. It's exquisite, but it's also $44.99.

"I don't know if we can afford to buy this set," I say, feeling deflated by the price. The combination of our recent trip to Denmark and a fireplace renovation has me feeling cash-poor. It's one of my few old-man traits. Even if there is enough in the bank, I still feel I should be saving money after large expenditures.

"We can buy it," says Kate. I cock my head slightly, an unconscious gesture mimicking our cat, Houdini.

"It's awesome. How could you not want this? I've wanted it since we first saw it at the store in Denmark," says Kate.

I leave the set on the shelf, but I'm delighted that Kate wants to build it as strongly as I do. I put it in the Christmas folder in my head, where I keep gift ideas. Whenever Kate mentions that she likes something, I store it away so I always have options when it comes time to look for presents.

The store is empty on a Friday night, the buzzing of the fluorescent lights the only sound other than the squeak of our cart's bad wheel on the linoleum. The toy aisle ends, and we come upon a series of entertainment centers. The shelves seem to be the right width apart, but all of the entertainment centers are too low. I try to imagine myself building on my knees, and it doesn't seem feasible. Some adult fans, like Wayne Hussey, have talked about putting down a towel or foam mattress pad to make it more comfortable if you're going to be kneeling for hours.

"I like the shelves, but I'm not sure about everything else," I tell Kate. She listens impassively, as noncommittal as I am when I'm waiting outside a dressing room for her to show me an outfit.

We look at bookshelves next. The particleboard and wood constructions are too tall or don't seem strong enough to support the weight of a dozen tubs of LEGO elements.

"Why can't I find anything that works?" I ask Kate.

"Probably because you don't know what you want," she replies. Kate's right. I don't know what I want. I'm the Goldilocks of grown men. Some storage bins are too short; other shelves are not deep enough. In my head I've invented a modular system of interchangeable squares or rectangles, something that could be updated or changed as my collection grows. It doesn't really exist. We've been inside Kmart for nearly thirty minutes.

Near the back left of the store is the kids' furniture section. Kate disappears briefly, but I don't notice. I'm by myself when I see the perfect storage unit. The white metal looks like a baseball rack, but it comes with nine pastel bins the size of shoe boxes. The bins are open, tilted upward. I envision grabbing bricks, and I think it would be the right height for where my arms fall from my five-foot-three-inch frame.

"Kate, I think I found something," I tell her. "These bins are a great size and I think they could even be swapped out."

I'm blathering on for close to a minute when I turn around and notice Kate is starting to cry.

"It makes me sad to look at this," she says.

I feel the hard bite of tears in the back of my eyes, and I blink once while blowing my breath out slowly. I look back at the box I'm holding and notice, for the first time, a smiling blond girl with pigtails in the picture of the product. *This is the best way for me to organize my toys*, she seems to be saying, *but you don't have kids like me who need to put away their toys*.

I'm an asshole. I leave the box on the floor.

"C'mon, we're going. That one doesn't work for me," I say. The emotion that I keep out of my voice leads me to push our cart too strongly, and the locked-up wheel sends it shooting off toward a shelf of children's coat hangers. We're surrounded by kid's items, and have been for at least fifteen minutes. It's a horror movie for the infertile.

I right the cart, but before I can push it farther, Kate asks the one question I'm not ready to answer.

"What if we never have a baby?"

I take off my Cubs hat and run my hand through my hair. I can feel my heart pulsing my blood.

"We will." And then I do the one right thing I'll do all evening: I hug Kate. These are the moments that are hardest for me, when I can't fix a problem.

"We're going to have kids, but first we are going to buy that Stegosaurus set." The words leave my mouth before I know I'm going to say them. Kate smiles weakly and I hold her hand, pushing the cart with my other hand. I don't know why I'm still pushing the empty cart; I guess I just don't want to let go of anything right now.

I grab the set and place it in the child seat. That memory will bring a rueful smile later, but for now I'm focused on two things: getting us home and finding a way to pierce my wife's sadness. While grasping for answers, I still realize that I'm buying LEGO to make Kate and me feel better. It's become a proxy for conversation. Instead of talking about that empty child seat, we're just filling it with LEGO sets.

We don't really talk on the car ride home, but we tear into that LEGO set as soon as we walk in the door to our house. The pieces fly together, but the answers that Kate and I are seeking will not come as quickly.

Kate puts the finishing touches on the Shipwreck Hideout, intently focused on the pirates, lest they try to escape or plunder.

21

Kate the Builder

Not many couples have life-changing moments in Kmart; even Novalee Nation decided to hide out in a Walmart. The next three nights find Kate snapping together the LEGO Stegosaurus. When she finishes, I pick up the set and move it to the bookcase in the living room.

And there it remains on display as a signifier of our decision that Kate didn't have to be sad and I didn't have to be frustrated at failing to get pregnant. When there is nothing left to build, Kate and I begin talking about what worries us, what excites us, and what could happen. Talking leads to crying, which leads to laugh-ing. A lot of emotions are inside that Stegosaurus. I don't know if we'll destroy it, like the fax machine in *Office Space*, or try to hang on to a set that provided a bridge toward the next phase of our relationship. I suspect it will be lost over time, like most objects.

The Stegosaurus also awakes in me a desire to build more with dinosaurs, especially when I find the DUPLO Tyrannosaurus Rex I bought at LEGOLAND Billund in the back of my dresser. For the first time, I sketch out a rough plan of what I want to build: a mad scientist vignette. When I'm finished, it looks like a three-walled diorama. In the middle of the room, a minifig in a labcoat is experimenting on a skeleton chained to a table. One wall is completely covered in turbines—repurposed LEGO car axles. The Technic motor from a garage sale becomes a gray, monolithic supercomputer.

The focus of the vignette is the left-hand wall where the snout of the Tyrannosaurus Rex appears to be bursting through it. Transparent 1×2 bricks surround the hole to give the illusion that the dinosaur is being pulled through the space-time con-tinuum. I even carefully select a minifig head to show surprise on the mad scientist's face.

I arrange the vignette alongside the Stegosaurus on the bookshelf. The whale, camel, and truck stand next to the LEGO vending machine. I cringe at the idea that all of these will be dis-played at our upcoming Halloween party.

"Are you sure you don't want me to put these away?" I ask Kate, trying to sound as if I'm asking for her benefit rather than to spare myself embarrassment.

"Nope. We've worked hard on these, we should show them off," answers Kate. Her pronoun choice tells me that she is invested: *At least we're in this together.*

Kate wants to build something for the party, so I suggest a square candy dish on a clear baseplate. It's the first freebuild she has attempted, and I try to be supportive. She builds in rainbow, in part because I don't have that big a collection of 1-by-bricks and also because she's just starting out—more worried about finish-ing than about matching colors.

So I don't hover over her with suggestions (it's hard to stop myself). I start piecing together a small 8 × 8 jack-o'-lantern out of orange safety bricks stolen from the LEGO recycling truck and green tiles from a Pick A Brick cup. I'm beginning to see how color differentials can give the appearance of shapes. I use brown bricks at the base to give the pumpkin a round silhouette. It's a cute little MOC, big enough to hold an unlit tea candle.

About an hour before the party, I'm filling Kate's LEGO bowl with candy corn. I'm definitely nervous. I haven't shown what I've built to that many people outside the AFOL community.

"Perfect," I say to Kate, holding up the bowl.

"Really. You think it's going to hold?"

I nod and place it on the bookshelf. I spend the first part of the party watching people to see if they're looking at the LEGO creations or straining to hear if they're making comments on what I've built. I tell everyone that Kate built the candy dish; I want her to get compliments on her creation. With our guests sipping wine from plastic cups, this is like a bad gallery opening.

Most people don't say anything, but those who do want to share about what they used to build as children. When surrounded by the potent combination of things they loved as a child and alcohol, more of my friends can relate than I would have expected. I learn that they were once space and town builders, and that a few of our friends have built Star Wars sets as adults.

"My husband would love to have a playdate with you," jokes an acquaintance.

"Anytime he wants to come over and play with LEGO, he's welcome," I reply, dead serious. She laughs, I don't.

The LEGO bricks fade into the background of the party. People are more confused by my decision to hang doughnuts on strings from the door frame, a holiday tradition at grade school Halloween parties, in lieu of bobbing for apples, that apparently never migrated from Connecticut to the Midwest.

I had put the LEGO mosaic of Kate and me away for the party, since I thought it would be little strange to have our dining room table covered with green baseplates. Now, it's three days later and I'm sorting through the pieces because I mixed up my bricks and plates in a last-minute rush to get ready. I've also been watching *Eight Below*, the second-best sled-dog movie of all time, for the better part of an hour. I'm moving 1×1 plates and 1×2 plates into tiny piles sorted by color, praying that all those poor dogs make it through the cold, barren winter.

I used to watch terrible action movies only when Kate was out of town. An evening between me, Paul Walker (*The Fast and the Furious, Varsity Blues, The Skulls*), and a few plates of Chinese food left me covered in a mild "shame glaze," as the stand-up comedian Louis C.K. would say. But now it's the middle of the day, and nobody's out of town. I didn't think men were hormonal. I also didn't think I'd get choked up when Paul Walker found those courageous little huskies left to fend for themselves in the Arctic winter.

My newfound self-awareness leads to a mini shopping spree later that afternoon and a bit more self-discovery. LEGO has just released the first in its new line of Pirate sets, bringing back the popular theme. LEGO Pirates were introduced in 1989, one of the sets I never owned but coveted when I went over to a more fortunate friend's house. The original pirates were bare-chested, mustachioed, bandana-wearing cartoons fighting a proper British armada. The new pirates have wooden legs, hook hands, and eye patches. The minifigs are more detailed, but the pirates still have a nineteenth-century adversary in the British armada.

I'm looking for the Shipwreck Hideout, a set that features the ribs of a wrecked pirate ship, cannons, and a lady pirate. But as long as I'm inside Toys "R" Us, I figure I may as well see all the sets they have in stock.

I've been sharing the LEGO aisle with a sixty-year-old woman, who has been turning a LEGO Ferrari set over and over for close to ten minutes.

"Can I help you?" I ask her.

"Do you work here?" she replies.

"No, ma'am, but I've been shopping for LEGO for a while," I tell her.

"My grandson loves cars. He's eight, I don't know if he would like this."

"That Racers set is a bit difficult, I think he might like this one a little more," I hand her a LEGO Creator set, the green Street Speedster. "It will probably hold up better if he's going to roll it around, too."

"This is perfect. Thank you," says the woman, leaving me alone in the LEGO section once again. I have just convinced someone else to buy a set, and I'm confident it's the right one. I decide to stop equivocating and grab the Shipwreck Hideout.

"Would you like a gift receipt?" asks the clerk.

"Nope, this one's for me," I tell him. I don't say that this is a mile-stone, the first time I've acknowledged that I'm purchasing a set as a gift to myself.

"Cool set," replies the clerk, whom I would peg at about seventeen years old.

Is buying LEGO winning me points with the younger generation? Am I cool? I get a text as I'm walking away from the checkout, and I put down my bag on a bench near the door to check the message.

"Wiffleball is cool," I overhear the clerk say to the customer who was behind me. He's probably high, and I'm not as cool as I thought.

I haven't built a set by myself in a while; it's tended to be joint building with Kate. But when I get home and open the Shipwreck Hideout box, I experience the old thrill of starting with a new set. I've developed a bad habit of stealing pieces from sets before I've even built any of the creations. I still read through the instructions, looking at building techniques and the elements mix, but I'm now looking at sets as raw materials rather than as finished products.

The closest feeling I've experienced to this was actually during my single semester in law school. Kate and I both like to joke that I'm one-sixth of a lawyer. Law school is about training you to think with a different method of logic, examining all possibilities in order to determine interesting ways to apply the law in an advantageous manner to your client. I think my LEGO thought patterns are starting to be altered in a similar fashion. The challenge and fun aspect of building with bricks is to figure out how to turn them into an unexpected shape or sculpture—something that other people might have thought impossible. It's about turning a yellow and black beach house into a zombie school bus. At this point, I'm a semester and a half into my LEGO education; but I won't be driving two hundred miles to my parents' house to tell them I'm quitting LEGO, as I might have done when I made the decision not to pursue a career in the field of law.

When Kate comes home and wants to join me, I find myself being a bit overprotective of the Pirates set. I then do something I'm not proud to admit to. I hand her an unopened Star Wars battle tank set, the latest mailing from my BrickMaster membership. It looks like a mechanized, gray hoagie on wheels.

"Could you please finish this for me? I've been meaning to build it, I just haven't gotten around to it," I ask Kate.

"No problem," she says, unaware that I'm just trying to buy more time with the Pirates set. I don't want to hurt her feelings, but I don't want to share. I'm kind of sick of being Kate's brick monkey, grabbing pieces for her while she builds.

But Kate is too adept at building, and the BrickMaster sets are really intended for children. She's knocked out the sixty-four-piece set before the first commercial break of *My Name Is Earl*.

The Pirates set has numbered bags, something that most adult fans feel is part of the continued juniorization of sets. The numbers on the bags correspond to sections in the instructions. It drastically reduces the build time from the previous packaging, which featured bags sorted by element type without numbers. On the first page of every instruction booklet are two illustrations. The first tells you not to put your LEGO on grass or a carpeted floor, but instead to use a table. It's charming if only because it makes you envision Smurfs or gnomes really angry that LEGO might be used as a housing material in nature. The second picture, which instructs you not to mix bags but instead to dump them out separately, is the one that sets most AFOLs off on a rant.

"LEGO is now trying to tell me how to sort. I mean, are you kidding me? All I do is build and sort," says Dave Sterling when I tell him I'm not sure how I feel about having numbered bags to guide my building.

In this case, however, numbered bags save me from an argument. I tell Kate that I want to finish the second bag, so I don't lose track of where I am in the building process, but after that, the set is hers to finish. I know that she doesn't need my help to build, and I no longer feel I have to constrain my desire to build in order to encourage her. I wonder if this is like when a dad decides to go all-out for the first time in a game of one-on-one with his son. He'll likely lose shortly thereafter; and I secretly think Kate would beat me in a speed-build competition.

But I don't wish to discover if that's true. I'm pretty sure it would be a damaging blow to my ego, based on my unsuccessful track record with brick building competitions. Also, I've avoided competitions with my wife for the better part of three years. We tend not to argue outside the arena of directions or household repairs. Yet we both are competitive people, the kind who were difficult to play board games with as children. Kate will no longer play Monopoly with me after our last game, when she believed that I refused to deal with her while tacitly colluding with her brothers to force her out of the game. I maintain that I am just better at Monopoly.

In reality, Kate and I are fundamentally different builders. She isn't really comfortable building outside the confined world of sets. She likes having a construct, lording over a world of miniature pieces. Kate not only has the patience to read the directions, but actually enjoys the sense of accomplishment that comes from checking a list. In contrast, I have embraced free building. I love not knowing what I may build when I sit down. She will likely always be a set builder, while I may build only those sets that I can't resist. Without reading too much into it, this fits the pattern of our relationship. Kate's organizational nature is what tempers my impulsive side. She builds the furniture. I experiment with strawberry soup. The furniture is always a safer bet than the soup, but we both appreciate what went on behind the scenes.

Since my new approach to LEGO building is a celebration, rather than a competition, I don't want to compare skills with my wife. Also, I like that we've managed to find a place for LEGO in

both our lives. It seems to fly in the face of the semi-serious admo-
nition from Joe Meno to make sure that we don't get a divorce
over my new habit. But in our relationship, LEGO seems to help
ease the tension and provide a break when we don't want to tackle
weightier things, such as infertility.

"LEGO lets you talk about an issue when you're unsure of where
to start. I keep seeing people that don't know how to communicate
find a way to tell their story through LEGO," says Serious Play
consultant Gary Mankellow.

The AFOL community attracts a multitude of engineers and
people with advanced science backgrounds. Typically, those with
a math or science bent can have trouble communicating their
ideas to a layperson or someone without a similar mind-set. But
LEGO seems to help cut down on the awkward silences. Adult
fans have an easier time connecting because LEGO bricks offer
them a common language and vehicle for self-expression. When
you've invested a piece of yourself in a MOC, you have a greater
incentive to make sure that another fan knows as much as possible
about it. *This isn't just a vignette of a dinosaur, it tells a story about who
I am.*

The joint layouts of Dave and Stacy Sterling work because
each of them has built a portion of their display. And that might
be one of the main differences between creating as a child and
creating as an adult. As we get older, it becomes more important
to have creations and possessions that reflect our identity. I was
comfortable at the Halloween party because building with LEGO
is part of how I identify myself when talking to people. That's why
it's time to acknowledge that there are two builders in our house.
I won't be the only one getting LEGO sets for Christmas.

My dad, Jeffrey, and I pose proudly with our LEGO constructions—the Sears Tower we built when I was in the fourth grade and Adam Reed Tucker's Brickstructures set.

22

You Can Go Home Again

It was after a visit to FAO Schwarz that I told my father I was going to be a master model builder. I had spent most of my time in the legendary Manhattan toy store staring at a towering giraffe made of LEGO. I was a ten-year-old with conviction. I made pronouncements. When you grow up in the state where the U.S. division of LEGO is headquartered, the possibility of working there doesn't seem far-fetched.

It's dark when I leave my childhood home to head toward my childhood dream job just four days after Thanksgiving.

And I have a nervous stomach as if I were showing up for the first day of work during the entire ninety-minute drive from Fairfield to Enfield, Connecticut. A pile of articles about LEGO Systems, Inc., the U.S. subsidiary of the LEGO Group, sits on the passenger seat. Thankfully, there is nobody to notice that I've been reading them at stoplights.

LEGO Systems is in Enfield, about twenty minutes north of Hartford and close to the Massachusetts border. As the buildings of Hartford give way to the bedroom community, I begin to see why LEGO executives might have chosen Enfield as their North American headquarters in 1975. It's an Americanized Billund, with Bradley International Airport only thirteen minutes away in Windsor Locks, Connecticut.

I know I've arrived when I see the familiar tumble of three giant primary-color LEGO bricks. Steve Witt meets me at the door to walk me through the two-story building that houses the sales and marketing offices for North and Latin America. He stops before we get into his office and hands me a small plastic bag.

"Just don't sell it, that's all I ask," says Steve, before I even know what he has given me. His request makes sense when I look down. In my hand is a chrome C-3PO, a limited-edition minifig randomly included in 2007 Star Wars sets. Only ten thousand minifigs were produced to celebrate the thirtieth anniversary of *Star Wars*. I now have one of them.

"I have no intention of selling it," I tell Steve. The metallic gold figs sell for about $100 apiece on BrickLink or eBay.

"Good, then you won't sell this one either," says Steve. He hands me the chrome Darth Vader, which hasn't even been released yet. Vader's chest plate is stamped with a sparkly silver. It will be included in the 2009 Star Wars sets to honor the decade-long partnership between LEGO and the movie franchise.

"You're kidding me. These are outstanding." There is no doubt that I'm going to accept these. I feel none of the unease that bubbled up when Jan Christiansen tried to hand me a set in Denmark. I guess maybe I am kind of a Star Wars geek.

From the smile on Steve's face, I can tell this is why he loves his job. For him this is like Wonka giving out golden tickets to the factory.

"It is pretty cool to know how happy this can make people," says Steve as he walks me from the main building over to a secondary site where the call center and model shop are located. These two buildings are all that remain of LEGO Systems; LEGO's presence in Enfield has shrunk considerably in the past several years.

The Enfield campus opened in 1975 and expanded to nearly 1.1 million square feet of commercial space by 2007. In January of that year, LEGO sold the 203-acre campus to Equity Industrial Partners for $58,880,848. In the wake of corporate restructuring, three hundred employees were laid off, and warehousing and packaging were moved to Mexico. The distribution center was relocated to Roanoke, Texas, and order fulfillment now originates in Memphis, Tennessee. As part of the sale agreement, LEGO leased back the two buildings we're walking between. Having seen the production plant in Billund, I wish now that I'd seen LEGO Systems in its heyday, when the packaging plant filled the ten million square feet of space inside the distribution center with its fifty-foot ceilings.

Steve stops in to visit with the head of the call center; I stand outside the office, listening to the calls coming in to customer service representatives.

"Sure, we can get you that tire right away. . . ."

"That's a nice birthday gift. . . ."

The voices float up from the rows of cubicles guarded by Bionicle creatures and minifigs. It's as if a group of schoolchildren came to the office one day to decorate and nobody ever took down what they built. Somewhere in the cubicles is Steve's wife, who has been working in the call center since they moved to Enfield from Texas.

We walk through another set of doors, and where I expect there to be offices is instead the bullpen of the model shop. The open studio could be an architect's office with elevated desks, were it not for the LEGO sculptures covering every bit of shelf and table space. LEGO model designers Steve Gerling and Erik

Varszegi are waiting for us. These are the same men who worked with Jamie Berard on the Millyard Project.

A row of life-size LEGO busts looks on as we are introduced. Steve Gerling notices my gaze, and the tour begins.

"The heads are still done by hand. The widths are within a six-stud range, and the eyes are usually four studs apart," says Steve, to give me a sense of the yellow head he's holding.

With a white beard and checked shirt, Steve, sixty, looks like an outdoorsman who's been trapped at a desk job for the last eleven years.

"I'm new to building, having only started playing with LEGO bricks again six or eight months ago. I think I'm a long way from one of these," I tell them.

"I never played with LEGO bricks before I walked through that door," says Steve.

"It's a generational thing. I might have had a few clone bricks when I was a kid," says Erik. He's tall and skinny with windblown brown hair. You wouldn't know he was forty years old, if not for the few flecks of gray that have snuck into his goatee.

It's surprising to learn that I've done more building than either of the two model designers did before setting foot in the model shop.

"There used to be a six-month training period, where you had to be taught building skills, repair, and regulations—like the height you can build before interlocking bricks," says Steve.

Model trainees were then promoted to model builders, and after a year of building could attain master model builder status. The model shop here has a function similar to the designer Jette Orduna's in Billund. They coordinate with marketing and sales to design and build models for publicity, charity, and corporate partnerships.

We've made it just fifteen feet inside the model shop when Steve Witt suggests we break for lunch. I only agree to leave when he promises we can return in the afternoon. Through a happy accident, we're joined by three other model designers, and I'm stunned to find myself sitting down to lunch with five master model builders.

"There's no cutting, altering, sanding, or carving," says Steve Gerling when I ask if they're LEGO purists.

I tell them the story of how I got started building with LEGO in the basement of my childhood home with my father. They all groan when I get to the part about my dad spray-painting the LEGO Sears Tower black.

"But he was the one holding the spray can," I offer weakly. Apparently I should have known better, even if I was only in fourth grade. This is not going well.

I try to move the conversation forward. "You know, when I was in fourth grade, I thought I wanted to be one of you guys."

"It's funny you say that, because it seems like kids are always excited to meet a master builder," says Dan Steininger, just back from leading the construction of an eight-foot pirate at the LEGO retail store in Orlando.

"You have kids walking around Disney with their autograph books, asking if they could get an autograph from the LEGO man," adds Steve Witt.

"But what about when those kids grow up to be adults? What's it like to build alongside adult fans?" I ask.

"When AFOLs come out for weekends, I look at them as coworkers. We've just worked a weekend together, but yet we have their dream job. We are those who are lucky enough to be paid by the LEGO Group," says Dan.

The model builders nod their assent.

"There's a real level of mutual respect. I love it too," says Steve Gerling.

"We'll pull up videos online, and what they build is amazing. You'll see cows' heads turning as a train goes by," says Erik.

"I guess we just speak the same language," says Dan.

"And yet we don't—what we call roof tiles are slopes to adult fans," counters Erik.

"Right, but everybody knows that a one-by-five is a hot girl at a LEGO event," cracks Steve Witt.

"Is that code, or is that because it doesn't exist?" I joke. LEGO only manufactures 1×4 and 1×6 bricks. They don't make

1×5 bricks, so it's the perfect way to acknowledge a hot girl without the public knowing.

Everybody at the table laughs. I feel like pumping my fist. When you can make people laugh, you speak their language. And once you speak their language, you're ready to be part of the group.

After lunch, I feel comfortable standing behind Steve Gerling's desk. This would be a good place to work. The shelf behind me has a LEGO bust of Scooby-Doo, a LEGO marlin, and a business card–size LEGO badge from BrickFest 2005, where Jamie Berard was offered a job by LEGO. Underneath the shelf is a series of gray bins with bricks sorted by color.

"My job isn't creating art; it's selling toys. I don't expect any of my pieces to end up in the Louvre. I'm just making this thing that shows people: look at the kind of stuff you can build if you try," says Steve, pulling up a three-dimensional image of a Cap'n Crunch model. The 3-D model is the cartoon picture of the cereal captain translated into a series of cylinders, cones, and squares.

"This program does not design a model for me, it makes designing a model faster for me," says Steve.

Model designers will typically sketch a version of a project on paper before using the virtual tools. That is followed by the first stage of model review, where other designers weigh in on the prototype.

"A big part of our job is to criticize models as they are being built," says Steve.

"If nobody is saying anything, then your model probably sucks," Dan chips in as he walks by. He still has the comedic timing from having been a professional clown for over two decades.

After the model review, the designer might make changes to the model before it is fitted for a steel interior structure. The final version is then built and glued. Model designers attempt to build with as many current parts as possible, in order to maintain the idea that anyone could build what they build. They have a digital inventory of all of the current elements in production.

"What's your favorite element?" asks Erik. I freeze up at the question.

"I call it a lunch box, it's perfect for micro monorails," I tell him. When I can't find the words to describe the part, I draw it for him.

"Ah, it's a one-by-two clamp," says Erik after searching for a few minutes on his computer. "We have a bunch of those in back."

The back of the model shop doubles as a parts warehouse. Shelves the color of old gray bricks have elements glued to the front to identify what is inside each bin. The Millennium Falcon sits casually on a table.

"It was broken in a shipment from a Denmark toy fair. Erik built that in a week with no instructions. All he had was a series of one-page photos," says Steve.

I whistle like the sound of a bomb falling. I have never made this noise in my life in response to a statement, but it seems apropos. That's the blind build on steroids. Putting together five thousand pieces without the instructions is impossible, like Luke Skywalker hitting the shot to blow up the Death Star.

Steve opens a door in the back left corner of the model shop, and we walk into a concrete storage room where I would not have been surprised to see the Ark of the Covenant. This is bulk storage, where plates and bricks are organized by color. An empty mail cart with a Red Sox cup holder is parked next to the shelves. I briefly entertain the idea of loading it with bricks and making a break for it.

"I think the company store is the last stop," says Steve, flicking off the lights on millions of bricks.

The company shop is a small room with off-white shelves and the feel of an outlet store. It's scratch-and-dent heaven. I tell myself I'm not going to buy much, seeing that I just spent $104 three days before on LEGO.com during the Brick Friday sale. *I need these three sets*, I said to myself. The first was the Custom Car Garage, which Joe Meno had told me about designing during my trip to Brick Bash back in March. The second was the Space Skulls set, another fan-designed set, which I had learned about from the New Business Group in Billund. And finally, Kate doesn't have a set to build, so I wanted to get her the Creator Cool Convertible set, an oversize white car with a top that folds into the trunk.

After a slow lap through the shop, I grab a small Creator and Batman buggy set.

"I'm good," I tell Steve after a few minutes.

"No, c'mon," says Steve, "you can get more. Go ahead." And there goes my willpower. I walk around the store like a contestant on Supermarket Sweep, blindly grabbing sets to take to the register. The total is $120, even with the benefit of a heavy employee discount. In the past four days, I have bought twelve LEGO sets; I'm officially a binge purchaser. I offer to give Steve a ride home, and we head out, the oversize LEGO bags rattling around in the trunk.

"You know that looks exactly like a LEGO half-pipe," says Steve, as we sit idling behind a truck in traffic.

"You do that too?" I say a bit too excitedly. "You find LEGO parts in real life?"

"I can't stop doing it. Some things just match up too well," says Steve.

This is like discovering that an acquaintance had the same childhood fear; it affords you a level of closeness that you probably wouldn't otherwise have based on the length of time you've known each other. Accordingly, Steve invites me up to see where he builds. This is only the second time I've seen another man's LEGO room, and it's intensely personal. These aren't just sets and bricks, they're memories and dreams. As Steve guides me through a moon base he's working on, which includes an intricate rock floor made of gray cheese wedges, he switches from employee to hobbyist. It's a subtle change, but it's nice to see. He's more relaxed, and the time passes quickly.

It's late when I get back to my parents' house on Tuesday night for dinner.

"Do you want to build?" I ask my dad nervously as we're clearing the plates.

"Sure, why not," he says.

I run up the stairs to my bedroom and grab the Brickstructures Sears Tower set I purchased at Brickworld. It's sixty-nine pieces; we can do this before he changes his mind.

My dad cuts the bag with a pair of scissors and lays out the pieces.

"That's not a stud," says my dad.

"Nope. There's a lot of new pieces since the last time we built together," I tell him; and as we sort parts, I teach him the name for each one. I draw confidence from the fact that I'm teaching him something. It must be rewarding to be a dad.

A pair of 1 × 1 plates are stuck together, and both of us try to pry them apart unsuccessfully.

"We both used nail clippers today," says my dad, noticing my short nails. I wish for a brick separator, and cringe when my father reaches for the pair of scissors to pry the plates apart.

"Don't use them—you'll ruin the integrity of the bricks," I scold him lightly. I briefly recall my conversation with the master model builders at lunch. I don't tell him that we have offended my gods by spray-painting our first attempt at the Sears Tower.

We fall into the comfortable rhythm of building, and my dad offers his first critique of the set.

"This is redundant, we're just stacking pieces on top of each other."

He's right, but I don't care. I'm building again with my dad.

"Ow!" He pinches his finger trying to snap the final brick into place. "It's good," he says, pronouncing it done.

We've finished too quickly, I want to tell him. The set has taken only thirteen minutes to build. My dad surprises me by taking the old shoe box with the first Sears Tower we built out of a cabinet.

"Let's see how we did," says my dad. He spins the model around 360 degrees. The first side is the only one that is close to right, with a tiered face. The back half of the building is completely transposed—almost the mirror image of the stacked-tubes tower design.

"So this was fourth grade?" asks my dad.

"The state fair. I think we would have won, if they had been giving out prizes," I reply.

I don't really want this moment to end, so I blurt out the first thing I can think of. "Do you want to build another set?"

"Sure, go pick one out," says my dad.

It's like Roy Hobbs telling the batboy Bobby Savoy to go pick him a winner in the final game of his career. I settle on the smallest set I've bought, a tiny Creator crane. The age range is seven to twelve years old. I think my dad can build it without getting frustrated. Neither of us is a patient man, but this is the first time I've wondered if my dad would have fun playing with something.

He starts putting together the crane while I fiddle with a small LEGO penguin model, a gift from the project manager of the model shop. Our silence is one of contentment.

"It spins, oh lordy," says my dad, noticing that the yellow cab on top of the crane rotates.

"When was the last time you said 'oh, lordy'?"

"I don't know, but I just did," says my dad. He starts laughing, and I join in. Fairly soon, I'm giggling like I used to do on the hourlong drive back from New York City to Fairfield, when my brother would make me laugh so hard that I cried—until my dad threatened both of us with pulling over the car.

That night I can't sleep, so I do what I always do when I'm staying at my parents' house. I watch terrible movies on cable, keeping the sound low so my parents think I'm asleep. I hit bottom around two-thirty in the morning with Jamie Kennedy in *Kickin' It Old Skool*, where he plays a break-dancer who awakens from a coma and attempts to reunite with his old dancing crew of the 1980s.

In one of the climactic scenes of the movie (one hour and twenty-two minutes in—please don't judge me too harshly), we find Jamie Kennedy's character, Justin, struggling with having never grown up.

Bartender: "Why are you smashing LEGOs?"

Justin: "These are a lie. They teach you that life is all fun and you can make anything you want, but you can't really make anything you want. You just get old, boring, and fat."

It's late enough that I find myself disagreeing strongly with a terrible Hollywood comedy. I can make anything I want. I can build again with my dad. I will build with my child when I'm a dad. These are my thoughts as I fall asleep to the static-y crackle of the television set.

23

My Christmas wish is granted. I challenge Darth Vader to a light-saber duel at LEGOLAND California in Carlsbad, California. We fight to a draw.

There Is No "I" in LEGO

It's just past midnight when my flight lands in Kansas City the next night. The traffic-congested Brooklyn-Queens Expressway on the way to LaGuardia Airport in New York City has been exchanged for a half-dozen cars marked by silent headlights on the roads home. I walk lightly when I enter the house, hoping not to wake the dog. She is our sleeping baby. Charlie whines softly from her crate in my office, and I stop, the carpeted stairs creaking in reply. She stays quiet, and I debate whether I should go in and check on her. I hear Kate turn over in our bed and head upstairs instead.

"I built with my dad," I tell her excitedly before launching into what it was like at LEGO U.S. headquarters. I am a seven-year-old who has just returned from his first sleepover. Kate listens sleepily, adding in "Uh-huh," at the right moments before drifting off to sleep. She stops just short of "That's nice, dear," the hallmark of any mom dealing with an overexcited husband or child. I shut my eyes too, content to be home. And I make the grown-up decision to sleep in my polo shirt and jeans.

I awake in bed to the gentle pressure of Kate's hand on my back. It's only been two days since I came home, so it takes me a second to remember that I'm in Kansas City and she's not in Fairfield.

"I'm pregnant," says Kate, holding up the test that echoes what she's saying in blocky capital letters.

"That's wonderful," I say thickly, turning over to pull her into my arms.

"I'm still in shock. . . . I didn't expect it. I've had so many negative ones and that's why when I took this one, I just thought there was no way," says Kate before sitting up to wipe her hands across her cheeks.

We finally have a use for that third bedroom.

"We can still keep LEGO in there, right?" I ask.

"What part of 'choking hazard' do you not understand?"

"They're not a choking hazard, they have the holes in the tops of minifigs," I offer weakly.

Kate gives me a single look that I can see will be effective when she is a mother. It says, *You're not being serious right now, because if you are, I will need to correct you in short order.*

"Right, I'll move the LEGO." I'm glad one of us has a basic understanding of babies. I will need a new LEGO room.

My office is the most likely candidate, although it currently looks like the back room of a Woolworth's department store that is in the process of closing. Sets and cardboard boxes are stacked behind the dog crate on the floor. Open sets are leaking parts—the concept of organization seems to have escaped a forgetful stockroom clerk.

I pick up a smaller set, Batman's Buggy, which features Batman and Mr. Freeze minifigures. I reason that the quickest way toward getting everything organized is to start building.

"It's about to get cold in here," I say in a vaguely Austrian accent as I tear open the bags. Governor Arnold Schwarzenegger would be mortified by my accent, but I think impressed by his minifig likeness.

The two miniature vehicles in the seventy-eight-piece set are done in just over four minutes. Joe Meno says I shouldn't worry about speed, but I'm still proud of the fact that I build faster with each set. It helps that I'm no longer surprised by parts or elements. Like a good chess player, I can see a few steps ahead during the build. While I'm not sure that Batman would utilize a buggy to fight crime, the set includes a cool flame element and rear fin that add a bit of style to the caped crusader's vehicle. Even in the short time I spend constructing the kit, I'm already considering how I might use the silver pistons in the buggy to build a muscle car, and how Mr. Freeze's helmet could be the cockpit for a mini retro rocket ship.

The Batman set inspires a mini LEGO building boom. Well, that and my need to channel all of the adrenaline I have in the week after learning that Kate is pregnant. I tackle five sets over the next five days, two of which are larger than the LEGO MTT Federation I've been avoiding since my thirtieth birthday. Suddenly that set doesn't seem so scary, but I still leave it untouched in what is rapidly coming to be known as the baby's room.

While I'm focusing on the sets in my office, Kate has become vexed by her search for a bedside lamp to put in the guest bedroom. I think we're expressing our need to nest in very different ways. However, this presents me with an opportunity to bring a bit of Denmark into the textured walls of our Tudor-style house.

It's easy to fall in love with Danish design. The neat, clean lines suggest that you will become not only more organized, but infinitely cooler. Yet, despite a few days in Copenhagen spent in the polished halls of modern design galleries and cosmopolitan museums, I just want a light that reminds me of the bell-shaped acrylic lamps that hung from the ceiling over the staircase leading to the entrance of LEGOLAND Billund.

At the height of Kate's frustration, I manage to convince her that we can emulate the clear lamps filled with monochromatic LEGO bricks. A local store sells empty, oversize jelly jars that have been wired as table lamps.

"We're going to fill the lamp with LEGO bricks," I tell the woman at the register (I'll admit with entirely too much enthusiasm).

"That will be . . . ," she pauses, ". . . nice." Her left eye squinches like a pirate as she ends the word "nice" with a long "s" to show her true meaning. She is not ni-ssss.

Kate is uncertain about the idea until the base is filled with white bricks and elements.

"It doesn't look half-bad," says Kate. She is being nice to me, but I'll take it.

The LEGO lamp satisfies the part of her that needs to cross it off the list before guests arrive for the holidays, while I'm pleased that we've managed to add LEGO to one of the few rooms in the house that didn't have any bricks.

By now there is no doubt that LEGO fans live in the Bender house. Since it's December, I can finally start to open the Castle Advent calendar I bought for Kate at Brickworld. It's agony waiting for her to come home from work each day so we can open the next window. A LEGO blog counts down to Christmas by unveiling the completed minifig or castle feature of the day, like a witch's cauldron. I find myself getting angry when I accidentally see one before we've had a chance to open the window; it is as soul-crushing as a television show spoiler.

Kate creates a holiday display on top of the entertainment center, having long ago surrendered the fireplace mantel to LEGO creations. She slowly separates the medieval minifigs into good guys and bad guys. I'm a bit disturbed that I think I bear a decent resemblance to a mine-working dwarf. If Kate notices, she keeps it to herself. I shave in the hope that she never reaches the same conclusion.

The creations continue to pile up in the living room, and despite submitting an extensive Christmas LEGO wish list to my wife and in-laws, I've still bought another two sets in December. It's as if the sets in my office have a tractor beam that keeps pulling in other sets from the toy stores in my area. For the first time, I consider hiding my purchases from Kate. That thought is quickly followed by the logical part of my brain telling me that's exactly how you get a divorce. My moral compass settles on a compromise, and I no longer justify my spending as research.

I also discover that LEGO purchases now come with a new form of guilt. I have only recently given up feeling guilty for purchasing a child's toy, when I find that buying toys instead of saving for my child feels terribly wrong. I imagine that all expectant fathers feel cash-poor; it's the same feeling that gives men an excuse to avoid getting engaged or buying new clothes.

I've never been one to store my purchases in mint condition in the hopes that what I buy will appreciate in price. Accordingly, my LEGO collection is purely functional and definitely out of the box. And while I am excited to see what my child will build with my bricks, it seems disingenuous to pretend that I'm buying things today with the idea that they'll be perfect when Wilbraham is six years old. (Wilbraham is the fictional, nonbinding name we gave our hypothetical first child during a road trip early in our relationship. Wilbraham happens to be a town in Massachusetts—a lovely town, I'm sure—but the name is a bit weighty for a child who is trying to learn to write it for the first time).

Yet I am buying for two. I've been buying for two all along—Kate and me. So now I guess I'm buying for three. Much as I had forgotten about the blue tub of LEGO bricks in the back of my childhood closet, I had conveniently ignored the fact that at some point I might want to pass on my collection. And that could happen sooner than I expected, once we pass the age where Wilbraham will try to eat LEGO pieces—this moment clearly being determined by Kate.

When you start considering the need for life insurance, you are forced to reconsider how your life is structured and what you would want done with what remains after you're gone. On Christmas Eve, I'm flipping aimlessly through instruction books

and cherry-picking minifigure accessories out of a parts box—
basically killing time until we go to church with Kate's family. But
then I come across the story of Ron Eaton in the *Everett Herald*, and
I start getting choked up over a man I've never known.

Eaton was an adult fan of LEGO who died on Christmas Day
in 2007 of kidney cancer. The retired software engineer from Mill
Creek, Washington, was a lifelong bachelor. His family gathered
a year later, after deciding to donate his extensive LEGO collection to Toys for Tots. This isn't just about finding a new use for
old toys, it's about a man who built his identity in LEGO bricks.
I know a lot of adult fans like Eaton, and I can see why it matters
to them what will happen with toys that have come to define their
lives.

LEGO bricks have become my default gift this Christmas. A Star
Wars fan gets a Republic airship, while a few of my friends get
small sets or basketball minifigs. I'm testing the waters to see their
reaction. It's not complicated. I'm hoping some of my friends
might want to come over and play with LEGO sets. And worst
case, they'll get the hint about the gifts I'm hoping to receive.

The past two years, Kate and I have driven over to my in-laws'
house on Christmas morning in our pajamas. These are special
Christmas pajamas, gifts from my brother and his wife—red long
underwear, the kind with the flap in the seat. So if we didn't
already feel like children, we would as soon as we unwrapped the
biggest boxes under the tree.

"No way. This is awesome," I yell. Kate has surprised me
by buying the LEGO Agents Volcano Base—a lava-spouting,
laser-firing, blast-door-opening 718-piece marvel. It is the best
version of a Bond villain lair I have ever laid eyes on. I jump
around before hugging her.

"But it was sold out. How did you get it?"

"I fought the masses on eBay and won it for you, dear," says
Kate.

I keep turning over the box to look at the parts included,
forgetting that there are other gifts to open. This will go on my
bureau in our bedroom, displayed as proudly as a child's model
car or a spinster's porcelain unicorn collection. I haven't been this

happy over a gift since a bowling party in fourth grade, when I received a soccer ball beanbag chair. I was a weird kid.

I've never been easy to shop for around the holidays. The most exciting gift I received the previous Christmas was a paper shredder. It was the top item on my list. But this year the LEGO gifts don't stop coming. I know that Jai Mukherjee from the licensing department at LEGO wouldn't like what I unwrap next. It's a Snack & Stack fork, knife, and spoon set. The three utensils are covered in primary-color, molded rubber shaped like a 1 × 7 LEGO brick (LEGO doesn't make 1 × 7 bricks, only 1 × 7 Technic pieces). They're a bit uncomfortable to hold, but they'll be perfect for the baby. My mind, after a slight delay, finally adds *in a few years* to that thought.

The last box I open is the biggest. It is the Green Grocer, the second in the line of modular buildings designed by AFOL Jamie Berard. All LEGO bricks are glossy, but this set gleams. The 2,352-piece monster has essentially been created for adult fans, with a recommended build age of sixteen-plus.

"That's a LEGO set?" asks my brother-in-law Ben.

"I know; it's a lot different than the tub of bricks you gave me." I explain the history of the set and what it means to adult fans. I would probably still be talking, but Kate reins me in, noting that there are still several more gifts for everyone else to open.

The architect in Ben can't get over the level of detail on the building's facade. The former LEGO builder inside him just thinks there are a lot of cool new parts. For my part, I chalk this up to the second time I have given Ben a chance to claim his tub of LEGO bricks—a repeat of the promise I made back in March. The LEGO has been offered and refused. Nobody can escape the logic trap of a one-sixth lawyer. This is important because Ben and his wife, Katy, have just had twins, who are here experiencing their first Christmas. I wouldn't have believed it had you told me, but I am actively stealing blocks from babies. Ben's bricks are going to my kid.

Everyone has Christmas traditions—the games or movies that occupy the day spent together. At my in-laws' house, we usually sit hunched over a puzzle for hours, inevitably searching for a single errant piece to complete the increasingly larger picture made of smaller and smaller pieces. I'm counting on the idea that the puzzle has been good training for constructing a Technic set. It's the one style of building I haven't tried, and I really wouldn't mind some help with the Off Roader set I purchased at the LEGO employee store in Enfield.

In a bit of hubris, I have selected a power-functioned Hummer look-alike, a behemoth at 1,097 pieces and the largest set (in any theme) I will have tackled to date. It has working headlights, hydraulics, and a motorized winch. The box is the size of a brief-case, and the tires are the size of limes. I bring the set in from the car.

"I was hoping we might all build this together instead of a puzzle this year," I say cautiously.

"Let's give it a shot," says my father-in-law, Bob.

We dump the pieces onto the living room floor, where we will sit in various combinations for the next three days while com-pleting the set. I get both my brothers-in-law involved early and establish a system wherein a parts monkey gathers the pieces for a given step in order to free up a lead builder to snap together the Technic elements. What starts out as a joint effort among four adults quickly devolves into an obsession for my father-in-law. I should have seen this coming. He is the one who continues to work on a puzzle long after the rest of us have quit.

"You have no idea what you've done to Bob," says Ann, Kate's mother, when we come back to the house two days after Christmas.

Bob waves hello from the floor, where he's sitting with the sec-ond of two instruction booklets. He's moved to the floor because his back is tight and sore from bending while on the couch. It's a rookie mistake.

"I was sitting at work, worried that the cats were going to get at the parts we had left out and we wouldn't be able to finish because of something they had hidden," says Bob.

I am amazed by how invested my father-in-law has become in seeing us complete the Off Roader. Later, when family and friends come over to see the twins, I keep seeing Bob demonstrate how the hydraulics work and the winch on the front of the Off Roader.

It strikes me that he is proud of what he has accomplished. And I'm proud of him.

When we're done, I realize that this is the mark of an evolved builder—someone who can help teach others how to build and has relearned the grade school value about the importance of sharing. The months spent building alongside Kate have been training, teaching me the patience to help somebody else put together a set and the joy of watching them succeed. They're the kind of skills that a father might want to have.

LEGO master model builder Gary McIntire works to repair the nose on a maxifig sculpture inside the mini golf course at LEGOLAND California before the park opens for the day.

24

Miniland Dad

D*ir-tee Brick-stur. Dir-tee Brick-stur.*"

The off-key chant fills the living room of the house in Oceanside, California. A LEGO witch minifigure keychain has just been stolen, and the crowd of men (and one baby) is yelling with enthusiasm. I'm a guest of the LEGOLAND master model builder Gary McIntire at the January meeting of the San Diego LEGO User Group.

To determine the order for opening the gifts, the meeting's host, Bill Vollbrecht, thirty-eight, a master model designer at

LEGOLAND, hands each person a different-color 1×1 cylinder. I want his collection, when it becomes apparent that he has enough colors for the fourteen men, one woman, and one baby participating. I draw sand green, which is the seventh pick out of the hat.

This LUG is stacked with high-skill-level builders because of its proximity to the park. On the coffee table rests a collection of models that have been featured prominently recently on the Brothers Brick, the most popular AFOL Web site. There's a red Converse sneaker and an upscaled Princess Leia minifigure, in her gold bikini from when she was imprisoned by Jabba the Hutt.

"I always steal from the kid, I love it," jokes Gary, nodding to the baby of one of his fellow LUG members.

An old McDonald's kit is opened early, along with a number of new Star Wars sets. Then my bag is taken from the pile. This time I'm prepared. I've brought a Creator set that is filled with cheese wedges and translucent pieces that I know serious builders would like.

"Oh, that's a good set," says one of the crowd.

"That's a really good set," confirms someone else.

Nobody knows I brought it, but I can't help smiling. I've solved the Dirty Brickster. Then my turn comes to pick, and I immediately panic, snatching a Stormtrooper set that I could get at any Toys "R" Us for $9.99. A few halfhearted "Dir-tee Brick-sturs" follow my theft.

"I've really wanted one of these," I mumble. Nobody will steal it from me. In a Dirty Brickster with four current LEGOLAND employees, the pickings are rich. I should not be the one guessing which is the Holy Grail if it ever comes to it, because I have chosen poorly.

I console myself as I always do, by buying more LEGO sets. One of the LUG members, Bruno Todd, is sharing the wealth from a recent clearance purchase. I grab two small starter sets, a classic space vehicle, and a street sweeper from the display that stands next to the couch. The street sweeper is for Kate. I know she'll appreciate that the James Lipton minifig continues to find work.

"Want to see something?" asks Bruno.

"Absolutely," I reply. I have never been disappointed when an AFOL has asked me that; it's some sort of code for "get ready to be amazed." Bruno holds up a small black box stamped with white writing that says "Modulex." Inside is a jumble of 1 × 4 sea-foam green bricks that look like miniaturized LEGO bricks.

"I just got these off eBay; the guy had no idea they were in the original boxes," says Bruno.

I'm looking at the predecessor to Adam Tucker's Brickstructures and an idea of Godtfred Kirk Christiansen's from the 1960s that was probably before its time. Godtfred was building a new house and wanted a scale version of his architectural plans. The 6:5 aspect ratio of the standard LEGO bricks didn't work, so Godtfred had bricks with a 1:1 aspect ratio molded for him.

The bricks produced were about five-eighths the size of a regular LEGO brick. This inspired Godtfred to launch a new company, Modulex A/S, in 1963. The specialty bricks were marketed to industrial planners and architects. Although the Modulex Planning System was primarily adapted by planners, the Finnish American architect Eero Saarinen, the designer of the St. Louis Gateway Arch, was known for creating prototypes out of Modulex and LEGO bricks. Today Modulex is one of the largest architectural sign companies in the world.

LEGO also released architectural sets aimed at the adult market. The sets, which consisted of only bricks and plates, included a ruler, graph paper, and instructions on how to design scale models. Adults weren't ready to be fans, though, and the architectural sets were discontinued in 1965.

Bill calls everybody back into his LEGO room. He's giving away some extra parts, and the grown men have descended like jackals on the plastic bags filled with minifig heads and specialty elements.

His models tell the story of how he has come to work at LEGOLAND. That makes sense for the self-taught artist.

"I've always been more comfortable expressing myself through drawing and what I build," says Bill.

He shows me the hieroglyphics he's drawn as part of his design for the Lost Kingdom Adventure—a new Egyptian-themed ride in the park. Above him, pirate minifigs peek out from among the shelves and models.

"It was Pirates that got me out of the Dark Ages in 1990. I'm standing in the [toy store] aisle for thirty minutes looking at the Black Seas Barracuda, thinking this was the most beautiful thing I've ever seen. The guy next to me says, 'It's okay. I'm a doctor and I do this too,'" says Bill.

There's the cartoon white bunny, made from his first bulk brick purchase in 1992, which he bought with half of a $9,000 Nevada slot jackpot. A two-foot-tall Mickey Mouse stands as a reminder of the two years Bill spent as a freelance LEGO artist, building customized cars and bar mitzvah centerpieces on commission.

"I love theme parks. I love to draw and I love LEGO bricks. I'm in the perfect place right now," says Bill.

So am I, I jot down in my notebook.

After the meeting, Kate joins us for dinner, back from her day-trip to Los Angeles to visit her brothers. Gary is animated, excited about an episode of *Mythbusters*, the Discovery channel show that uses science to prove or disprove urban legends, that he recently filmed in San Francisco.

"What were the myths? That if you put together LEGO and MEGA Bloks, they'll explode?" asks Bill.

The table erupts in laughter, mostly my own. I look at Kate, who is also laughing, and I find that at the intersection of my two worlds, I'm pretty content.

I can't wait until we head home, so I give Kate the street sweeper set the next morning. I've been up for several hours, excited that we're going to LEGOLAND California. We've arranged to meet Kate's brother Sam and his girlfriend, Tai, when the 128-acre park opens at ten o'clock.

We pull into the parking lot and wander over to the Volvo family, a set of four life-size LEGO figures that are next to a blue Volvo XC90 made entirely from LEGO bricks.

"Jack, that's what happens to naughty children, they get turned into LEGOS," says a mother as she pushes a little kid in a stroller past his LEGO counterpart.

And I have my first parenting lesson of the day. Kate and I laugh, not at that relatively terrifying threat, but about the construction stories that Bill and Gary told us the night before at dinner.

"There is no C cup when it comes to LEGO. So she was either getting an A cup or a D cup," said Gary, who helped put together the LEGO mom.

"It's a weird thing to be holding the butt of a model as you work on the front and having people watch," added Bill, who worked on the LEGO dad.

We wander inside the park while waiting for Sam and Tai to arrive. I immediately ask Kate to take a picture of me dueling an eight-foot Darth Vader with a LEGO light saber. The setup is designed for a ten-year-old, as evidenced by the line behind me, so the photo shows me in a hunched over fighting stance.

"You're going to be a daddy," says Tai, shortly after they arrive. It's the first time I've ever heard anybody call me that.

The next day feels a bit like Groundhog Day, as I'm headed to the park again early in the morning. It's just after seven on Monday morning when I pick up Gary to make the thirty-mile drive north from San Diego to Carlsbad, California. It's early, but Gary still looks cool in a leather jacket. With a neatly trimmed beard and brown hair that he clearly takes time to style, Gary is a "LEGO rock star," according to Steve Witt. He's extroverted—an animated storyteller and a natural as a representative of LEGOLAND. He was also a finalist in the master model builder competition of 2004, becoming friendly with the set designer Jamie Berard.

I'm shadowing him in an attempt to find out what life is really like in the model shop at LEGOLAND California. I've been wondering if adult fans can find happiness working at the park since I met Mariann Asanuma at BrickCon in Seattle back in October. With long, straight black hair and a need to speak her mind, she seemed destined to be one of those tough little old ladies who runs her neighborhood.

Mariann, thirty-one, had been a master model builder. She was the first American woman hired in the model shop at

LEGOLAND. She got used to being the odd one out in a club
reserved for boys.

"The first few months were not that fun," Mariann told me
when we talked at BrickCon. "I'm kind of an outspoken woman,
and they didn't know what to do with me yet."

Her voice got notably softer. This is what Mariann must have
been like as a child, I thought. I wasn't surprised that she remem-
bered telling her elementary school teacher she wanted to be a
master model builder.

"She said, 'That's nice, dear, but you have to have a real job.'
But I knew it was a real job—I'd seen it in magazines. So, it's
almost like I wanted to prove it to her," said Mariann.

She applied to be a model builder five times in the first three
years the park was open, before landing a retail job in 2003. She
stocked shelves for three months at a Toys "R" Us before being
transferred to the park.

"Working in retail really opened my eyes to LEGO as a
business. All people don't love it; to some it's just a job," said
Mariann.

When I hear adult fans talk about the business side of LEGO,
it feels like a loss of innocence. They're not naive; it's more like
willful ignorance. But that doesn't stop so many of them from
wanting to wear a red polo inside the LEGOLAND model shop.
While working at the park, Mariann befriended some of the
model builders and began showing them her portfolio. When a
model gluer position opened, her knowledge of LEGO elements
and her relationship with the model builders helped her get the
job. She was promoted to model builder right before the Master
Model Builder Search in 2004.

"You quickly learn the company value of a brick as opposed to
the value perceived by an adult fan. A model builder would just
build with old brown—and I'd be like, we can't do this, it's not
available anymore," Mariann told me.

Her last project was working on Miniland Las Vegas, where she
spent three weeks building the MGM lion. A LEGO mouse is hidden in the lion's stomach.

"It was a nice way to say I was here, I did this," said Mariann.

But it wasn't enough. Mariann left the model shop in 2007 to pursue a career building models on commission, in the hope of becoming the first female LEGO certified professional. Even for someone who had dreamed of working at LEGOLAND since the age of six, being a master model builder wasn't a dream job. On some level, I'm sure that's because no job is perfect, especially when compared with the freedom the average AFOL has to build whatever he wants. Thinking of my conversation with Mariann prompts me to wonder how Gary feels about working at the park.

"Do you have to separate your world as an adult fan from your job at LEGOLAND?" I ask him.

"You have free rein as a hobbyist, you're only limited by your patience. Whereas as a professional, you always have the limits of a budget and time constraints," he replies.

Gary flicks on the lights in the model shop. It's weird to be on the other side of the huge plate-glass window that has been set up for park visitors to watch models being built. When I later visit the new Sea Life Aquarium exhibit, I realize that the model shop is not unlike a human LEGO fishbowl.

Four solid wood tables painted green, each with four grates, sit in the center of the room. Gray vacuum tubes snake down from the ceiling like Doctor Octopus's tentacles. The grates and tubes remove the fumes from the solvent used to make models. Large gray shelves span the entire width of the room and are covered with primary-color bins that hold bricks and elements. A tan skull and limo sit behind Gary's workstation, where he is in the middle of putting together a bust of Oprah Winfrey.

"Let's just grab some bricks and the repair list, and then it's off to do park check," says Gary.

He consults a repair chart on his clipboard that keeps track of the model, its location, the reported problem, and whether it has been fixed.

On the cement pad outside the shop, Gary points to what is essentially a yellow adult tricycle. "Usually I'll take that, but we'll take the cart today," he says. A short walk takes us behind the administrative offices, where we climb onto an electric golf cart.

As we ride, Gary waves to a cleaner walking through Miniland. The cleaner is using a leaf blower and a brush on a long stick to sweep away leaves and pollen from the streets and buildings of the miniature cities. He'll also do the job that Mariann once did, when she was nicknamed "Miniland Mom": overseeing the daily maintenance and repair of Miniland. She used to spend two hours every morning walking around with a small glue bottle and a loose mix of bricks. I recall her telling me what it was like to walk around inside a miniaturized world.

"The fence, even though it's only a foot high, is like a magical barrier," she said. "I was able to walk across that fence and walk through the cluster. I got to kneel down and see what the actual models were. It was like I walked into Wonderland."

The park is quiet just after 9 a.m. The whine of our golf cart is the only noise as we putt across the concrete walkways.

"There are some models that will always be issues. I just want to make sure that there are no sharply broken bricks or exposed steel," says Gary. A pizza chef model is missing an earlobe. A DUPLO mechanic has lost several buttons from the front of his shirt.

"We have firefighters everywhere," says Gary, as we stop in front of a fire truck in Fun Town. A bolt has jimmied loose, popping up the black LEGO bricks from the right foot of a firefighter model.

"I don't have the right bricks," says Gary, as he tries to find a way to repair the foot.

"Do we have to go back to the shop?" I ask.

"Nope, this will just take a minute." Gary holds up a 2×10 black brick that he proceeds to saw in half with an X-Acto knife.

"You made a 2-by-5 brick," I say. "You're creating LEGO. It's like the 1-by-5 brick."

"Where did you hear about that?" asks Gary.

"Maybe Steve Witt. Why, you know it?"

"I coined it, along with [LEGO certified professional] Dan Parker. He used to work as a bag boy in a grocery store and they'd say, 'We need a cleanup on aisle twenty-seven.' So, we tried to figure out what we could say about LEGO," says Gary.

He checks his clipboard, jumps back on board, and hits the accelerator. Gary points out a LEGO dog where someone once thoughtfully left a real leash. Our next stop is the Wild Woods Miniature Golf Course.

"I'm not sure golf clubs and LEGO models were the best combination," says Gary, bending down to look at an upscaled minifigure that is missing a nose. After drilling a hole, he attaches a new yellow 2×2 brick with a screw. A 2×2 plate covers the head of the screw, and we head back to the model shop. Motorized carts aren't allowed in the park once guests are inside.

The paved road of the back lot gives way to a rutted dirt one. As the cart bounces across dirt moguls, we come upon a large white tent. Miniland trucks sit stacked outside the entrance, along with flamingos and leaping fish. The tent is where models are sprayed with crushed walnuts in order to extend their life at the park. The sunny conditions turn translucent and white bricks yellow, and chrome tiles gray or translucent. Most models have a life span of ten to fifteen years, except clear bricks, which usually need to be replaced or repaired within five years. The mild abrasiveness of the shells helps to wear away the exterior of the models that has been dulled by the elements. A blasted model has softer corners and rounded studs that no longer say LEGO on them.

Those models that can't be polished or are being retired end up in the adjacent model graveyard.

"This is where AFOLs usually get the most upset," says Gary, gesturing to the open wooden crates that look like Hollywood missile containers.

An oversize Hagrid leans on his side against a lizard in blue-and-white shorts. Loose park brick and prototypes that have been written on in black marker are stacked inside the wooden bins. I gently finger the top half of a friar's head.

Gary drives us back to the concrete loop, and as we get closer to the park, I hear the sounds of children screaming from the Dragon roller coaster.

"You get to work in a place that has "Darth Vader" stenciled on a crate. Not too shabby," I tell Gary as we whiz into the storage area amid replacement coaster cars and the park's on-site hardware warehouse.

In the middle of a cul-de-sac is the model shop storage tent, what looks like an open-ended hangar filled with seasonal models. Pumpkins and Christmas ornaments are waiting to be packed away. Gary hops off the cart and stops a forklift operator moving a LEGO Santa and his sleigh into a crate. The base is too low and the model is about to be crunched.

"Santa tried to kill me once," says Gary. In his first year at the park, he was in the flatbed of a golf cart. Another model builder was driving, and Santa was riding shotgun. When the driver got up out of his seat, Santa's foot slipped onto the accelerator and the cart took off with Gary in the back.

"So, I'm standing there holding on to Santa's head as we take off. Thankfully, the other guy caught us after about a dozen feet."

He waves me over to a set of metal double doors outside a room the size of a cargo container. Here the blasted models receive a clear coat for ultraviolet protection.

"I do repair and maintenance with an emphasis on LEGO," deadpans Gary as he eyes a butler with a surfboard that needs a new access panel in his foot.

"Would you mind unscrewing that screw?" says Gary, gesturing to a button that has come loose on the butler's tuxedo. Gary needs both hands to hold the swaying model on top of a wooden pallet.

For literally two seconds, I'm a master model builder.

"You could try to make it perfect, but you have to let it go. That's a hard thing for AFOLs to adjust to," says Gary.

His cell phone beeps. It's Gary's boss, Tim Petsche, and we're headed back to the model shop. They are the only two model builders in the LEGOLAND model shop. They maintain the existing models and install new models. The majority of designers work in the development shop off site, which opened in 2007 to design and animate new models as part of the park's expansion.

An unmarked door off the left side of the model shop leads to the animation room.

About ten feet inside the room, a row of yellow panels features maps that correspond to each Miniland layout. The panels are next to banks of switches that remind me of an airplane control panel. A series of lights flash green and make small clicks like your tongue hitting the roof of your mouth.

"Each time those lights go off, somebody is playing in that part of Miniland or a car is moving," says Gary.

The cars in Miniland run between a series of charge points. The computer tells the cars when to stop in order to power up and when to continue.

"This is the story of the park," says Gary.

When we step back into the model shop, Gary is called into a meeting, and I have the park to myself. I wander into Miniland and begin jotting down the proportions of the figures. The feet consist of two 1×2 plates and the arms are each two hinges.

I take my calculations over to the Pick A Brick store inside Fun Town, where I'd been only a few hours earlier with Gary. I begin filling a bag with parts. I have a secret plan to build a Miniland version of myself and place him somewhere in Miniland New York, since they haven't gotten around to building Miniland Kansas City just yet.

I'm sorting bricks on a table, watching American children navigate according to the rules of the driving school, when Kate calls.

"I've got my street sweeper on my desk. How's your day going at LEGOLAND?" she asks, having flown home the previous day.

"Well, I'm talking to you from Fun Town. I'd say pretty good."

"Is this still your dream job?" asks Kate. I take a moment to consider my answer.

"No, I really don't think so."

A minute after we hang up, I'm walking back toward Miniland when I fall into step behind an employee wearing a red LEGOLAND polo shirt. I reconsider what I told Kate. *Well, maybe, I could just work here for a little while,* I think. I pass by the parade floats that roll through the miniaturized French Quarter of New Orleans.

I'm sitting on a bench snapping together the legs of my mini-me model when Gary calls to let me know he's off work. It's 4:45 p.m. and the park closes in fifteen minutes.

"Want to hit a few rides?" asks Gary.

I really don't, but I agree to get on the Dragon. Plus, I'm not sure it really counts; it's the same coaster I rode in LEGOLAND Billund.

"This is only the third coaster I've ridden in my life. You owe me," I tell Gary. My seat is right behind his, and we're both strapped in. The ride starts up with a jerk, and I decide to let go. Gary turns back to make sure I'm okay, and I lift my arms with my palms up in the traditional roller coaster posture of one who is happily along for the trip.

After we get off the ride, we check out the kiosk where they show you your picture from the camera set above the coaster. It's been turned off for the night, but I'd bet I was smiling on the tape.

"We can walk around if you want," says Gary.

"I was hoping we could spend some more time in Miniland," I tell him. The race cars stop circling the track at the Daytona Motor Speedway as we approach, since the power has been shut down for the night.

"If the park's closed, that means we can do this," says Gary, stepping over the black, wrought iron fence that surrounds the racetrack. I look at him uncertainly.

"C'mon." We spend a few minutes next to the grandstands. I can barely hear what Gary is saying, because I am *walking around inside Miniland.*

"This is my favorite part of Miniland," says Gary as we climb the hills of San Francisco. My head swivels, trying to take in all of the details that I couldn't see when I was forced to stand fifteen feet away behind a fence. There are elements in colors I have never seen, teal and gold. A woman hangs out the back of a building with two minifig heads on her chest that look surprisingly like a filled-out bra.

My feet are the size of the frozen trolleys.

"Do you ever make Godzilla noises?" I ask him somewhere near Coit Tower.

"No, but I've thought about it," says Gary.

He stops me at a brownstone where a man sits on the steps, a bouquet of flowers by his side.

"I love these little scenes because they are reflections of life. We're making these figures say so much without being able to give them facial expressions," says Gary.

I'm about to get up when I see what Gary means. A female figure peers out from behind a curtain in a window to the left of the stairs.

"I wonder what she's thinking," says Gary.

It's in New York City that I finally confess my plan to Gary to hide a Miniland version of myself. It's easier to admit my plan since I've abandoned it.

"I was going to do the same thing when I got here, but I never got around to it," says Gary.

The light begins to fade, and we both take out our cell phones, using the blue glow from the screens to illuminate our way as we talk about the buildings in front of us. Our footsteps are the only sounds in the park, and it's peaceful. We move through a newly redesigned New England town, walking the short distance between the lake and the farm area in about fifteen steps. Gary talks about how the landscaping was redesigned after all of the old boats were removed from the New England harbor. The very boats that Dan Brown bought at auction and I admired in a classroom in Bellaire, Ohio.

It's close to eight o'clock when we reach the Inauguration scene in Washington, D.C. Gary was interviewed by nearly every major international news outlet in the several weeks leading up to President Barack Obama's swearing-in.

"It's been amazing. I think it was just the idea of possibility that captured people's imagination," says Gary.

A flashlight washes over us, freezing Gary against the backdrop of the Lincoln Memorial and me just steps from the presidential motorcade. Gary waves to the security guard, and the beam of the flashlight continues down the path.

My eyes don't adjust back to the sudden dark, and I hear a small click next to my shoe. I kneel down. In the blue wash of my cell phone, I see I've kicked over a woman pushing a baby stroller.

"Don't worry about that, we'll fix it in the morning," says Gary.

"No, I got it." I set the female Miniland figure and her stroller back upright.

In the year that I've spent challenging myself to build, I've succeeded. I just didn't expect to be building a family.

"You ready to head home?" asks Gary.

"I am."

He snaps his cell phone shut, and the last of the lights go out in Miniland.

Epilogue: August 17, 2009

Kate has gone three days past her due date, and the joy of anticipation has clearly given way to the frustration of waiting. It's a difficult thing not knowing when your child is going to be born, and yet, it turns out that it might be even harder to adjust to the idea that she will be born at a specified time.

Kate's doctor had scheduled an afternoon ultrasound to determine the size of the baby. In the small, darkened room, I saw the computer's prediction for the first time—8 pounds, 15 ounces.

"How's your fat little baby?" asked Kate's doctor when he came in to discuss the results. And just like that we were discussing when our child would be born, via caesarean section—two days hence, on the morning of August 19.

The evening of August 18, we tried unsuccessfully to find things to occupy the hours. And then I thought of the one thing left for me to accomplish before we added another person to our family.

"Two words," I say to Kate.

"And they are . . . ?"

"MTT. Federation," I reply.

She gives me a puzzled look, until I bring in the briefcase-size box from the dining room. The model of the droid army attack vehicle from the most recent *Star Wars* trilogy is not just a LEGO set—it is *the* LEGO set.

I've owned it for over a year. My thirty-first birthday has come and gone. And for too long, this box has sat acquiring dust—a lucky totem and a weighty anchor. It recently migrated to the dining room after the third bedroom in our house was transformed from a brick room into a nursery. This set isn't going to put itself together.

"Yes," says Kate, excitedly. "I was like, I know what that is, but I just can't place it."

The standard relationship patter suggests that men have difficulty envisioning the future or thinking ahead, and I've been having trouble picturing what it will be like when our baby is born. I understand objectively what will happen, but I can't see the moment. What I have pictured is this night when we conquer this set together.

We approach the Trade Federation MTT like a surgical team. Kate grabs some storage containers and I grab two green cereal bowls—one for each of us to have parts handy. I cut the tape on the side of the box carefully, taking a deep breath.

Kate lays twenty-two bags of LEGO pieces out on the ottoman, while I begin to flip through the instruction manual to see what's in store. I quickly pass it to her, once she's done.

"We're not building on grass, so we're okay," says Kate, opening the second page of the first instruction booklet. It's an old joke, but a good one, especially coming from my wife. AFOLs like to poke fun at the first step of every kit, which informs new set owners to not mix the contents of the bags and to avoid putting the set together in the grass.

"This is not going to be good for color-blind you," says Kate as she looks at the various shades of brown, gray, and black in nearly every combination of brick, tile, and plate. I have a mild form of color-blindness, but while Kate makes sure my ties and socks match, she likely won't need to give a lot of help with this set.

For a long while, there are just the happy sounds of LEGO bricks being shuffled around in cereal bowls. We don't need conversation. I don't know if you can grow old together playing LEGO, but right now that sounds pretty great.

As Kate works on the main body of the droid ship, I begin to snap the droids themselves together. I outfit them with laser guns, which makes them topple, and I try hard not to dance them around the coffee table.

"It's like the game of memory—I know I've seen a piece, I just can't find it," says Kate, beginning to show frustration that the ship is taking so long to come together.

I imagine that some of that frustration stems from her inability to bend particularly far, her belly pushing out her T-shirt. *Mad Men* plays in the background, adding a soundtrack and style to our living room. I pay attention only when the conversation at the fictional advertising agency focuses on the pregnant wife of one of the characters.

"I've done my part. Now it's just up to her," says media buyer Harry Crane.

"Don't pay any attention to that due date. It will just drive you crazy," replies a coworker.

Amen to that, I say to myself.

Right about then, Kate finishes Step 2 and announces she's done. We're not even halfway through the first of two instruction books. It should feel as if we're quitting, but instead it feels just right. We spent our last evening as a childless couple happily playing with LEGO bricks.

Now all I want is for us to try to get some sleep before we have to leave for the hospital. Kate's C-section is scheduled for eight tomorrow morning.

The sun has started to come up as I clean the car and put in the hospital bag. I sweep LEGO bricks from beneath the floor in the backseat and put them away in the Creator mini train set box stuck in the back pocket of the driver's seat. Between that and the car seat, it looks like we already have started our family.

Everything runs smoothly until it's time to change into my scrubs. I hold up the package, an extra-large.

"Ma'am, I'm not sure these are going to work," I tell the nurse. She gives me a quick look, one that says I'll be her second priority all morning.

"Yeah . . . "—she pauses—"probably not. . . . I'll go get you a large." Her efficient nurse walk carries her out of the room before I can ask if they have a medium or, ideally, a small.

Kate laughs at the idea that I'll be wearing a large, and I'm glad for the break in the tension that exists in hospital rooms. But I'm not laughing when the nurse hands me the large scrubs and I step into the bathroom to change.

The top is a V-neck that hangs closer to my knees than my waist, while the pants pool around my sneakers, even after I've cinched them as tight as I can.

"How's this?" I ask proudly, stepping out of the bathroom and showing Kate and the nurse entirely too much chest hair. Kate laughs; the nurse does not.

"Do you have a T-shirt?" the nurse asks, with not a little concern in her voice.

"Yes. I wasn't sure if I should wear anything under it," I reply, not wanting to disobey any sort of hospital protocol regarding operating room attire.

"I think that you should wear the T-shirt," she replies.

So, hospital johnny issues resolved, we proceed into the operating suite. My eyes are drawn to the two massively oversize surgical lamps pointing down on the operating table. I can't help but think that they look like the headlights from the Power Miners sets. I tell myself that that is the last LEGO comparison I will allow my mind to make.

After Kate is prepped for the surgery, my chair is placed next to her head and before I'm even aware I've moved, I'm holding her hand.

"Are you ready to meet your baby?" I ask her.

"Yes. Are you?"

"Yes."

I feel her squeezing my hand, and suddenly I hear the doctor saying that if I want to see our baby, I should stand up now. The nurse puts a hand behind my back—I think she's waiting to see if I'm going to pass out.

And then our daughter appears, beautiful and screaming, her tiny red fists clenched and a mass of hair slicked against her skull.

"Whoa," I say. "That's a lot of hair."

"Look at all that hair," says the doctor.

I kiss Kate's cheek roughly and am caught briefly between following the baby to the corner of the room where she will be tested and weighed and staying with Kate to make sure she is fine.

"Go," mouths Kate, and I leave without asking if she's sure.

They stretch the baby's legs out to measure her, and she is placed on the scale: 8 pounds, 9 ounces appears on the red digital readout. A nurse places her beneath a warmer before swaddling her in a blanket.

"You can take her to your wife now," she says. I lift the baby from the warmer and walk over to my wife.

"Would you like to meet your daughter?" I ask Kate, my voice cracking for the first time.

"Hello, Charlotte," says Kate, kissing her, as I hold them both cheek to cheek. "Hello, little Charlotte Ann. I'm your mama."

That night, I lie on a foldout cot, attempting to avoid any movement and the associated awful grinding noise made by the plastic cover, which I'm convinced will wake the baby sleeping in the bassinet at the foot of Kate's hospital bed. I try to imagine what life will be like from now on, but that proves as difficult for me to do now as it was before the baby was born.

I try not to worry each time Charlotte makes a noise or when she is silent, but that still doesn't stop me from checking on her several times throughout the night—the cot protesting each time with the screech of plastic. It then threatens to collapse each time I try to climb back in.

It's hard leaving the hospital room two days later, but I sneak home to gather some additional baby clothes, the carrier, and a much-needed shower. I turn on my desktop computer out of habit and zone out briefly, the lack of sleep making me forget that time is passing.

While still on autopilot, I wander to the online LEGO Shop and click on the search function, which allows me to view sets by age. There's a section for ages zero to two; I open it. *This is baby stuff*, I think, forgetting that I'm not shopping for myself.

At the thought of "baby stuff," my mind re-engages and I remember that *our* baby is waiting back at the hospital. I click through pictures of houses and trains and large pails of bricks. I momentarily wonder if there is a baby toy I can order, but after a quick scan I see that newborns are not quite ready for LEGO. Only two days in and I'm making the right call as a parent. The recommended age actually begins at one and a half years, and that's for DUPLO bricks.

So, it looks as if I've got a playdate in 2011.

Index

Page numbers in *italics* refer to photos.